FREEDOM MOVES WEST

Freedom Moves West

A History of the Western Unitarian Conference 1852-1952

Charles H. Lyttle

James Freeman Clarke Professor of Church History Emeritus
Meadville Theological School

edited by Lynn Gordon Hughes
with a foreword by Rev. David A. Johnson

Blackstone
Editions
Providence

UNITARIAN UNIVERSALIST
HISTORICAL SOCIETY

Blackstone Editions, Providence, Rhode Island 02906
© 1952 by The Beacon Press
Revised edition © 2006 by Blackstone Editions
All rights reserved. Published 2006
Printed in the United States of America

ISBN: 0-9725017-6-2

THIS BOOK IS DEDICATED TO THREE UNITARIAN LAYMEN
"PILLARS" OF CHURCHES I HAVE SERVED
LOYAL CO-WORKERS
INSPIRING FRIENDS

Henry A. Farnell
Second Unitarian Church
Brooklyn, New York

William Fales Baxter
First Unitarian Church
Omaha, Nebraska

Warren A. Smith
The Unitarian Church
Geneva, Illinois

Contents

Illustrations

Foreword

Dr. Charles Lyttle and his wife Marcia were a devoted and passionate team of Western Conference partisans, determined that the story of Western Unitarianism not be lost, forgotten, or overrun and obliterated by new ideas and new people "who knew not the fathers" and mothers of our Israel. Charles Lyttle, long professor of Unitarian Church history at Meadville Theological School, gathered the stories, the characters, the contexts, the courage and convictions, the fierce contests and theological battles, church by church, preacher by preacher, partisan by partisan, town by town. He was determined that the reader should feel the soul-searing struggles, the immense devotion and fortitude it took to plant the seeds of liberal religion in the raw unsettled West. He wanted readers to flush in the heat of the conflicts and cheer for victories won, and never, never forget what it meant to the cause of liberal faith.

I was privileged to know the Lyttles and share their hospitality when I studied at Meadville/Lombard Theological School, though Charles was long retired. There was much he knew that no one else had even studied. Charles was in his nineties then, and one had the feeling that he had known every one of these figures who march through *Freedom Moves West*, personally. Of course he wasn't *that* old. But he had known every major and most of the minor Western figures of his long lifetime, and many of these had known the pioneers, the founders. Charles was a vital link to a past mostly forgotten even then; and there was virtually no one and no important issue on which he did not hold heartfelt judgments and fierce convictions.

It is no simple thing to write a history, fair and balanced, when you are and always have been so personally partisan. Charles tried hard! He was also a man of infinite detail and grand generalizations, and they too could be a problem. He was hardly ever fair to other denominations in his wide-cast nets of generalization. The American Unitarian Association and its fearful conservatives and centrists were not too badly mauled. Western Unitarians, whatever their positions and particularities, generally fared better, for he always found much to praise. In wrestling with the overall meaning of times, crises, ministries, events, Charles could overreach and speak beyond his knowledge. And in the thick of thousands of details he could make mistakes. One sentence has six mistakes in it; I know because I know that tiny corner of history intimately. There are doubtless several of these.

Dr. Charles Lyttle reminds me of the old story Mark Twain used to tell on himself. His redolent art of cussing was always an offense to Livy, his wife. She tried through the years everything she could think of to bring a halt to it. Finally one day in the wake of a particularly florid display of pyrotechnical cursing by Twain, Livy repeated slowly and quietly every word he had said. He stood stunned for a moment, then replied, "You got the words, Livy, but you ain't got the melody." Charles Lyttle always had the melody. Words, facts, generalizations might miscarry, but he had the melody. He knew what Unitarianism meant in the lives of the pioneers, preachers, prophets, and the tough local folk who, in season and out, kept those tiny outposts of faith going. He knew how and why the Ethical Basis brethren and sisters saw the world differently than most Unitarians of the long-settled East, and why they fought so doggedly for the freedom to live their vision. He well understood why the Western Unitarian Conference was orphaned by the A.U.A. and had to argue and fight its way back into the denominational tent – without compromise!

He lived the religious humanist revolution and knew the bitter warfare waged against it in the A.U.A. He wanted to tell its story with sympathy and conviction, and he did.

No one ever could write another history like this one, based on so much research in records no longer extant, on lives and memories no longer among the living. It is a vivid testament to a pioneer era of Unitarianism. It deserves to be passionately and compassionately read.

David A. Johnson

Editor's Preface

The text of this edition is substantially the same as that published by Beacon Press in 1952. Although this is a new edition, not a reprint, the original pagination has been retained.

In preparing this edition, our aim has been to make it as easy as possible for readers to navigate through the text and references. For this reason, the subheadings within chapters are listed in the table of contents, and some new subheadings (marked in the text with square brackets) have been added. The book has been newly indexed, including a new Index of Works Cited – an alphabetical listing of all of the books, periodicals, articles, essays, poems, reports, tracts, and sermons referenced in the book, with pointers to the pages on which they are mentioned. This brings together, in one list, the sources mentioned in Lyttle's Bibliographical Guide, in the mini-bibliographical essays elsewhere in the book, and in passing throughout the work. Since all of Lyttle's sources are, of course, over fifty years old, we have consulted library catalogs to confirm that the works cited are still in existence and available to be consulted. Except for those few marked "[not located]" in the Index, all of them were found among the holdings of some academic or research library. (As in Lyttle's day, most are to be found in the libraries of Harvard University and Meadville/Lombard Theological School.) Minor inaccuracies in titles, authors' names, and publication dates have been silently corrected, both in the index and in the main text.

Changes to the 1952 text, other than those mentioned above, are marked with square brackets. These changes are of two kinds. First, there is material that has been added to the text, mostly for the purpose of identifying people who were mentioned only by surname in the original text. When discussing the cultural context within which Western Unitarianism developed, Lyttle often listed persons whose deeds or writings helped to shape the intellectual climate of the time. The passage of time has made some of these references obscure; names such as Boulanger, Bradlaugh, Lecky, Buckle, and Froude (p. 170) may have been household words in 1952, but they are no longer. The added information will make it easier for readers to seek further information about these people in reference works and library catalogs. Finally there are a small number of corrections. Aside from verifying the bibliographical information, we have made no attempt to fact-check the book. However, in a few cases where corrections were brought to our attention, we have incorporated them in this edition.

Acknowledgements

The Unitarian Universalist Historical Society is fortunate in having access, via the Internet and personal contacts, to a worldwide community of scholars and local historians with an interest in Unitarian and Universalist history. Several of these people have generously shared their own special expertise. The section dealing with the works of Kristofer and Drude Krog Janson and the church which Kristofer Janson founded in Norway (p. 152) has been revised on the basis of information supplied by the Norwegian Unitarian, Knut Heidelberg. Andrew Hill of Edinburgh provided information about about the British Unitarian, John Campbell, and straightened out the confusion between John Campbell and John Sherman (pp. 17-18). Local church historians, Walter Herz of Cincinnati and Audrey Geer Masalehdan of Pittsburgh, searched their institutional memory and archives for the full names of people mentioned in the book only by a surname or title.

All but one of the illustrations in this book is from the 1952 edition. The atmospheric but indistinct photograph of the

Unitarian Church of Meadville, Pennsylvania, taken during a snowstorm, has been replaced with a clearer photograph of that historic church, supplied by Kate R. Walker, current minister of the Unitarian Universalist Church of Meadville.

Finally, we thank Naomi King and David Bumbaugh, who patiently scanned, edited, and typed the text of the 1952 edition into the electronic files used for this publication.

Lynn Gordon Hughes

Author's Preface

THE HEARTY INTEREST and ungrudging helpfulness of many friends within and outside of the denomination have supplied both information and encouragement for my efforts to create an accurate and a tolerably lucid conspectus of a significant stream of religion in our country.

Consultation with Randall S. Hilton, Secretary of the Western Unitarian Conference, and with Curtis W. Reese, its President, has been frequent, genial, and rewarding in terms of factual knowledge and value judgments. Their assistants, Mrs. Carl A. Schaad and Mrs. Earl F. Cook, have been embodiments of gracious and efficient aid. The same is true of Dr. Margaret Boell, Librarian of the Meadville Theological School and of its Assistant Treasurer, Mrs. Mary K. Randall, who have spared no pains in searching for hidden data. Mrs. Frederic M. Tileston, of the First Unitarian Church, Chicago, has been equally obliging. The painstaking ingenuity and artistry of Mr. Wolfgang Hoffmann of Geneva, Illinois, and Mr. Henry D. Green of Chicago in making the best of time-stained prints and photographs are self-evident.

Information on difficult point has been provided by Mrs. Martha D. Watts, Librarian of the American Unitarian Association; Miss Helen M. McFarland of the Kansas State Historical Society, Topeka; Miss Mabel Dean, Archivist of the University of Chicago; Miss Elizabeth Baughmann of the Chicago Historical Society; Mr. Paul Bixler, Librarian of Antioch College.

Prompt and understanding response from historians of local churches has helped me greatly. Among those to whom I am indebted are Mrs. Edgar G. Braun, Detroit, Michigan; Mrs. Ethel E. Brown, Toledo, Ohio; Mrs. Albert Capella, Cincinnati, Ohio; Mrs. Nina Moore Tiffany, St. Paul, Minnesota; Miss Bertha Pauschert, Shelbyville, Illinois; Dr. Allen C. Austen, Kansas City, Missouri; Mr. Frank M. Keezer, Denver, Colorado; Mr. H. Hadley Grimm, St. Louis, Missouri; Dr. E. B. Montgomery, Quincy, Illinois.

The pleasant surmise that this history has been regarded as a co-operative venture by the whole Conference has been confirmed by the ready response of ministerial colleagues to sometimes bothersome inquiries and requests. For such response and reassurance I am especially grateful to E. Burdette Backus, Indianapolis, Indiana; Preston Bradley, Chicago, Illinois; Thaddeus B. Clark, St. Louis, Missouri; Benjamin H. Clark, Marietta, Ohio; John R. Heyworth, Chicago, Illinois; John Haynes Holmes, New York City; R. Lester Mondale, recently of Kansas City, Missouri; Edwin C. Palmer, Kalamazoo, Michigan; Philip Schug, recently of Lincoln, Nebraska; Carl A. Storm, Minneapolis, Minnesota; Ellsworth C. Smith, Cincinnati, Ohio; Kenneth J. Smith, Duluth, Minnesota; Von Ogden Vogt, formerly of Chicago, Illinois; Kenneth J. Walker, Bloomington, Illinois; Robert W. Lawson, Dayton, Ohio; Glenn O. Canfield, Syracuse, New York.

My greatest good fortune has been the unusually rich knowledge of Unitarian history, thought, and literature possessed by my wife, whose father, Dr. Lewis G. Janes, and whose minister, John White Chadwick, were friends and staunch allies of Jenkin Lloyd Jones, William C. Gannett, and other spokesmen of Evolution and Free Religion – as she herself has been of John Haynes Holmes and other social prophets. We have greatly enjoyed writing this book together.

Charles H. Lyttle

NOTE: In places where the frequent repetition of the full titles would become tiresome, the following abbreviations have been used: A.U.A. (American Unitarian Association); W.U.C. (Western Unitarian Conference); F.R.A. (Free Religious Association).

Introduction

ON FRIDAY, THE SEVENTH OF MAY, 1852, about forty lay and ministerial delegates assembled in the Unitarian church of Cincinnati at Fourth and Race Streets, and after four days of prayers, sermons, discussions, and collations, got the Annual Conference of the Western Unitarian Churches organized. Reporting the meeting to *The Christian Inquirer* of New York City, the minister of the church, Rev. A. A. Livermore, rejoiced

… that our doubt and anxiety are dispelled and our best hopes fully made good … we have had a well-attended, harmonious, spirited, delightful Conference … not one unkind remark nor discordant incident. It is a serious reflection that we have, in this Conference, planted an institution which will endure for many years … will probably measure its twenty, one hundred, one thousand years.

Before adventuring the next nine centuries of the prophecy, it has seemed desirable to the Board of Directors of the Conference at the present time that the history of its first century should be recorded in fairly full detail and that this record should be published in book form to ensure a permanence and a wider distribution than previous retrospects had attained. Livermore himself summarized the first twenty-five years in 1877; Rev. T. B. Forbush extended and somewhat reinterpreted this summary in 1882; Rev. R. R. Shippen furnished a half-century review (1902); and in 1910 *Unitarianism in America*, by Rev. G. W. Cooke, contained many references to the Conference and much information, but no consecutive narrative. Much the same may be said of Rev. E. M. Wilbur's invaluable but very condensed work, *Our Unitarian Heritage*, of 1925. In all these cases the necessity of extreme condensation excluded material that gives lucidity, logic, continuity, and vividness to all historiography. It is hoped that this study with its broader canvas and more generous inclusion of names, places, writings, and pictures will enhance the significance of Western Unitarian history by increasing interest in it.

At the outset of our century journey, a charting of its stages and their salient phases may be helpful.

In the *first period* the conditions – physical, historical, and religious – presented to the immigrants an opportunity for a new civilization unprecedented in history. The Unitarian missionary effort began with the coming of the English Unitarian, Joseph Priestley, to Philadelphia in 1774. Spontaneous and unorganized though it was, its forth-puttings reached as far as Pittsburgh and Harrisburg, Pennsylvania, before its impetus slackened. Responsibility for the missionary effort was then assumed by the American Unitarian Association, formed in 1825 largely for the purpose of missionizing the West with the Gospel according to William Ellery Channing.

The *second period* begins with the courageous establishment of churches in the Ohio River and Mississippi River basins by ministers trained in the Harvard Divinity School. Their enterprise was paralleled by similar activity in central New York and the southern ports of the Great Lakes. Scarcity of ministers, however, and brevity of pastorates made necessary the foundation of a Western theological school at Meadville, Pennsylvania, in 1844.

In the *third period*, expansion proceeded so satisfactorily that its integration into a Conference of Western Unitarian Churches was brought about in 1852. The effects, however, were partially nullified by the intensification of the anti-slavery issue in the following decade, as well as the conflict developing between the conservatives in the denomination committed to Channing's Christian – rather than his questing – spirit, and the radicals who were responding to Theodore Parker's Theistic faith with its strong emphasis on social reforms. With the onset of the Civil War, nevertheless, both wings heartily collaborated in the cause of Union and Emancipation, as well as the work of the two Sanitary Commissions, and hope was felt that the pre-war tensions might be surmounted by the formation of a National Conference of Unitarian churches in 1865.

The hope was futile, since dissensions over the Preamble and Articles of the Conference served to render the *fourth period* one of deeper tension, though of more vigorous missionary activity, since, by the aid of the new railroads, preachers could conveniently reach Denver in the Far West, Portland on the Pacific coast, and St. Paul and Minneapolis in the Northwest. But this promising advance, led by Rev. C. A. Staples, was halted and even unity endangered by renewed efforts of the conservatives to fixate Unitarianism within Christian doctrines and terminology. The defeatism of the early eighteen-seventies was, however, reversed by the rallying of the "*Unity* men" under the leadership of Jenkin Lloyd Jones. The Conference reaffirmed as its basic and unitive principles: intellectual Freedom and Fellowship in the quest for truth; Character, in the sense of moral integrity and human service, as the test, proof, and fruit of genuine, universal religion; no uniformity in speculative doctrinal opinions on the part of members and ministers was required.

This position was accepted by the National Conference in 1894.

In the *fifth period* the Conference asserted its individuality as a Western institution, having manifestly outgrown its previous status as a projection of liberal New England religious culture. On the new Ethical Basis of fellowship and co-operation, a fresh impetus was given to missionary expansion as well as to literary and educational activity. The Ethical Basis facilitated also the constructive assimilation of the Spencer and Darwin hypotheses of evolution, Huxley's agnosticism, Haeckel's materialism, the rival attraction of Ethical Culture, the disturbing parallelisms of the non-Christian religions with Christian mythology, moral teachings, theology, and rites. This dynamic and dramatic period of Conference history rose to a climax in the World Parliament of Religions in Chicago in 1893, which was conceived and arranged largely by Jenkin Lloyd Jones. That the harmony of the second half-century of Conference history has not been broken by disagreements over Socialism, pragmatism, pacifism was due to the lesson learned in the conflicts of the early years. The emergence of Humanism and of Scientific Naturalism, with their fresh critique of supranaturalism and tradition, virtually coincides with the leadership of Rev. Curtis W. Reese, whose steady loyalty to the Conference position – spiritual comity in agreement on ethical values and goals, with mutual tolerance of opinions on speculative theological subjects – has done much to bring the Conference to its centennial year united and thriving. Thus far, at least, its long, troubled, yet persistent fidelity to the free spirit and the free mind has demonstrated the feasibility of the principles. As never before, freethinkers in religion, united in spirit and work for the promotion of Truth, Righteousness, and Love in the world, have created an enduring union.

That the name "Unitarian" is appropriate for the development under consideration may, for some readers, require explanation, for, up to about 1841, it commonly denoted a heterodox position within the Christian tradition. Its chief tenets were the Unity and Fatherly Character of God; the perfect divine and human nature of Jesus, God's Son, the Messiah foretold by the prophets and authenticated by miraculous signs and powers; the Savior of sinful man by the perfect holiness of his life, the superhuman wisdom of his precepts, and his perfect obedience to God's will even unto crucifixion.

The term "Unitarian" also signified those who rejected all other doctrines of Calvin as non-Scriptural save the sovereignty of God, the benefits of divine grace, and the necessity of Holiness as a *sine qua non* of salvation. Such was Unitarianism as proclaimed by William Ellery Channing (1780-1842). Much of the power of his preaching, however, derived from his fearless application of his faith to the reform of the social evils of his day – slavery, intemperance, poverty, war – as well as to his pleas for Christian unity on the non-creedal, non-sectarian bases of simple Gospel faith and life.

In Channing's spirit, Theodore Parker (1810-1860), influenced greatly by the Transcendental philosophy of Emerson and the Higher Criticism of Griesbach, De Wette, and Strauss, discarded "evidences" of the miracles and prophecies as well as the supra-natural Messiahship of Jesus, whom he revered as a supremely good and wise human being. Parker held that the Nazarene's office as the Exemplar and Teacher of absolute truth and morality to his people and age had analogies in other great religious leaders of history and might be reproduced by future prophets within the Christian tradition. This faith of Parker seemed to him to reassert Channing's stress on the dignity and the potential if not the actual goodness of human nature. It gave his attacks on the crying social evils of his day – slavery, industrial exploitation, mercenary politics, aggressive war – a passionate earnestness and eloquence.

Underlying the non-conformity of Channing and Parker, as well as of Priestley and the whole body of British (Latitudin-arian), Dutch (Arminian), and Polish (Socinian) liberals, even as far back as the Florentine and Erasmian liberals of the Renais-sance – who discovered it in the Greek and Roman philoso-phers – is the principle that the human intelligence ("reason" in the classic terminology) is entitled to guide and check religious feeling; to investigate its sources and authorities; to criticize its ideologies by the light of contemporary secular knowledge; to rectify its moral codes, to ethicize its institutions, its use of power and wealth.

By the use of their free, bold, keen minds, Luther and Calvin reformed Roman Catholicism back to what they deemed apostolic Christianity; then they denied the use of reason to the Anabaptists and anti-Trinitarians who believed that the Reformers themselves ought to be reformed. The Puritans claimed this right and liberty of reasoning – the same, indeed, that the Apostle Paul had used to refute the Jews – in order to point out the un-Scriptural usages of the Church of England; yet when the Baptists and the Quakers made free to criticize them, the Puritans did their best to harry them out of the land. When Channing and his liberal colleagues took the liberty of reasoning against the Calvinist system and the Calvinists became hostile, the Channing Unitarians complained of bigotry and mental bondage; but when, in the course of time, Parker took the liberty of reasoning away some of their cherished beliefs, the *soi-disant* followers of Channing sought to excommunicate Parker. And before our history closes, we shall see followers of Parker endeavoring to dis-fellowship those of their Unitarian brethren who had emulated Parker's free spirit and had advanced beyond Parker!

History presents few aspects more ironical than that of heretics becoming heresy hunters, prophets becoming persecutors, reformers becoming reactionaries! The phenomenon occurs in all fields of thought — science, art, literature, education, as well as religion. What progress has been blocked, what strife created! Yet the very survival of our race depends upon keeping free, sensitive, alert, bold, and creative the human intelligence.

The justification of the use of "Unitarian" to denote the continuum of teachers and churches dealt with in this history derives from the fact that, although the grand principle of spiritual and intellectual freedom was sometimes betrayed by a few, it was always retrieved by the majority of the members; its sanctity and primacy were acknowledged by all in their higher moments of unity and co-operation. The *dénouement* of this history consists in the decision made and maintained by the Conference through all the unseemly contentions of the period from 1875 to the victory in 1894, to keep the principles of freedom of thought and conscience paramount, sacred, and inviolable.

Twelve churches, some fairly strong and large, some not so at all, met in Cincinnati in 1852 to form the Conference. Today the Conference includes fifty-five churches, two institutions, twenty Fellowships. In 1852, however, there were no sharply defined boundaries for Western Unitarianism. Syracuse, New York, and Northumberland, Pennsylvania, were its Eastern outposts. Reports were submitted for decades concerning the progress of new societies on the Pacific Coast. New Orleans, Louisiana; Mobile, Alabama; and Nashville, Tennessee, were regarded as within its constituency. Were all the Unitarian churches now existing in this vast area members of the Western Conference, its gains would appear far more impressive than they do. But six large regional conferences now subtract both area and churches from their mother Conference. Even so, the increase and the losses are at first glance disappointing in terms of numerical success. What have been the deterrent factors? Some will become obvious as our study progresses. One, in particular, deserves to be clearly understood at the outset.

The Unitarian reformation of Puritan Calvinism occurred in churches of the Congregational order located chiefly in eastern Massachusetts and Maine, with its spiritual and cultural center in Harvard College and Boston. Regular intercourse between the New England seaports and Europe had opened the minds of these eastern New Englanders to the arguments of British and Scotch theologians that ecclesiastical Christianity had subordinated the ethical and spiritual teachings of Jesus to doctrinal orthodoxy; had divided mankind by its intolerance; had chilled beneficence by the doctrine of election; had impeded intellectual progress by obscurantism. As early as 1765, Rev. Jonathan Mayhew of Boston was preaching not only this liberal critique of Calvinism but also the positive duties of Christian tolerance, morality, and non-sectarian charity.

In the wake of the wars that agitated the colonies from 1740 to 1783 came an unprecedented undertow of infidelity, licentiousness, intemperance, and profanity, as was to be expected. But the orthodox leaders, without a trace of justice, seized the opportunity to impute responsibility for such spiritual and moral decadence to the Unitarian liberals. Their hostile propaganda to this effect was taken up by the Presbyterians of New York, Princeton, and Philadelphia and even permeated the Baptist pulpits in the South. Liberalism was charged with promoting moral indifference or anarchy, with cryptic designs of atheistic and bloody revolution after the manner of the French Jacobins.

Such was the reputation of their faith that the Unitarian immigrants from New England found rampant in the West. Their denomination was the largest to arrive on the scene; they had been preceded by far greater numbers of Calvinist Congregationalists, Presbyterians, and Baptists, who had churches well established in virtually every community a decade before the Unitarians reached the spot. If the last were steadfast and forthright in their faith, they encountered unfriendliness and discrimination. If a group of them drew together for the exercise of their constitutional right of freedom of worship, for the provision of liberal religious education for their children, or for the morale of fellowship and nostalgic consolation, they were met by the cold disapproval of a united orthodoxy. Pulpit invective, social ostracism, political and economic boycott beset the church members, even their friends, especially their ministers, to a degree almost inconceivable today. The records and recollections of early Unitarianism in the West are full of testimonials to such antagonism, usually instigated by orthodox clergymen.

For such reasons the founding and maintenance of a Unitarian society in a small settlement was more difficult than that of a church of any other denomination save possibly the Universalist. The venture involved in most cases really heroic independence and sacrificial loyalty. Even the utmost measure of these was not able to save dozens of little Mayflowers from foundering, to the joy of the conservatives and the lingering disrepute of Unitarianism in the regions roundabout. The West is dotted with the graves of these faithful failures; the traces of their brief existence are hard to find. Historians of the extension of the orthodox denominations exult in the fast-increasing number of presbyteries and conferences, each with its scores of new churches. The annalist of Western Unitarianism must count in gains by single societies, widely separated and for decades struggling for existence.

The biographies of those churches that have survived and are thriving today have been sketched in some detail in order to remind present and future generations of Western Unitarians of the price their precursors have paid for spiritual freedom. The inscription on the monument of Governor William Bradford atop Burial Hill in Plymouth is the message of this History:

Quod patres difficillime adepti sunt
Nolite turpiter relinquere.

(That which the fathers did with such difficulty achieve,
let us not shamefully surrender.)

PART I

FRONTIER CONDITIONS
AND PIONEER CHURCHES
TO 1844

CHAPTER ONE

Settling, Civilizing, Missionizing the West

How beautiful to think of lean, tough Yankee settlers with most occult, unsubduable fire in their bellies steering over the western mountains to annihilate the jungle! Oh, if we were not a set of cant-ridden blockheads there is no myth of Athene or Hercules to equal this fact, whenever the Greek, Semitic and other multifarious cobwebs are swept away!

Carlyle to Emerson, 1849

CARLYLE'S ENTHUSIASM over the epic grandeur of Western settlement is readily understandable, but most of his rhapsody otherwise is highly unfactual! The honor of Clio requires that we set Carlyle right on certain points, to wit:

The prospect before one of Carlyle's mythical "Yankees" as he paused on a peak of the "western mountains" to train his binoculars on the Rocky Mountains over two thousands miles away would not have been that of a "jungle" in any commonly accepted use of the word! Sweeping his gaze from Kentucky, south of the great basin of the Ohio River, "pathway of empire," to the noble forests, boundless prairies, and inland seas of the states of the Old Northwest north of *la belle rivière* – Ohio, Indiana, Illinois, Michigan, Wisconsin – he would have surveyed the greatest area of fertile land, navigable watercourses, mineral riches ever opened to mortal man in the history of the world to enter and enjoy. Nor would he have glimpsed any "jungle" beyond the silver band of the Mississippi bisecting his panorama, but rather endless grasslands, pinioned at the south by the mountain domes of the Ozarks and in the north by the sharp peaks of the Tetons. Does a jungle possess the mineral wealth of the West – the iron ore of Wisconsin and Minnesota, the lead of the driftless area of southwestern Wisconsin, the coal of southern Illinois and western Pennsylvania?

Whatever Carlyle meant by "steering over the western mount-ains," the fact is that after 1775 there was little if any need to go over any mountains at all to get into the West. Immigrants were able to get into Kentucky from the Piedmont regions of western Virginia and the Carolinas through the Wilderness Road of Daniel Boone's making in 1775; through the Adirondacks and the Catskill Mountains by fair turnpikes after 1795; into the heart of the Lake Plains by the National Road which had been put through from Baltimore to Wheeling, West Virginia, on the Ohio River by 1818, to Columbus, Ohio, by 1833, and to Vandalia, Illinois, on the river of that name, by 1850. The post roads through the Alleghenies from Philadelphia to Pittsburgh were, indeed, a trial not only for express coaches but even for "Conestoga wagons," commonly known as "prairie schooners"; but by 1834 the incredible Pennsylvania portage and canal system carried passengers and freight the 320 miles to Pittsburgh in four days. At Pittsburgh the poorer immigrants to the farther West could get flatboats and sailboats for the thousand-mile journey down the Ohio to St. Louis; after 1811 the richer travelers could go by steamboat. Light-draught stern-wheelers waited at river junction points to take them up the broad shallow tributaries of the great river – the Muskingum and the Miami in Ohio, the Kentucky River in its own state, the Wabash in Indiana, the Illinois in that state, the Cumberland and the Tennessee Rivers in western Kentucky – sometimes for a distance of one hundred miles. The Mississippi above St. Louis was navigable as far as the Falls of St. Anthony in Minnesota, where Minneapolis now stands.

The Ohio River waterways were paralleled in the North, after 1825, by the Erie Canal through New York state to Buffalo. Large steamers gave daily service on Lake Erie between Buffalo and Detroit after 1831; to Chicago via the Straits of Mackinac after 1838. To be sure, there was not much immigration to Chicago, northern Illinois, and southern Wisconsin until after the Indians had finally been driven across the Mississippi by the Bad Axe River massacre of 1832. Soon thereafter the ancient Indian trail from Detroit to Lake Michigan was improved into a "corduroy" road for stagecoach service, with connections by steamer at Michigan City for Chicago. The latter became, after 1835, a focal point for transportation routes north, west, and south: highways to Milwaukee, Wisconsin, and Galena in the northwest of the state [Illinois] near the Mississippi; the Illinois and Michigan Canal from Chicago on the lake to La Salle on the Illinois River, with steamboat service thence to St. Louis.

Scarcely had the elaborate and ruinously costly systems of canals between the waterways of the Central States opened the hinterland to settlement and industry than the construction of railroads began, using the labor, in many cases, of the Irish and German immigrants who had built the canals! But the capitalists and executive staffs of the new railways were mostly Yankees and New Yorkers. By 1855 New York was linked (by eight different roads, necessitating that many changes of cars!) with Chicago; Chicago had access by rail to Madison, Wisconsin, on the north; to Rock Island, Illinois, and Davenport, Iowa, on the west; to Cincinnati, Ohio, and St. Louis, Missouri, on the south. By 1867 one could reach Council Bluffs, Iowa, and Omaha, Nebraska, on the Missouri River, by rail from Chicago; Denver was accessible through Kansas City. Duluth and the Twin Cities of Minnesota had railroad service from Chicago by 1873. Long before this – in 1857, indeed – our "lean, tough" Yankee could have traveled around in Pullman cars – if not too parsimonious!

But all the immigrants to the West were not Yankees – far from it! Up to 1825 or 1830 the majority of the pioneers were "Southrons" – folk who came from the Piedmont regions of Virginia and the Carolinas by foot, horseback, oxcart along Boone's Wilderness Road through the Appalachian Mountains into Kentucky, which they entered into and possessed so effectively that it had enough people for statehood in 1792. Then they moved across the Ohio River into the southern regions of Ohio, Indiana, and Illinois, which, by virtue of their numbers and of Connecticut Yankees pushing into the southeast and northeast parts of Ohio, gained their statehood in 1802, 1816, and 1818 respectively. The Southrons brought their social patterns with them as clearly as did the Yankees later in the North. Kentucky, to which the Northwest Ordinance's prohibition of slavery did not apply, had its plantations, its log-cabin tenant farmers, its plethora of lawyer-politicians, its Episcopalian upper class,

Presbyterian middle class, and Baptist (later Christian) and Methodist worker class. The Southrons were mostly Jeffersonian in their political philosophy; hence the constitutions of the new states, excepting Kentucky, contained not only the bill of rights of the great Ordinance of 1787 (freedom of worship, jury trial, habeas corpus, etc.) but also the Jeffersonian principles of manhood suffrage, the supremacy of a popularly elected legislature, an elective judiciary; while in Wisconsin (a state in 1848) small homesteads were exempted from seizure for debt, married women could control their own property, and the foreign-born immigrants could vote on simply taking an oath of allegiance. As the result of this blending of the political idealism of Thomas Jefferson and Manasseh Cutler, the Connecticut Congregationalist, "the society thus newly organized and constituted is more liberal, enlarged, unprejudiced than a society of unique birth and character who bring all their early prejudices as a common stock." All the differences and the tensions of Western Unitarianism and New England Unitarianism are epitomized in this observation of Timothy Flint, the West's first philosophic historian.

To return to Carlyle: whatever could have been the nature of that "most occult, unsubduable fire" in the Yankees' bellies? Pioneer determination and hardihood? No doubt of that! But for what goal? Let a pioneer Unitarian minister of St. Louis, Missouri, speak his mind:

> The grand motive which actuates all who come here is to make money, – not liberty of conscience, not intellectual improvement, not the desire to do good, but to better our own condition, to make ourselves rich and influential members of society. And in the universality of this motive I discern our greatest danger: that religion and learning and morality and education and everything which makes a people truly prosperous shall all be forgotten, all made to bow to one god, Mammon.

Thus Rev. W. G. Eliot, Jr., in 1835, admonished the Franklin Society, a corporation to promote the Lyceum movement of lectures and study classes. It should be added that he himself wrought valiantly to put Christ in place of Mammon. What allies had he in the ranks of religion, orthodox and liberal, in the West of the frontier period?

Never in recorded history had any religious faith so free and unobstructed an opportunity to plant and extend its institutions and culture as the West offered American Protestantism from the very first. Few vestiges remained in 1787 of the religions of the West's previous occupants except the awe-inspiring creations of the Mound Builders, the grotesque ceremonials of the decadent Indians, the vacant stockade chapels and graveyard crosses of Spanish, French, British forts and trading posts. In old Cahokia and Kaskaskia on the west bank of the Mississippi above St. Louis, in St. Louis itself and Vincennes on the Wabash River, in Detroit and a small hamlet at the Sault Ste. Marie, the Roman Catholic mass was still celebrated. These poor relics of primitive piety were not molested by the advancing legions of pioneers; was not the Republic the first state in history where practically complete religious freedom obtained? Its citizens could decide for themselves whether or not they would attend church; what church they would attend; what church they would organize if they felt inclined. They were even free to say or print whatever they thought about religion, barring blasphemous or obscene utterances; on the same conditions preachers could criticize the government from their pulpits with immunity. As a result of such freedom the American spirit created within seventy-five years of the pioneers' entrance into the West the most vital and powerful segments of both Protestantism and Roman Catholicism on the face of the earth.

Of the conservative Protestant denominations, the Presbyterians from western New Jersey, Pennsylvania, Virginia, and the Carolinas came first – the faith of the Scotch-Irish farmers and middle-class folk. Unless they brought their parsons with them, however, churches had to be organized and ministers called from the East – from Princeton College especially, since the Presbyterians maintained high educational standards for their leaders: the Bible languages, the Latin classics, Calvin's exegesis and theology they must know well, and they must be able to speak and write the English language correctly. Their strict and somewhat oligarchical polity virtually ensured the morality and orthodoxy of their clergy; for the same reason heresy trials and schisms were more frequent than in other bodies. Saving the Roman Catholic cathedrals, the Presbyterian churches after 1830 were the most costly and imposing of any in the Ohio and

Mississippi River ports. The Synods of Pittsburgh and of Transylvania (Kentucky) were established in 1802, that of St. Louis
in 1817, and that of Illinois in 1831.

Were there no Presbyterian churches in the North, from
Albany, New York, through to Chicago? Many, of course, but
until about 1835 the Presbyterian missionary effort was combined
with that of the Calvinist Congregationalists of Connecticut and
western New England by virtue of an agreement known as the
"Plan of Union," from which sprang a curious kind of "Presbycongregationalists." In 1826 missionary giving and spending
were centered in the American Home Missionary Society which
aided hundreds of churches and supported as many or more
missionaries in northern Ohio, Indiana, southern Michigan, and
central and southern Illinois. In southeastern and northern Ohio,
however – the "Western Reserve" – the expatriate Connecticut
Congregationalists held to their native polity and name. Growing
Yankee colonization of central Illinois inspired a "Yale Band"
of seven ministerial students to come west and found Illinois
College in Jacksonville, Illinois; an "Andover Band" from the
Congregationalist seminary of that name in Massachusetts
missionized Iowa after 1842 and stimulated the foundation of
what is now Grinnell College. With similar enterprise and devotion the work was carried on in northern Illinois and southern
Wisconsin. By 1850 the Society (now no longer approved or
supported by the conservative Presbyterians) was supporting
119 settled ministers or evangelists in the above states.

In spite of their kinship in social status, New England origin,
church polity, and cultural interests, there was slight comity
between the Unitarians and the Congregationalists in the West,
owing to the rancor of the old days of division in New England
and the present necessity for the Congregationalists to disavow
with forensic indignation the Presbyterians' taunts of Unitarian
leanings in the growing latitude of Horace Bushnell and Henry
Ward Beecher. But on the part of the Episcopalians a more
friendly attitude toward the Unitarians existed, for Western Epis-
copalianism up to about 1850 was markedly "Low Church." Its
pioneer missionary had been the Vermont farm boy, Philander
Chase, to whose indomitable initiative was due the organization of the Diocese of Ohio in 1818, the foundation of Kenyon

College in northern Ohio (1824), the Diocese of Illinois in 1834, and Jubilee College in that state. Bishop Kemper took up "Farmer Bishop" Chase's work in 1835, and by 1841 there were 131 Episcopal ministers in the West. The literary beauty of the Prayer Book, the distaste of the Episcopalians for the indecorum of revivals, the high cultural qualities of their clergy, their emphasis on Christian morality and charitable work, and their willingness to co-operate in the same with heretics and infidels – all made the establishment of a Unitarian church doubly difficult in any city and, in the opinion of some Unitarians, unnecessary – until Low Church latitude and democracy were extruded by Anglo-Catholicism.

Of the Baptist and Methodist denominations in the West, the paucity of Unitarian contact with them either in co-operative efforts or in controversy leaves little to be said. In point of time the Baptists came but slightly later than the Presbyterians; but in type of membership and church polity and doctrine there was a vast difference. The Baptist preacher was usually a farmer or small artisan who immigrated with his people, supported himself, won his leadership by fluent Bible memorization and naïve exposition, gloried in river baptizings and revivals – "camp meetings" as they were called, since they often lasted a week. Unless he was a "Free Baptist" he was a bibliolater, retaining enough Calvinism in his doctrines to confine salvation to the newly converted who had undergone "believers' baptism," and to condemn all other humans to hell-fire forever. In the main, the Baptists were to be found in rural districts and country towns. Seldom did they run afoul of the Unitarians save in Fundamentalist denunciation of the latter in their religious press.

Because of the implicit Arminianism of the Methodists, as popularized in their doctrines of "free grace" and "free will," as well as their warm-hearted and generous participation, without sectarian restraint, in works of public charity, their relations with the Unitarians were in most cases hospitable and cordial, as befitted the followers of the tolerant John Wesley. By 1850 the efficiency of their discipline and polity, operating through their system of methodical circuit-riding, class meetings, and episcopal oversight, made them the most numerous denomination in the West. Perhaps the hearty support given by the

Unitarians of Boston to the Methodist "Father Taylor" and his Seamen's Mission there – where Dr. and Mrs. Channing often went to kneel at the altar rail for Communion – opened the Western Methodist heart to the Unitarians. Father Taylor twice came west to attend the meetings of the Western Unitarian Conference and in each case his welcome to the Unitarian pulpit of the city where it gathered was not less enthusiastic than to those of his own persuasion.

The Progress of the Liberal Christian Denominations in the West

We now come to a situation so paradoxical as to be well-nigh incredible. Before the missionary work of the American Unitarian Association began in earnest in 1826, there were three bodies in the West professing Unitarian conceptions of God's Unity and parental love to mankind; of Christ's work of reconciliation and perfect obedience rather than of vicarious, sacrificial Atonement; of man's individual responsibility for sin, his moral competence to seek and to respond to the regenerating influences of the Holy Spirit. These bodies were, first, the "Christians" or the Christian Connection led by Barton W. Stone and Burton Eastin of Kentucky; second, the Universalists; third, the Society of "Liberal" or "Hicksite" Friends. With the last two groups the Unitarians of today are on terms of mutual friendship and collaboration. (In the centennial year of 1952 the virtual unification of the Universalists with the Unitarians was about to be ratified.) But with the Christians (who united with the Congregationalists in 1931) – with whose liberal elements the Unitarians were in close rapport and co-operation for three to four decades after 1826 – the relation today is one of friendliness and respect, but scarcely of such mutuality as can be measured by free pulpit exchange, dual ministerial fellowship, and organizational federation. An explanation of such surprising changes is essential to a right understanding of the evolution of Western Unitarianism.

Before 1826 or 1827 the liberalizing movement in the Society of Friends that Elias Hicks initiated was still under way in the West, into which Friends had migrated from Virginia and the Carolinas as soon as the Ordinance of 1787 guaranteed religious freedom and forbade slavery north of the Ohio River. Thereafter the local ("monthly") Meetings multiplied so rapidly that the regional Ohio Yearly Meeting was formed in 1812, the Indiana Yearly Meeting in 1821, the Iowa Yearly Meeting in 1843; and an educational central focus, Earlham College at Richmond, Indiana, was founded in 1844. By this time the opposition of Elias Hicks to creedalism and bibliolatry, which he made a definite issue at the Baltimore Yearly Meeting of 1817, had established itself strongly in the West, so that the Quakerism with which the early Unitarian missionaries and ministers there came into contact was popularly known as "Liberal." The liberalizing influence of Hicks was almost as potent in New England, where Emerson made its acquaintance in New Bedford. Moreover, the Friends' opposition to slavery dates well back into the eighteenth century and was continued particularly in their enlightened communities at Mount Pleasant, Ohio, west of Steubenville on the Ohio River, and at Fountain City in eastern Indiana. In Mount Pleasant, Benjamin Lundy transformed *The Philanthropist* of Charles Osborne, the first periodical in this country to advocate the abolition of slavery, into *The Genius of Universal Emancipation* which, transferred to Baltimore in 1827, employed William Lloyd Garrison and converted him as well. In 1826 in Fountain City, Levi Coffin inaugurated the "Underground Railroad," whose efficient organization eventually extended throughout the Ohio River valley and up to the outlet cities on the Great Lakes, an undertaking in which many Western Unitarians co-operated.

Considering these many points of sympathy, even of affinity, as well as the encouragement and hospitality shown Unitarian missionaries in such centers as Wheeling, West Virginia, and Steubenville, Ohio, the aloofness of the Unitarian leaders in the East can only be explained on the ground that, owing to the absence of preaching ministers in the Meetings as well as other conventional ecclesiastical features, the Society of Friends was not taken seriously as a liberal religious organization.

More serious reasons account for the lack of fellowship and co-operation with the Universalists, whose movement was well advanced in New England, New York state, and northern Ohio before the Unitarians appeared on the scene. Like the Unitarians, the Universalists could claim the distinction of having been for a millennium and a half of Christian history a severely persecuted heresy. Through the influence of his *Treatise on Atonement* (1805), Hosea Ballou divested the Universalist movement in Philadelphia and New England of every trace of Calvinism, including the doctrines of the Trinity, the vicarious sacrificial Atonement, the eternal alienation of the non-elect, unregenerate sinner from God, and his punishment in the fires of hell. In the Universalist Profession of Faith, adopted in 1803, its adherents affirmed the ultimate reunion of all mankind in the forgiving love of the One God and Father, whose nature is manifested in the divine goodness of his Son, Jesus Christ, "who will finally restore the whole family of mankind to holiness and happiness." To us moderns the general purport, if not the specific premises of such a version of Christianity seems eminently humane, optimistic, and consistent with the universal compassion of the Man of Nazareth. The early Unitarians, however, retained enough of their old Calvinistic legalism and Puritan authoritarianism to cause them to object severely to the omission of any condign and terrifying punishment for unrepentant sinners. Ballou, anticipating Emerson's theory of Compensation by thirty years, taught that the sinner is punished in this present life by the forfeiture of the supreme happiness that comes with holiness; in his next he would be given another chance to learn that the only true happiness is the holiness required by God and exemplified by Jesus Christ. Ballou could not conceive how an infinitely loving God could inflict eternal torment on a frail human being, regenerate or unregenerate. He found plenty of texts in the New Testament to support this view – although there are just as many to refute it! Lest, however, such a denial of hell-fire should encourage sinners – and saints, as well – to lapse into moral anarchy, the Winchester Profession, and Universalist preachers generally, urged that "believers ought to be careful to maintain order and practice good works."

Since the time of Tertullian, however, the Christian Church has made the claim that by right divine it was the aid and adjunct of the state in maintaining private and public morality – the spiritual policeman of the *forum internum*. This was the major premise of all state churches, of which the Standing Order of Massachusetts was one until its abrogation in 1833. Scarcely without exception, therefore, the Unitarian clergy – and leading laymen –

joined with the Trinitarian Calvinists to condemn the Universalists as allies of Satan; Universalist churches were "the Devil's insurance offices."

To make matters worse, the early New England Universalists were recruited from the country and small-town folk chiefly, and took the political position of Jeffersonian anti-Federalists; the early New England Unitarians were notoriously committed to Federalism. Not until the issue of Federalism faded and, concomitantly, a distaste for social obloquy moved sundry Universalist ministers about 1830 to oppose Ballou's theories with "Restorationism" did Unitarian hostility begin to moderate; for the new position rehabilitated the "sanctions of morality" by conceding the possibility of a few millennia of torture for reprobates before God regarded them as worthy of restoration to his favor!

The changing attitudes of the Eastern Unitarians were of course carried into the West by missionaries and periodicals. Ballou Universalism made rapid progress in New York state and northern Ohio, whose State Association was organized in 1821; those of Indiana and of Illinois came in 1837. In the latter state there were thirty Universalist churches in 1850 to eight Unitarian. Eventually the lack of tested and trained ministers retarded seriously the further spread of Universalism. Although as the years passed the number of Universalist students in the Unitarian seminary at Meadville increased, it was not until 1850 and later that the theological affinities of the two denominations began to assert themselves and the early hostility turned into amity and co-operation.

Even more anomalous than their aloofness from the Friends and their censoriousness toward the Universalists was the sympathetic interest of the Unitarians in the Christians after 1825 and their undiscourageable efforts to work with the latter in educational projects. The enigma is underscored by the fact that the Christian movement began, as had Universalism, right under the noses of the Unitarians of northern and western New England, in virtually the same years and social classes, and that it was equally anti-Federalist and anti-Calvinist. Abner Jones, a former Baptist revival preacher, came to reject the doctrines of the Trinity and Predestination and on this broader basis organized a church of his followers at Lyndon, New Hampshire, in 1801; he called it a "Christian" congregation in token of their repudiation of sectarianism and creeds. Elias Smith, previously a Congregationalist, later a vehement critic of the Standing Order clericalism, with its title of "Reverend," its gown and bands, its social pretensions, joined Jones in 1803, and founded *The Herald of Gospel Liberty* in 1805; by 1814 a Christian Church was organized in Boston. The new reformation spread swiftly across the Green Mountains and the western lakes into New York state where a General Conference was held in 1820, followed by the demarcation of local conferences which extended, by 1840, to the Mississippi River. As an indication of the general character and tendencies of these New Testament Christians, their convention of 1827 condemned both Universalism and instrumental music in church services!

Meanwhile there had been developing another "Christian" movement in Kentucky and the Ohio River valley. Barton W. Stone, a Presbyterian revival preacher of great effectiveness, came to the conclusion that the doubts he had felt at his ordination concerning the Trinity, election, and reprobation were the promptings of the Holy Spirit; he was forthwith dismissed by his Presbytery. Soon after he joined other revivalists in forming the Christian Church of Cane Ridge, Kentucky – the very place where the famous camp meeting of 1801 was held! *En passant* we recall that since the days of George Whitefield (about 1740) the liberal precursors of Unitarianism had been firmly opposed to the "enthusiasm of revivals." After Barton W. Stone had brought himself to accept adult baptism as the Scriptural requirement for Christian church membership, the inroads made by his views in the ranks of the Calvinist Baptists of Ohio, Indiana, and Kentucky were impressive. But Stone's chief emphasis was on Christian Union, by which he meant the abandonment of all sectarian tenets and names; "Unitarian" was no more acceptable to him than to Channing! Of his ideal catholic Christianity the main principles were the following: Christ as the only Head of the Church; the sufficiency of the plain Scriptures as the sole, divine source of Christian truth; the centrality of Christian character and conduct for church membership and the pulpit message;

frequent and unrestricted celebration of the Lord's Supper, with no sacramental interpretations.

Since for over thirty years the Unitarians, especially in the West, were closely colligated with the Christians, as an official missionary policy, it is well that we know and ponder their thought and ways. Of equal relevance are their requirements for the ministry, beginning with a licensed evangelist: a conversion experience, habitual piety, an ardor to save souls, a fluent knowledge of the Bible, ability and willingness to support himself and to devote his spare time to itinerant evangelism. There were no educational tests even for the elders, who were temporarily elected to preside at the annual conferences and settle questions of ministerial and lay discipline. The Christians had neither regular ecclesiastical officials nor missionary funds. Their periodicals were organs of pious exhortation and missionary notes, without literary pretensions or theological disquisitions. In comparison with *The Christian Register, The Christian Examiner, The North American Review* of Unitarian provenance, the Christian publications were elementary – though sincere and kindly.

When the tocsin for open battle between the Trinitarian and the Unitarian Congregationalists in New England finally sounded in the economic implications of the Dedham Case decision of 1820, the Untiarians looked about for allies. Partly because of their delusion that the common people would gladly hear their rational, practical version of Christianity, partly owing to the taunts of the orthodox that theirs was an aristocratic movement, the Unitarians proceeded to inform themselves concerning the non-Trinitarian, anti-Calvinist Christians and to explore the feasibilities of co-operation with them, in New York state and the West. The sincere, warm-hearted, catholic piety of Barton W. Stone and his associates won the admiration and confidence of the Unitarian emissaries, particularly because Stone's Christology and general doctrinal position were singularly like Channing's. With this type of Christians both missionary and institutional co-operation seemed feasible; and had Stone's spirit and leadership remained in the ascendant, the later Unitarian-Christian relations might have been more trustful, fraternal, and constructive than they actually became. But in 1832 Alexander Campbell, the protagonist of the Disciples of Christ, appeared on the scene; by dint of his oratorical power, theological erudition, assertiveness, and executive efficiency he displaced gentle Barton Stone; he openly opposed the vague Unitarian Christology of Stone and the "Old Christians" of New York state and the East; he swept a majority of the Southern Christians into his own sect, with its Bethany College and seminary in West Virginia. The more liberal "Old Christians" remained on terms of generally friendly co-operation with the Unitarians, who went more than half-way in the joint ventures of founding the Meadville Theological School and of sustaining Antioch College. But a latent sensitiveness on the part of the Christians over Unitarian "intellectualism" – which developed into outright Fundamentalist opposition to the latter's open-mindedness to the Higher Criticism of the Bible – eventually nullified an *entente cordiale* from which the beginning, save for the transient rapport with Barton W. Stone, was essentially factitious and unsound.

Apart from the extensive missionary work of the Universalists, the Hicksite Friends, and the Christians, there were but two settlements west of the Allegheny Mountains where Unitarian churches had been established before 1826: the village of Barneveld in the central Mohawk Valley in New York state, and the thriving city of Pittsburgh at the forks of the Ohio River. Each of these churches owed its inception to foreign-born individuals who had suffered from state-church persecution in the Old World and who came to the New resolved to avail themselves of its opportunities of pioneer initiative and religious freedom.

The United Protestant Religious Society of Barneveld (1803)

After Congress had repaid loans made to it during our War of Independence by Amsterdam bankers, the latter formed the Holland Land Company and then purchased vast tracts of land in west central New York and western Pennsylvania. Their agent, Colonel Mappa, established his land office in a pleasant valley north of the present city of Utica, which he named Barneveld in honor of the Dutch liberal, Jan van Oldenbarneveld, a staunch friend of the Arminian Remonstrants against High Calvinism in the early 1600's. In 1803 Colonel Mappa and his close friends, Francis van der Kemp and Dr. Luther Guiteau, were prime movers in organizing the United Protestant Religious Society, which by 1806 felt strong enough to extend a call to Rev. John Sherman, a Congregationalist minister of Connecticut who had been extruded from his ministry for uttering Unitarian views. With Sherman's assistance, Articles of Association were framed for the church, whose Unitarian character is attested by the third Article which declares that "Liberty of conscience shall be preserved inviolate … every member shall be maintained in his right of free inquiry." For the next seven years, in spite of Sherman's self-denying labors, the existence of the Society was precarious, owing it its poverty and to the defection of some of its members who capitulated to the venomous attacks of the Calvinists. The able captaincy of Rev. I. B. Peirce – to whose aid in 1826 came the Secretary of the newly formed American Unitarian Association, Rev. Henry Ware, Jr. – enabled the little group to weather the storm of the Finney revival campaigns. He stayed at the helm with laudable devotion till 1840 and assured the Barneveld church of permanent existence in the quaint white structure of colonial design still in use.

[Unitarianism in Pennsylvania and the Middle Atlantic States]

The fact that British Unitarian friends of Van der Kemp sent contributions to the Barneveld church in its early years introduces us to the important role that the missionary zeal and theological views of Great Britain's most eminent Unitarian, the distinguished chemist Dr. Joseph Priestley, played in the founding of churches not only on the Atlantic seaboard but in western Pennsylvania – even as far down the Ohio River valley as English Prairie in Illinois. This venture, though of small moment in our history, deserves notice because undertaken by an Englishman of the Priestley school of Unitarian thought, George Flower. About 1820, to confute objections by frontier revivalists to their settlement as infidel and godless, Flower built a Unitarian chapel where he or his friends read Priestley's sermons to a more or less attentive audience; while his associate, Morris Birkbeck, held Common Prayer services in an Episcopalian church nearby.

Of no such dilettante character, however, was the formation of the Unitarian church of Pittsburgh, Pennsylvania, in 1820 by a circle of British Unitarians. It had its Colonel Mappa in the person of Benjamin Bakewell, a pioneer manufacturer of flint glass; its John Sherman in [John] Campbell, a [British]

Unitarian minister and, like his friend Dr. Priestley, a scientist of high merit. His public lectures on astronomy augmented the appeal of his preaching to such effect that in 1823 a neat brick chapel was erected in the heart of Pittsburgh. Shortly afterward a friend of Bakewell, the Western agent of the Holland Land Company, Harm Jan Huidekoper, came down the Allegheny River to Pittsburgh from his home in Meadville, Pennsylvania, and was taken to hear [John Campbell] preach. Huidekoper was so impressed by the preacher's argument for the *duty* as well as the right of independent study of the Scriptures that when he went home to Meadville he promptly put the sermon into practice – with the result that after [Campbell's] death in 1824 his spirit went on to greater creation in the Unitarian church and Theological School in Meadville that Huidekoper led in founding. But the Pittsburgh congregation, unable to secure a preacher equal to Dr. Sherman, finally withered and died in the sulphurous air of Presbyterian Pittsburgh. The present vigorous Unitarian church there dates from 1890.

Joseph Priestley, motivated largely by his abhorrence of the reactionary, persecuting Church of England, was – like Rev. William Hazlitt, who had visited Boston in 1784 and converted the Episcopal congregation of King's Chapel to Unitarian views – a forth-putting, not a passive, Unitarian. Scarcely had he arrived in Philadelphia than he instigated the founding of the First Church of Unitarian Christians – the earliest to bear the Unitarian name in this country. No sooner had he built his house on his estate in Northumberland, Pennsylvania, than he gathered a small congregation of family and friends about him – of which the present Priestley Memorial Church is a continuance. Had the great minister-scientist not been halted and disheartened by the extension of the political antagonism of the New England Federalists to his theological views, he might have communicated something of his missionary zeal to them. Save, however, for the tacit appreciation of such liberals in New England as William Bentley and Professor Andrews Norton of Harvard, Priestley got neither hospitality nor sympathy from New England. Had he not been made an (honorary) Citizen of the French Republic – even though this had been done in the period before the Terror? Was not Thomas Jefferson his friend? For his theological system they cared as little. His "Socinian" conception of Jesus Christ as a perfect human being rather than a sort of secondary Deity (Arianism); of the human will as bound in the cosmic chain of cause and effect unless liberated by its recognizance of its divine nature, reason, and freedom; of death as an everlasting sleep, unless and until the First Great Cause, the universal, all-benevolent Providence, should determine at Judgment Day to re-create the personality unto eternal life – all these ingenious, though earnest, hypotheses for the reconciliation of the physical science of that day with Christianity only accentuated the disapproval of him.

With the political changes after 1815, dramatized by the friendly correspondence of John Adams with Thomas Jefferson, and followed by the coming of many British Unitarians to the Middle Atlantic seaports, the situation was altered, for the latter were disciples of Britain's Channing-like Theophilus Lindsey rather than of Priestley. A group of such immigrants in Baltimore, convened and liberally financed by Henry Payson, organized the First Independent Christ's Church in 1816 and called on Rev. James Freeman of King's Chapel, Boston, to dedicate their imposing new building. To their ministry they called a protégé of Freeman and of Professor Andrews Norton of Harvard – Jared Sparks. His historic ordination by Channing and a constellation of New England liberal divines marked not only the *rapprochement* of the New England with the British Unitarians but also the transfer to the former of the missionary vision and impulse of the Priestley and Lindsey tradition. The Baltimore ordination was the first missionary sortie of New England Unitarianism beyond its native soil.

A fitting culmination of these developments was Jared Sparks' persuasion of Thomas Jefferson to ally himself explicitly with the Unitarian movement – a decision now commemorated by the Thomas Jefferson Memorial Unitarian Church in Charlottesville, Virginia.

CHAPTER TWO

New England Unitarianism Organizes for Missionary Work

ON MAY 26, 1825, THE CONSTITUTION of the American Unitarian Association was adopted in the vestry of the Federal Street Church in Boston, of which the "great Dr. Channing" was minister. The meeting consisted largely of clergymen to whom Rev. Henry Ware, Jr., had presented a proposal the day before for

... a new organization ... the chief and ultimate object [of which] will be the promotion of pure and undefiled religion by disseminating the knowledge of it where adequate means of religious instruction are not now enjoyed. Its operations will extend themselves throughout the whole country [and] will chiefly consist of the publication and distribution of tracts and the support of missionaries.

Though there were many opponents of such action among the older clergy and laity, who distrusted the move as a rash project of theological sectarianism, they were either absent from the meeting or abstained from voting, for the proposals were adopted unanimously; their phraseology was virtually repeated in the Constitution, save for the substitution of "pure Christianity" for "religion" and the references to the distribution of tracts and the support of missionaries:

(2) The objects of this Association shall be to diffuse the knowledge and promote the interests of pure Christianity throughout our country.
(3) Unitarian Christians throughout the United States shall be invited to unite and co-operate with this Association.

The reiteration of the national scope of the new Association in both the Proposals and the Constitution as adopted is significant. It represents a transcendence of New England provincialism by the young men who pushed the project through –

20

Henry Ware, Jr., Ezra Stiles Gannett, James Walker, John Pierpont, Samuel Barrett – all of them ministers of Boston churches.
All of them, moreover, had been students in the Harvard Divinity School of Professor Andrews Norton, the editor of that
outspoken defender of liberal Christianity, *The General Repository
and Review* (1812), whose articles on the progress of infidelity in
this country are strongly reminiscent of the forebodings of Dr.
Priestley in his many writings after his arrival in this country in
1794: "I find nothing but the extremes of infidelity and bigoted
orthodoxy … there is something very remarkable about the
progress of infidelity in this country …Volney and Dupuis are
read everywhere."

Priestley's Missionary Zeal

The Calvinist Congregationalists and the Princeton Presbyterians thought so, too, and blamed such progress – as well as the
decline in church-going, the increase of popular political radicalism, even the relaxation of Puritan moral standards – on the
liberals of Boston and Harvard. Priestley, however, had held
"the absurdities of orthodoxy" responsible for such indifference
and irreligion, and argued that if Christianity could be freed
from its "corruptions," of which he regarded the dogma of
the Trinity as progenitor to all the rest, the intelligent leaders of
society would return to the faith and thus, by example and pre-
cept, reform morality. Acting on this belief, he had no sooner
landed in New York (1794) than he envisaged founding a
Unitarian church there; in fact he later encouraged an abortive
attempt by an Englishman, John Butler. In Philadelphia he had
inspired, as we have seen, the formation of the First Society of
Unitarian Christians by a group of young Englishmen whom
he persuaded to try the experiment of a wholly lay ministry
(including the administration of baptism and the Lord's Supper).
In Northumberland, Pennsylvania, in 1800, he had organized a
society in his own library, with preaching and an adult Bible-study
class. In fact, this Unitarian evangelist practically pigeonholed
his scientific studies in his later years!

But the birthright New England liberal, John Adams, who
while Vice-President had been a cordial, regular attendant on
Dr. Priestley's preaching, in 1794 and 1795 quietly stopped

coming! His action is representative of the Federalist disapproval of the honorary Citizen of the French Republic. It connoted, also, a distaste for Dr. Priestley's brand of forthright, proselytizing Unitarianism, with its socially pernicious doctrine that even for unrepentant sinners death is just a long sleep – not a slow roast. Priestley died in 1804; but Federalist dislike of his ideas lingered as long as Federalism itself was a vital issue. By 1825 circumstances had so altered that the dynamic Priestley spirit seemed timely. The conservatives had taken the offensive; they were denouncing the liberals as Unitarians and then defining Unitarianism as infidelity or Deism. After the Dedham Case decision in 1820, which gave possession of the church buildings and other property to the liberals if they were in a majority, they began to withdraw from the old town churches to form separate Calvinist churches of their own. Priestley's own voice is heard in John Pierpont's ringing words: "We have and must have the Unitarian name. Organization is necessary to maintain it and organization there must be!"

Moreover, it was Priestley's own rationale of the function of Unitarian Christianity that furnished the stimulus of the new missionary Association. Long years of quiet indoctrination by Professor Andrews Norton of his Divinity School students explain why they voted so unanimously for the Association. While Norton never accepted Priestley's theology, he had made his own Priestley's thesis that rational Christianity could and must serve as a *via media* between Calvinism and infidelity, between fanaticism and skepticism, so as to save the superior minds in every area of social leadership from irreligion – which, in his logic, inevitably entailed moral cynicism, with all its potentialities of ruling-class tyranny and licentiousness, of lower-class revolution, vice, and crime. To the highly intellectualized Norton, religious conviction meant rational persuasion, first of all; its expression was in words, written and spoken. To Channing, religion meant exalted, expansive feeling; its primary form of expression was in conduct. "Pure Christianity" signified for him a quality and way of life rather than a verbal formula. Besides, he knew only too well, from the history of Christianity, that the opinionated theologian could be as intolerant and imperious as the mercenary ecclesiastic or his dupes, the superstitious, fanatic crowd. To Channing, therefore, and far more to some of the older clergy and laymen, the drive of Norton's students to form the Association suggested theological sectarianism in the making. In 1825 Channing was much more interested in the project of Dr. Tuckerman for a Ministry to the Poor of Boston; by 1826 he had succeeded in persuading the new Association to adopt it as a "Domestic Mission."

[Early Missionary Efforts of the American Unitarian Association]
It is imperative for a right understanding of the difficulties of the Association from the very first in raising money for missionary work that the objections of the "Old Liberals" to sectarianism should be explained. They conceived of their churches and themselves as parts of what was until 1833, nominally at least, a state church (the "Standing Order"), seceders from which, like Baptists, Universalists, *et id omne genus*, were lopsided "sectarians." Their liberal views they regarded as merely left-wing Congregationalism; indeed, there are many Unitarians in New England today who like to think of themselves as "Liberal Congregationalists" – the cognomen which Rev. Samuel K. Lothrop, president of the Association from 1851 to 1858, avowedly preferred to "Unitarian." Moreover, long experience with bitter Calvinist wranglings over abstruse doctrines had taught them to distrust all doctrinal controversy, since it distracted attention from Christ's main emphases: righteousness and love in *life*, not just *words*. Channing himself, contrary to the impression given by theology-minded church historians, very rarely preached doctrinal sermons of a Unitarian cast; and when he did he made it entirely clear that his end – the Christian life – was more important than his means – a theology reformed back to "pure," that is, non-Trinitarian, even pre-Pauline, simplicity and practicality. So strong were such objections to "sectarianism" that the Executive Committee of the new Association saw fit to circularize in the winter of 1825-26 the conciliatory assurance that

…We value our doctrines only so far as they evidently are the revelation of the will and character of God and so far as they tend to improve the religious, moral and intellectual condition of mankind … The great end of this Association is the promotion of pure morals and practical piety.

Nevertheless, the militant motor force of the organization was expressed not by the last sentence of this declaration but by the first; and such doctrinal evangelism, so akin to that of Priestley, was inspired by Professor Andrews Norton acting through his closest disciples and former students – Henry Ware, Jr. (his successor in the Divinity School faculty in 1830), and Ezra Stiles Gannett, Channing's colleague. Norton was elected first chairman of the Executive Committee; Ware later took his place; Gannett acted as Secretary for the first six years. In fact, all the Secretaries of the Association until about 1870 were former students of Norton. The first missionaries to the West were likewise his students – notably Ephraim Peabody, James Freeman Clarke, W. G. Eliot, Jr., George W. Hosmer, John Pierpont.

"Tracts ... missionaries ... throughout the whole country!" The Executive Committee lost no time in implementing these objectives as best it could with small means. Henry Ware, Jr., was the author of the first tract published, *The Faith Once Delivered to the Saints*, a masterly exposition of Norton's Lockean Unitarianism. To the only visible missionary in action, the Priestleyan James Kay in Northumberland, the committee granted one hundred dollars and the same amount to the Harrisburg society for a church building. To satisfy much mutual curiosity between Christians and Unitarians and to make an unbiased estimate of promising places for Unitarian missionary work, a sturdy theological student from Cambridge, Moses G. Thomas, was dispatched on a five-month "mission of inquiry" to the West.

After traveling between four and five thousand miles through twelve states, covering half this distance on horseback, Thomas rendered his report in the fall of 1826. It is the first of three such surveys made over a period of twenty-five years (Secretary Briggs' in 1837, Secretary Holland's in 1850 follow the pattern); it not only is interesting as a colorful frontier travelogue but approves itself as the product of a percipient and shrewd yet honest and tolerant mind with a deep instinct for genuine religion such as he found among the Christians: "I never was among a class of Christians who better lived up to their profession!"

More relevant to our purpose are his recommendations as to "towns and cities favorable to missionary efforts ... where the establishment of Unitarian preachers would be most useful to the cause of religion." Listing these places according to the

degree of confidence he felt in each, we have: Cincinnati, Steubenville, and Marietta, in Ohio; Paris and Louisville, in Kentucky;
Pittsburgh, Pennsylvania; St. Louis and St. Charles, in Missouri.
The eastern part of Indiana and the southern part of Ohio were
recommended for further investigation, since both sections were
dotted with flourishing settlements of liberal folk. Since Thomas
used the Ohio River valley as an axis of his explorations, he
penetrated no farther to the north than Vandalia, Illinois, and
Indianapolis, Indiana, the state capitals, and Cleveland, Ohio,
which he thought "important only for its local situation." He
did not visit Meadville, the most promising place of all at that
time in the West.

Throughout the report, apart from his warm enthusiasm over
the Christians, Thomas displays the shrewd perspicuity and cool
caution of a Yankee business prospector. Not even to the hospitable Christians did he once preach a sermon! Was this reticence
due to orders from the Association or to the traditional diffidence
of a theological student? In any case, his advice to young or older
ministers considering the missionary field is amazingly prescient
of the future's major problems:

> Because I have mentioned the foregoing places as favorable for mission-
> ary efforts I would have no person think that a preacher would immediately
> step into a fine meeting house or into ample means of support or even into
> a church already organized; but rather into places where some have neglected
> religion because they have heard it presented in a manner repugnant to their
> reason and their conscience, others because they have seen it made a matter
> of "experiences," confessions and creeds, an austere, exclusive and gloomy
> system; into places were one must labor as becometh a minister of the gospel
> and reap the reward of his labors in seeing a church grow up around him.
> Preachers at first may promise themselves hearers in all these places but it
> will depend on their own powers whether they interest and retain them.

Nothing seems to have been done for more than a year to
develop the opportunities suggested, not even in Pittsburgh or
Steubenville or Marietta, which were not so *very* far west! One
reason undoubtedly was the lack of funds, due to the continuing
attack on the Association as a sectarian agency. Another explanation lies in the small number of men graduating yearly from "the
school in Cambridge, to which the Unitarian churches almost
invariably look for a supply." By the autumn of 1828, however,

the reaction produced by the Finney revivals in New York state coupled with the opening of the Erie Canal and the consequent stimulus to emigration from New England into the cities along its course, brought Henry Ware, Jr., of Boston, and his brother, William Ware, minister of the First Congregational Unitarian Society of New York City, to preach in such promising centers as Utica, Watertown, Ogdensburg, Buffalo, and Rochester. In the last city, Rochester, William Ware's message was so convincing, and a young man from Massachusetts, Rev. James D. Green, came and preached so effectively, that a First Unitarian Congregational Society was formed on March 16, 1829, and a call was extended to Green. He declined the call, however. Although the new Society at great sacrifice bought a church building, it had no better luck with two other ministers, so that by the end of the year 1830 the church building had to be sold. The story of the continuance of Unitarian preaching in Rochester by a devoted and gifted layman must be reserved for the following chapter.

The Calvinist attack on Unitarianism had been growing in divisiveness and bitterness ever since the decision of the Supreme Court of Massachusetts that the theology of a religious society was determined by the vote of the majority of its supporters, to whom on the same principle the church property belonged and the choice of ministers as well. The withdrawal of the Trinitarians to form new churches resulted in controversy and recrimination, which were exacerbated by the financial strain involved in supporting two churches instead of one. Furthermore the American Home Missionary Society (1826), controlled largely by Connecticut Calvinists, was sending ministers into Massachusetts to aid in the formation of the new Trinitarian churches, an objective that could only be attained by fostering sectarian bigotry and hostility toward the Unitarians. The latter's resentment and concern reached a climax in the Association's annual meeting of 1829, in Channing's dramatic defiance of such Calvinist attacks – a theme that was continued in his sermon "Spiritual Freedom" in 1830:

> There is a coalition extending far and wide to put Unitarianism down. A voice has gone forth from this city to distant parts of the country, that the Unitarians *must* and *should be, put down*; that men of property [are]

willing to sacrifice it to this object and that distant parts must in some way or other lend a helping hand. No political coalition was ever formed among us of a more determined character than this religious one. Let this engine once succeed and what security have we against similar conspiracies to crush other opinions?

Channing's protest, particularly its references to the aggressions of Trinitarianism in "distant parts of our country," was as catalytic in its effect as had been his Baltimore Sermon of a decade before. Forthright, militant, eloquent John Pierpont went to the West, accompanied by a publication agent of the Association, Frederick T. Gray; and as result of Pierpont's successful meetings, the First Congregational Church of Cincinnati was incorporated on January 21, 1830 – the term "Unitarian" having been omitted in deference to the objections of the well-known author Timothy Flint, a former Presbyterian missionary. Then Pierpont went down the river to Louisville, and again his earnestness and eloquence moved a group of expatriate New Englanders – some of them former students of Dr. Holley of Transylvania University – and Old Englanders as well, to organize the First Unitarian Society on July 3, 1830, with Secretary Bernard Whitman of the Association as mentor, not only for this action but for the building of a handsome neo-Doric church.

No wonder that Pierpont and Gray reported optimistically on their Western reconnaissance to the Association's meeting in May, 1830. Pierpont offered a resolution:

That in the opinion of this Association the country lying west of the Allegheny Mountains presents a field for missionary labors peculiarly interesting and encouraging to Unitarian Christians.

In support of the resolution he made the observation that

… Society in the Western country is marked by strong features … They are direct and prompt in their intellectual movements. They are further distinguished by intellectual activity and energy. Freedom of religious inquiry is encouraged. *They* will examine and understand and appreciate our faith!

CHAPTER THREE

Starting Churches and Settling Ministers along the Ohio River and Mississippi River Axis

"LIBERTY, HOLINESS AND LOVE" was the motto devised by Rev. Henry Ware, Jr., for the new Unitarian Association. Since "Christo et Ecclesiae" was the traditional battle cry of the conservatives, the summarization of the principles and objectives of the new Unitarian movement in secular terms was unique; it was likewise practical. Ware sought to correct any notion that the Unitarians were a sect concerned rather with theological beliefs, than with Christian character and life. Theological contentions were not overlooked but subordinated to moral values. Fifty years later the Western Unitarian Conference was similarly to state its faith in three words: "Freedom, Fellowship and Character in Religion" – equivalent in practical purport with those of 1826 but with a different theological underpinning – with what results later chapters will reveal. But in 1826 *The Christian Register* cordially adopted "Liberty, Holiness and Love" for its editorial caption; and it became a denominational slogan for over three decades.

"Liberty" denoted the right and duty of free inquiry in religion, especially in the interpretation of the New Testament; the liberty to reject traditional doctrines of the Christian Church as reason and conscience dictated; the liberty to welcome new wisdom and knowledge, to create new concepts of truth, goodness, and beauty as the Spirit led. Such powerful sanction for spiritual liberty as expressed by Channing in his "Remarks on National Literature" (1824) and his sermon on "Spiritual Freedom" (1830), as well as by Emerson in "The American Scholar" (1837), proved a mighty stimulus to the rapid liberation, expansion, and progress of the New England mind which gave its literary activities and educational institutions national leadership up to 1850. Rev. Samuel Gilman, the Unitarian minister at Charleston, South Carolina, immortalized this challenge to spiritual liberty in the second stanza of his Harvard Bicentennial Ode (1836):

Let not moss-covered error moor thee by its side
As the world on Truth's current glides by;
Be the herald of light and the bearer of love
Till the stock of the Puritans die.

"Holiness" betokened the Unitarian emphasis on Christian character as the goal, the fruit of the true piety, attainable by all repentant, aspiring souls, not solely by the small minority of the Calvinist elect.

"Love" in the sense of universal human sympathy and beneficence was not admissible according to High Calvinism. Love could properly exist only among the elect, regenerate "saints" on earth. The non-elect, unregenerate sinners were beyond the pale of sympathy or charity. Channing's insistence on the spiritual dignity and perfectibility of every human soul, however lowly or degraded, as well as on the Christian's duty to emulate Christ in helping and healing the poor, the bruised, the blind, the bound, was not only consonant with American democracy but a veritable *reveille* to the New England conscience. In direct opposition to Calvinism he did indeed "breathe a humane spirit into theology"; he breathed it also into the hearts and minds of men and women who proceeded to pioneer in much-needed social work and reforms. Rev. Joseph Tuckerman inaugurated the Ministry to the Poor (later known as the Ministry at Large), the precursor of modern social work; Samuel Gridley Howe modernized and humanized the care and training of the blind, deaf, and dumb; Dorothea Dix performed the same service for criminals and the insane.

In the cities of the East, particularly of New England, where slums and the poverty, unemployment, misery, and degradation of the "lower classes" were obtrusive problems, such practical humanitarianism soon became a distinctive feature of the Unitarian message and church life. In the West, however, where such unfortunate conditions had not yet developed, Unitarianism was at first identified with advanced intellectual culture – a characteristic manifested not only in high standards of sermonic thought and literary production but in the promotion of popular education through a free, non-sectarian public-school system and the encouragement of Lyceum lectures, public libraries, and evening classes for working people.

The Association's first missionary prospector in the West, Moses G. Thomas, had reported such intellectual interests in Louisville, where he had found a "number of literary men who entertain liberal views of religion [but] at present seldom attend any church." From persons of the same type in Cincinnati he found encouraging response. Mrs. Trollope, who must at least have known of John Pierpont's preaching if she did not hear him, gave a similar estimate of the Unitarians in her witty description of the denominations in Cincinnati: "The Methodists are regarded as the most pious; the Presbyterians as the most powerful; the Episcopalians as the most stylish; the Universalists as the most liberal; the Swedenborgians as the most musical; the Quakers as the most amiable; the Unitarians as the most enlightened."

In general, the organization of Unitarian churches in the West was motivated by one or both of the following desires: (a) to refute by pulpit message, Bible-study classes, and the distribution of liberal literature the attacks and abuses of revivalist fanaticism and obscurantism; (b) to provide a fellowship and to support preaching committed not only to Unitarian views of Christian truth but to high standards of intellectual culture and uncircumscribed works of charity and general social betterment. Progress in such church organization centered in (a) the larger cities on the Ohio River axis of travel to the Mississippi; (b) the Erie Canal and Great Lakes axis to the Mississippi; (c) Meadville, Pennsylvania, where Harm Jan Huidekoper was a miniature Unitarian Association in himself.

The First Congregational Church of Cincinnati [1830]

To show his continuing interest in the Cincinnati movement, and perhaps also as a salute to the literary *forte* of the members, John Pierpont sent a ten-stanza ode for the dedication of its neo-Gothic building, May 23, 1830. The Association sent one of its militant younger ministers, Rev. Bernard Whitman of Waltham, to give the sermon. Heading the list of subscribers to a "covenant of communicants in the Lord's Supper," which affirmed belief in "Jesus Christ the Son of God, exalted to be Prince and Savior, Mediator between God and Man," was Timothy Flint, a Harvard graduate who had been a Presbyterian missionary on the lower Mississippi, then left the ministry and became a noted novelist, geographer, historian of the West, and editor of the admirable but short-lived *Western Monthly Review*. Nathan Guilford, a lawyer and bookseller who played a leading part in getting state taxation for a public school system, was another signer of the covenant. Dr. Daniel Drake, the "Franklin of the West," an indefatigable promoter of medical science and the Lyceum movement, was not a signer, though a regular attendant and supporter of the Society.

In fact, the language of the covenant was so much more conservative than the original basis of organization drawn up by Rev. Charles Briggs of the Association that we can sense the existence from the first of a more or less serious theological tension between those who construed Unitarianism as the "pure" (that is, the only Scriptural, rational) form of supranaturalist Christianity, and those who deemed it the highest extant form of natural religion, "pure and undefiled." Comparing the covenant's definitely creedal language with Flint's general remarks on religion in the *Western Monthly Review* for that very month of May, it appears that he may well have held the "salutary superstition" theory: that for the sub-philosophic minds which need to have spiritual and ethical truths given them in oracular, personalized, mythical, and mystical forms, liberal Christianity is the most practical medium. It was with such "pragmatic" Christianity of the Locke-Norton type of apologetic that the Transcendentalists, notably Emerson and Parker, took issue on the ground that it was not only intellectually untenable but dishonest as well. The Lord's Supper was inaugurated and the covenant drawn up by the church's first minister, E. B. Hall, a young graduate of the Divinity School, who went back east after eight months; but the discord within the society was not so easily disposed of.

After a year of pulpit supplies and candidates, another young

Harvard graduate was called, Ephraim Peabody; and as if to re-emphasize the Association's concern for the welfare and prestige of the Cincinnati church, two outstanding Boston preachers came to install him – James Walker, later president of Harvard, and Francis Parkman, father of the historian. Peabody stayed for four years. There followed two years more of supplies and candidates. The situation was growing ominous when James Handasyd Perkins, a young layman of the church, joined with James Freeman Clarke of Louisville and W. G. Eliot, Jr., Unitarian minister in St. Louis, to persuade their magnetically eloquent and incorrigibly visionary friend William Henry Channing – nephew of the great Dr. Channing – to venture west. His sermonic cascades of classic diction and poetic imagery packed the church; but his efforts to solve the problem of the Lord's Supper by transferring the rite to Sunday afternoon and organizing the communicants as a "Church of Christian Brethren" for charity relief planning – the main interest of his friend Perkins – were not so well received. Still less so were his vehement attacks on alcoholism and slavery. When he voted for Cincinnati's stormy petrel of anti-slavery agitation, James G. Birney, editor of *The Philanthropist* and author of *The American Churches the Bulwarks of American Slavery* (1840), there was so much criticism that Channing resigned and returned to the East.

At this juncture Channing's friend of boyhood days in Massachusetts stepped into the breach. From ethical scruples James Handasyd Perkins had abandoned a mercantile career with his uncle, Colonel Thomas Perkins (founder of the Perkins Institute for the Blind), and had come west to go into farming. In Cincinnati he had been persuaded to try the law, had initially done well – and then had abandoned that vocation from ethical scruples! With high respect for a young man of such talent yet such unworldly conscientiousness, the trustees of the Unitarian church offered him the position of Minister to the Poor (later called Minister at Large) – though he was not an ordained clergyman and had never had ministerial training. "Gladly will I consecrate my life to this ministry," he told them; and his success in administering and organizing charity relief work in Cincinnati substantiated their confidence and his pledge. As in the case of Robert Collyer two decades later in Chicago, who also began as Minister

THE OHIO RVER AND MISSISSIPPI RIVER AXIS

to the Poor, Mr. Perkins was drawn by his devoted friends into the full ministry of the church (1841-48). Like Robert Collyer, again, his sermonic power and literary talent were the natural outflow of "a lighted mind and a loving heart." When he died in 1849 he left a strong and united church to Rev. Abiel Livermore.

The latter was not only a winning preacher but an adroit organizer, as his conduct of the inaugural meetings of the Western Unitarian Conference in 1852 demonstrated. Though Livermore was as unequivocally opposed to slavery, war, and intemperance as Channing before him, his sermons were persuasive rather than peremptory. In the same spirit he tried to extinguish the smoldering strife between conservatives and radicals by rallying most of the members around the original bond of union that committed them merely to "believe in the Christian Revelation and the cause of pure and undefiled religion." Like his neighbors, Eliot in St. Louis and [J. H.] Heywood in Louisville, and in keeping with their efforts to interpret Unitarianism primarily in terms of Christian unity and charity, Livermore increased the religious and philanthropic activities of the church to their highest point for four decades. His successor, Moncure D. Conway (1855-62), though fully maintaining the church's traditions of pulpit and literary excellence, was a forthright Parkerite as well as a militant Abolitionist. As a result, the conservatives drew apart in 1859 to organize the Church of the Redeemer, calling to its ministry Rev. A. D. Mayo, a staunch believer in Christian miracles, evidences, and sanctions. Rev. Thomas Vickers, on the other hand, the new minister of the "Old First," accepted the anthropogenic origin of religion and ethics, the Higher Criticism of the Bible, and evolution. Not until 1876 were the two churches reunited under the leadership of Rev. Charles W. Wendte.

The First Unitarian Society of Louisville (1830)

After dedicating the new Cincinnati church in May, 1830, Rev. Bernard Whitman, the Association's emissary, went down the river to Louisville and made a round of calls on certain individuals who had been deeply inspired by John Pierpont the preceding autumn. Some of them had been students of Dr. Horace Holley, president of Transylvania University in Lexington,

and had greatly resented his forced resignation under Presbyterian attacks on his liberal views. Others were editors (Fortu-
natus Cosby, Jr.), lawyers (Judge S. S. Nicholas, Judge Henry
Pirtle), industrialists (S. S. Goodwin), educators (Mann Butler).
With George W. Merriwether as chairman and S. S. Goodwin
as secretary, the Society was organized on July 3, 1830, and a
church built after a year and more of money-raising and hearing
candidates. Then down the river from Cincinnati and Peabody's
installation came James Walker and Frances Parkman to dedicate
the trim neo-Doric brick structure. Their first minister, a young
and delicate Harvard Divinity School graduate, Rev. George
Chapman, wrestled for about a year with the task of wringing
two sermons a week out of his soul, then went back to Boston.
Then the church appealed to Whitman in Waltham to send them
another skipper – a sturdy and staying one, if the Society was
to survive!

Whitman's choice was momentous for Western Unitarianism. He selected from the School's graduating class of that
year a young Boston Brahmin, James Freeman Clarke, the foster
grandson of James Freeman, first Unitarian rector of King's
Chapel. With his brothers William, Abram, and Samuel, who
later followed him to the West, he was destined to do more for
the extension of Unitarianism to the Mississippi than any other
person before Jenkin Lloyd Jones. The first sermon he ever wrote
he preached in the Waltham church on the text "Whatsoever thy
hand findeth to do ..."; in the afternoon of the same day he
was ordained, Henry Ware, Jr., making the Prayer; and within a
week he was on his way, by stage from Boston to Providence,
steamboat to New York, steam carriage to Philadelphia, stage
to Baltimore, stage over the mountains to Wheeling, steamboat
to Louisville.

For six years (1833-40) he worked in Louisville with not
much encouragement. Though Clarke, by nature and principle,
was too democratic and genuine to be successful in what his
friend Emerson called "the great religious shows" with their
climax in fervent pulpit rhetoricals, he soon impressed his competent auditory as being "the finest writer of English the city
had ever known"; while his unaffected concern for fraternal,
practical Christianity eventually transformed the church from a

coterie of critics of orthodoxy into a constructively ethical and spiritual institution, with a large Sunday school and adult Bible class. For free public schools Clarke worked hard and long and in 1839 was appointed superintendent of the city's system of schools. His editorship of *The Western Messenger,* which he took over from Peabody in 1836, made it famous for the contributions he solicited from Margaret Fuller, Channing, Emerson, Christopher Cranch, and other literary lights of the East. Every summer he went back to New England to replenish his intellectual resources; and in 1838, while staying in Meadville to see Huidekoper on *Messenger* business, he met the latter's daughter Anna, whom he married in 1839. His missionary industriousness was quite as out-reaching as his literary enterprise. He sought to organize churches in Jeffersonville and Lexington; he traveled down to Mobile, Alabama, to establish a church there among Unitarian migrants from New England, New York, and Kentucky – as well as several local freethinkers, with whom he was signally effective. Meanwhile he had been instrumental in inducing his Divinity School friend, W. G. Eliot, Jr., to come out to St. Louis.

In 1840 Clarke left Louisville to return to Boston, where, by the aid of his wife's father's wealth, he realized his long-cherished dream of an unconventional, laity-centered, humanitarian "Church of the Disciples." Another young Harvard graduate, John H. Heywood, came to take over Clarke's ministry at once, and though his long record (1840-79) was less notable in literary and missionary achievement it was more so for church growth and civic service. He continued Clarke's work for the public schools, and as president of the school board promoted the opening of two high schools in 1856. In the foundation of the nonsectarian Kentucky University at Louisville in 1847 his parishioner Judge Henry S. Pirtle had a leading part. A Minister at Large, assisting Heywood in family relief and rehabilitation, was appointed in 1845.

Heywood's irenic and catholic spirit carried the church through the violent controversies over Parkerism and Abolition without any such division as befell the Cincinnati church. Though Louisville never enjoyed the financial prosperity of St. Louis, nor had Heywood the ability of W. G. Eliot in soliciting great wealth for religious, philanthropic, and educational purposes, their ministries have many points of resemblance; and both churches kept the banner of Channing Unitarianism aloft through the Civil War period and the theological storms of the seventies and eighties.

The First Congregational Society of St. Louis (1835)

A dramatic braiding of coincidences leads to the founding of this most vigorous and influential of the Western churches in the early period. We take note first of the interest in the West aroused in a young collegian of Washington, D. C. His father, W. G. Eliot, Sr., an incorporator of the Unitarian church there, and a government official, had secured for his son summer work in the Post Office. Young Eliot while sorting mail from the West had his curiosity awakened by newspapers from St. Louis – and he dreamed dreams! We note next that in 1833 John Pierpont visited St. Louis and preached to a small group of New Englanders which included not only Christopher Rhodes, James Smith, and Wayman Crow, but William and Abram Clarke. The group decided that if Louisville could start a Unitarian church, they could do the same. The brothers Clarke then wrote James in Louisville, and James wrote his close friend in the Divinity School, W. G. Eliot, Jr., who had already been corresponding with him about the possibilities of missionary work in St. Louis. "Let them know," answered Eliot, "that a youngster is ready to come there to live, to spend his life among them if they will provide food and lodging; for if I come I come to remain and to lay my ashes in the valley of the Mississippi." Clarke wrote Christopher Rhodes to this effect, and when the latter went to Boston, Professor Henry Ware, Jr., recommended Eliot so heartily that the latter was straightway engaged. He was ordained in the Federal Street Church in August, with his friend Clarke preaching the Sermon, Professor Ware, Jr., giving the Prayer, and Doctor Channing himself the Charge and a blessing.

In November, 1834, Eliot reached St. Louis. Twenty-five years later he wrote: "It never entered into my head that failure was possible. I was determined to persevere. My faith in the power of Christian truth was such that I felt sure … By faith we may become one with God and receive from him power to do all things." It may be interesting to the reader to know that Eliot was twenty-three years old when he reached St. Louis and of rather slight physique.

The church was organized on January 26, 1834, but for the first two years of its history met in more or less seemly halls and lodge rooms. During this period, Eliot needed all his faith. "I could not calculate upon an audience of more than twenty-five or thirty even in pleasant weather." Yet in 1836, with what they had subscribed and $3,200 donated by Eastern friends, the Society built a stately stone church with four massive Doric pillars and a basement room for the growing Sunday school. In 1840 this building had to be enlarged. Meanwhile the philanthropic activities of the Society had grown to the point where a Minister at Large was appointed for non-sectarian relief work and the conduct of a free public school. The year 1843 found Eliot undertaking the establishment of the Academy of Science, a technical school and library for young men. Less than ten years after Eliot's coming to St. Louis, Charles Dickens visited the city and found reason to sweeten his otherwise rather sour *American Notes* with this comment:

> The Unitarian Church is represented in this remote place, as in most other parts of America, by a gentleman of great worth and excellence. The poor have good reason to remember and bless it; for it befriends them and aids the cause of liberal education, without any sectarian or selfish views. It is liberal in all its actions; of kind construction and of wide benevolence.

The educational work kept on expanding, and the philanthropies as well. In 1849, a terrible year of cholera, fire, and flood, Eliot, who was then president of the school board, persuaded his fellow citizens to impose a heavy tax on their property for school purposes; in 1850 he instituted evening classes for working people; in 1856 the Mission Free School was founded for handicapped children. In 1853, Eliot, while president of the State Association for the Blind, requested his devoted parishioner, Wayman Crow, then state senator, to secure a grant of $20,000 for relief and training of the unfortunates. Crow got the grant and at the same time he got from the legislature – and this climaxed the early series of coincidences – the charter of what is now Washington University!

It was done quite nonchalantly. Crow brought back to St. Louis and presented to his astonished minister a charter establishing "Eliot Seminary," the incorporators of which were W. G. Eliot, Jr., president; Wayman Crow, secretary; and seventeen of the leading laymen of the Unitarian church as trustees – none of whom had any previous knowledge of their new responsibility! The charter was also remarkable for the fact that it gave the widest latitude of powers and complete exemption from taxation of its property – in perpetuity.

In that same year the Society occupied its new "Gothic" church, seating over twelve hundred persons and costing almost $150,000.

The evolution of "Eliot Seminary" into Washington University and Eliot's part in the process must be postponed to Chapter 8. His work in creating and sustaining the Western Sanitary Commission must be similarly deferred. Nor is there space to do more than briefly indicate his missionary work which, in spite of all his other labors, was more extensive than that of any other Western minister – or Association official – before 1865. He preached at St. Charles and Burlington, Iowa, on the Mississippi, and up the river as far as Galena; he went down to New Orleans to hearten lonely Theodore Clapp. He went up the Illinois River (by steamboat) to Peoria, where he fostered the organization of churches; to Chicago, where he reorganized the finances of the faltering Unitarian church there; to Milwaukee – on the plea of Abram Clarke – where he revived in 1856 the movement begun there in 1842. To his inspiration and continuing counsel and oversight are due not only the origins but the survival of the Unitarian churches in Alton and Quincy, Illinois – as we shall now see.

The First Congregational Church of Alton (1836)

"Every measure for which I work, I must originate," Eliot once confided to his diary. But what are pioneers for? Such was Dr. William S. Emerson in Alton, Illinois, a town up on the bluffs of the Mississippi above St. Louis, a river terminus for liberal migrants from New England. In 1836 they twice invited Eliot to preach for them, with such good effect that in December a church was formed and a call extended to a special protégé of John Pierpont, a Divinity School graduate of 1827, Charles A. Farley. His opening sermon in Alton leaves little to be desired for liberality of thought and literary finish, and it was undoubtedly with confident hopes that he was ordained in St. Louis in the summer of 1837. But Farley was an Abolitionist like Elijah P. Lovejoy, who had removed his press from St. Louis to Alton in 1836. Lovejoy's differences with the "slavers" in Alton, culminating in his murder on November 7, 1837, exposed his friends of the Unitarian church, particularly Farley, to the threats of the rowdy element. Moreover, Dr. Emerson died two weeks after Lovejoy; perhaps this was the last straw for Farley, for he left Alton and the church expired. Not until 1853 was Eliot able to rally a new liberal group headed by Edward Keating, chairman of the library board, to persuade them to form a church with the St. Louis name, and to call a young graduate of the Meadville Theological School, William D. Haley. During his ministry of three years, the church (with $3,500 in aid from St. Louis) bought and remodeled the former Roman Catholic cathedral – which it still uses. Suffering, perhaps, from the shell shock of the experiences of 1837, the congregation in 1856 criticized the vehemence of Haley's preaching, and he resigned. But after a soul-searching session the trustees refused to accept his resignation, assuring him that "as a Society we will never condemn a person for upholding the cause of truth and morality."

Haley's eventual departure for the Washington pulpit led to a call to Rev. Jacob D. Forman, who continued his predecessor's record of "eloquent sermons and the promotion of the philanthropic and literary interests of our community" – the latter clause referring particularly to the public library, public schools, and poor relief. With Eliot's support he gave his assistance to Dorothea Dix's inspection of the state prison at Alton and her dramatic presentation to the legislature at Springfield of the horrible conditions she had found. After Forman resigned in 1864, Eliot preached without salary until another minister was secured. Before his death in 1887 he had the satisfaction of seeing the Alton church in a flourishing condition through the joint efforts of Rev. Judson Fisher and Mrs. Anna D. Sparks, an indomitable and extremely capable treasurer.

The Second Congregational Church of Quincy, Illinois (1839)

The early defeat at Alton did not daunt the enterprise either of
W. G. Eliot, Jr., or of a band of expatriate New Englanders in
Quincy, north of Alton, part of a large number who had come
into western Illinois from the Old Colony after 1835. Robert
Benneson and Edward Everett – a nephew of the famous orator
– were active in inviting Eliot to travel up the river in April,
1839. They responded to his message by forming a church
with simply the name "Congregational," like those they knew
at home, in May of the same year; Rev. W. P. Huntington came
over from Hillsboro to preach for them and assist in getting a
small frame building for meetings. Huntington then (October,
1840) returned to Hillsboro to start a church there (1843),
and Rev. George Moore, a rather frail young graduate of the
Divinity School, was sent to Quincy by the Association. Had it
not been for the determination of a foursome of laymen, the
church might have gone under, owing to the minister's recurrent
illnesses. After his death in 1847, Eliot sent a convert he had
made from Judaism, Rev. Mordecai DeLange, just graduated
from the Meadville School. DeLange revived the languishing
enthusiasm to the extent that a new building was acquired and
dedicated by Eliot in 1850. After another leaderless interim, Rev.
Liberty Billings, of the class of 1848, Meadville School, came
to rally the faint-hearted and to build the Society's third home
in 1857-58 – a massive, brick, neo-Gothic structure in downtown Quincy which, with the annex built in 1869, housed the
vigorous educational and cultural activities of the church until
1914. Billings enlisted as a chaplain in 1861, then became lieu-
tenant colonel of a regiment of colored infantry, not returning
to preach in Quincy until 1865.

After that time there was never any doubt about the continuance of the church. Its ministerial roster through the last
three decades of the nineteenth century contains the names
of men of marked literary talent – F. L. Hosmer, James Vila
Blake, Charles W. Pearson. For seventeen years its Unity Club
contributed richly to the cultural life of the city. By the natural
logic of such intellectual progressiveness, however, it swung
out of the orbit of Eliot's Christian Theism into that of

the "Ethical Basis" of fellowship which so seriously divided the Western Unitarian Conference in the seventies and eighties.

Conclusion

The Alton and Quincy churches were but two of the many efforts Eliot made to organize Unitarianism along the upper Mississippi and the Illinois Rivers before 1860. By dint of his frequent visits and sermons, unfailing encouragement, and generous financial aid, churches were started in Peoria (1839, revived 1849), Hillsboro (1841), Tremont (1849), all in Illinois. Along the upper Mississippi, Eliot preached at Burlington, Iowa Territory, with such success that in 1840 a charter was granted by the legislature for a Unitarian church to which, in 1843, came the Rev. Charles C. Shackford; his ordination in South Boston in 1841 had been made famous by Theodore Parker's sermon on "The Transient and Permanent in Christianity." As far as settlement in the Western ministry went, however, Shackford represented the transient aspect, for he retreated to the East in 1846 and the church expired. Though Eliot paid several visits to Davenport, no society was formed there until 1868; those at Warsaw and Galena, Illinois, struggled on into the fifties, only to give up the ghost for lack of a settled ministry. Eliot wrought valiantly, but his best efforts were not equal to the need.

His faithfulness to his ordination vows as an evangelist to the West, as well as his devotion to his work in St. Louis, pass all praise. In 1847 he declined to serve as General Secretary of the Association in Boston, and the same year he refused a call to King's Chapel. What had he written in 1834? "If I come, I come to remain and to lay my ashes in the valley of the Mississippi!"

CHAPTER FOUR

Starting Churches and Settling Ministers along the Erie Canal and Great Lakes Axis

WHY DID NOT THE UNITARIAN ASSOCIATION dispatch a scout to report on the needs and openings for missionary work in central New York and western Pennsylvania just as it had sent Moses G. Thomas to survey the situation of liberalism in the Ohio valley and its environs? Great numbers of New Englanders had crossed the Berkshires and the Green Mountains to settle along the Mohawk River and in the rich farmlands of the Finger Lakes region. The proportion of immigrants from the western sections of Massachusetts and Maine, the chief habitat of the Unitarians, was, however, very small. We are entitled to conjecture that the Association officials were not in correspondence with any nostalgic Unitarians beyond the Hudson – except the Dutch group at Barneveld; and since Thomas' report of his "mission of inquiry" deals largely with Christians of the Barton W. Stone following, it would seem that the leaders in Boston were well enough informed as to the numbers and, very likely, the revivalist sympathies of the Christians in New York state.

It appears that the early Unitarian churches there owe their origin largely to the reaction caused by the revival excesses of Charles G. Finney and his imitators. The Universalists, of whom there were many in northern New York especially, came in for savage tongue-lashings from the revival preachers, not so much for their denial of the Trinity as for their outspoken disapproval of the Calvinist emphasis on the torments of hell awaiting the unconverted. The only other "Unitarians" the evangelists took cognizance of were the Deists of the Thomas Paine tradition, whose property and even whose lives were sometimes endangered by the hatred incited against them. Finney finally polarized his activities about 1829 in Rochester, where Rev. William Ware from New York City had been preaching in the autumn of 1828 while on a missionary tour that took in Watertown, Ogdensburg, Oswego, and Buffalo as well. When he left them, the embattled group of liberals appealed to his brother, Rev. Henry Ware, Jr., in Boston. He responded by sending them "a young and talented preacher" who kindled their enthusiasm to the point of organizing a church.

The First Unitarian Congregational Society of Rochester, New York (1829)

The new Society bought a frame church from the Episcopalians and gave [J. D.] Green a call to their ministry. Why he declined it, went down to Cincinnati, preached to the group there, then returned to Boston is all a mystery – unless he used his candidating fees simply to get a vacation and business tour in the West! After many trials and disappointments the church was sold in 1830. Liberal meetings and religious ministrations were, however, carried on for the next decade by an eloquent, enlightened and highly honored philanthropist of Rochester, Myron Holley. To continue his work after his death in 1841 a new organization was formed and another young minister was called from the East – Rev. Rufus Ellis. He stayed a year, got another church built – then took wings and soared off to a bride and a parish in Northampton, Massachusetts!

Thrice during the next thirty years the storm-tossed church was rescued from shipwreck by Rev. Frederick W. Holland (1842, 1865, 1869). The six years of "good, steady growth" he gave it (1842-48) were followed by twelve years of short, stormy pastorates. As an intense Abolitionists (though theologically conservative), Mr. Holland requested at the outset of his ministry a pledge of pulpit freedom, which he was generously given: "We leave [you] free and unfettered in the performance of your duty, amenable only to conscience and God." Such freedom Mr. Holland himself used wisely; but such was not always true of the five young men who followed him. Abolitionist extremism was the major bone of contention, with Frederick Douglass publishing in Rochester and the Underground Railroad in flagrant operation. A lesser issue was that of Women's Rights; an historic first convention was held on August 2, 1848, in the church to which Susan B. Anthony's Quaker-Unitarian family belonged.

This meeting was not attended, perhaps not even countenanced, by young Rev. Rufus H. Bacon, whose pretentious ordination (F. L. Hosmer, S. J. May, John Pierpont, S. K. Lothrop, and Holland participating) was followed by his unlamented departure after seven months. Ten years more of turmoil – and the church building was destroyed by an incendiary in 1859. After the war Holland returned, like Nehemiah to rebuild the walls of Zion, and again in 1870 to inaugurate the happy era of the ministries of Newton Mann and William Channing Gannett.

The Unitarian Congregational Church of Syracuse, New York (1838)

In the early period, all of the state of New York west of the Hudson River was regarded as within the area of Western missionary work, and Rev. Samuel J. May regularly attended the meetings of the Western Unitarian Conference until his retirement. Fortunately, not only the pioneer period, but seventy-five years of the life of this church were undergirded by three pastorates linked each with each in natural harmony: that of Rev. John P. B. Storer (1838-44), of Rev. Samuel J. May (1845-69), of Rev. Samuel R. Calthrop (1869-1911). The magnitude of the pioneering services of these ministers and their people – to Negro freedom and post-bellum education, to prison reform, Cornell University, and on the community level to the Orphans' Home, the Onondaga Indian School, the Society for the Prevention of Cruelty to Children, the Women's and Children's Hospital, the Boy Scout movement, and the Art Museum – is comparable with that of the benefactions of the St. Louis Unitarians and their equally beloved and honored leader, Rev. W. G. Eliot, Jr.

The First Unitarian Congregational Church of Buffalo, New York (1831)

The militant resolution on Western missionary work that John Pierpont offered at the annual meeting of the American

Unitarian Association in Boston, in May, 1830, had no sooner been reported in *The Christian Register* than a group of New England Unitarians in Buffalo, headed by Noah P. Sprague, wrote Pierpont for counsel in forming a church and securing a minister. Not until December 2, 1831, however, was organization effected. Rev. William S. Brown, a British Unitarian of much culture and ability was secured, as the early acquisition of a neat neo-Doric building, dedicated by Pierpont in 1833, seems to demonstrate. Health failing, Brown left in 1834. A recent graduate of the Harvard Divinity School came, stayed two years and deserted to the Episcopal church. Was Buffalo's church to share the fate of the first effort in Rochester? Though the Association appropriated funds in 1835 for five missionaries to the West, only two volunteered and set forth. But one of them, a hearty, deep-voiced, richly gifted Harvardian, a very successful minister in Northfield, Massachusetts, Rev. George W. Hosmer, stopped to preach at Buffalo. They begged him to stay with them. Sprague and his associates hinted at the possibility of a University of Buffalo – or a Unitarian theological school – on the rosy horizon of the future. Such prospects seemed to shift duty from Northfield to Buffalo. Hosmer consulted the elder statesmen in Boston. There was no indecision about Dr. Channing's opinion: "I often think of the West and its wants … I cannot conceive a nobler field for Christian efforts … with enlightened and fervent ministers we might cover the country with churches." The others responded in like fashion, and Hosmer accepted the call.

That very year (1837) came the great bank depression; for the next six years only his steadfast loyalty sustained the church, for the fortunes of Mr. Sprague and many members were swept away and his own salary was far in arrears – when not voluntarily renounced. No University of Buffalo now – though Hosmer and his friends were chiefly instrumental in starting Buffalo's public library and public school system; and Hosmer himself had a prominent part in the founding of the Meadville Theological School, where he taught Homiletics and Pastoral Care in conjunction with his ministry in Buffalo. On the subjects of slavery, temperance, and peace, his pulpit message was the bravest and clearest in western New York. In 1848 he sponsored a monster petition to Congress to end the Mexican

War, for, like most Unitarian ministers of the early period – disciples of Worcester, Channing, and Norton – Hosmer forswore war "except in the very last extremity for the defense of life and liberty."

His personal disapproval of the Compromise of 1850 affected in no way, however, his pastoral friendship with his parishioner, President Millard Fillmore. His unfounded benignity of spirit and a radiantly noble pulpit presence and message gave him wide and warm popularity, attested by his re-election annually from 1855 to 1868 as president of the Western Unitarian Conference.

What of the prospects of planting Unitarian churches west of Buffalo now that, in 1831, steamboats daily traversed Lake Erie? Rev. Charles Briggs, Secretary of the Association, together with an observant companion, Rev. A. D. Jones, went prospecting as Thomas had done in 1826 and reported to the Annual Meeting in 1837 that it was extremely important to send preachers to Erie, Pennsylvania; Cleveland and Toledo, Ohio ("which has no organized religious society of any kind"); and Detroit, Michigan. From Detroit, Briggs went by stage, horseback, and steamboat to Chicago, which he described as a "large and flourishing place on Lake Michigan where a society has been organized and a lot procured for a church." This arouses our curiosity, for never before had Chicago been recommended for missionary work. How did it happen that a Unitarian church developed spontaneously, as it would appear, in the brash new center of lake and canal traffic, a paradise for land speculators and immigrant labor contractors?

The First Unitarian Society of Chicago, Illinois (1836)

When Harriet Martineau, noted British journalist and suffragist, and Dr. Karl Follen, recently dismissed from Harvard for Abolitionist fervor, stopped at the low-lying, treeless settlement of nondescript business buzzards, mixed with a small contingent of decent professional and business folk from New England, they were met by the Clarke brothers, William, Samuel and Abram, who had just moved from St. Louis and set up a small book and stationary store on Lake Street. The Clarkes had known Dr. Follen at Harvard. He was a Channing enthusiast, a Fichtean Transcendentalist, a passionate Abolitionist. The

Clarkes persuaded him to preach on Sunday morning in an unfinished hotel parlor, and so thrilling was Dr. Follen's emphasis upon the innate capacity of the soul for infinite perfection and immortality that immediately after the meeting the group raised twenty thousand dollars – in subscriptions – and invited Dr. Follen to remain and be minister of the society they forthwith organized, June 29, 1836. He declined to stay; and the lot they bought stayed vacant until Samuel Clarke came from the East with Rev. Joseph Harrington, Jr., a former pupil of Dr. Follen. Harrington, who was a paragon of manly beauty, musical gifts, elocutionary skill, missionary zeal – and good principles – persuaded the pastorless group of Universalists to join with his congregation and, with the aid of $2,500 he had raised in the East, a trim neo-Doric church was built in 1841.

Meanwhile he had been preaching in Milwaukee, Wisconsin, to which a state highway had just been built from Chicago. Let us follow him to Milwaukee and then make a detour to Rockford and Geneva before retuning to Chicago.

The First Unitarian Society of Milwaukee, Wisconsin (1842)

In Milwaukee, Wisconsin, a society was formed in 1842 and a church built in 1843. During the next six years young ministers from Harvard Divinity School came, stayed, and departed. By 1850 the building had to be sold to pay debts. But when W. G. Eliot was in Chicago attending the Western Unitarian Conference of 1856, he was besought by his former parishioner, Abram Clarke, now of Milwaukee, to go to that city and try to resuscitate the church. A meeting of the loyal few was held at the home of Mr. and Mrs. W. H. Metcalf. Eliot spoke impressively – and started a subscription list for a new church with $500! It would appear that the earlier movement had been weakened or destroyed by controversy over Parkerism, since the sponsors of the second effort stipulated that the structure be called the "Church of the Redeemer." The first minister of the New Dispensation, Nahor A. Staples, a recent graduate of the Meadville School, was all that could be desired for earnest piety and thoughtful, beautifully composed sermons. But in 1861 he went into the chaplaincy and never returned to Milwaukee. With a deep sense of responsibility for his brother's first church, Rev.

Carlton A. Staples left his position as colleague to Eliot in St. Louis and steered the church safely through the Civil War years to 1868.

The Rockford, Illinois Unitarian Church (1841, 1845)

West of Geneva and Elgin, Illinois, both of which lie in the Fox River valley, there stretched as late as 1850 a treeless and trackless prairie. Then one came to the wooded banks of the Kishwaukie and Rock Rivers, whose rapids and falls gave the towns of Belvidere and Rockford ample power for mills.

From 1841 on, attempts had been made by Universalists, then by Unitarians, then all together, to get a liberal church started in Rockford. To the pulpit of the First Unitarian Society (1841) came missionary preachers, [A. H.] Conant from Geneva, Elder [John] Walworth from Belvidere, Joseph Harrington, Jr., from, Chicago. The last caused "great religious excitement" in 1843 by gathering a "Church of Christ" inside the larger society for the exclusive reception of the Lord's Supper – the old, invidious New England pattern of division between the "unco' guid" and the average good. A reaction followed. Some friction between Universalists and Unitarians appeared. The Unitarians withdrew and in 1845 formed the Rockford Unitarian Society for Unitarian worship and preaching by Unitarian and Christian ministers only. By Conant's and Walworth's aid, together with lay reading of tracts, they held together for years, though two Meadville students came for short periods – John Murray and John Windsor. Under the capable direction of Melanchthon and Lucretia Starr, a stone neo-Gothic church was built in 1855, with Murray's ordination following the church dedication – a canny saving of ministerial traveling expenses! Conant came from Geneva to Rockford in 1857 to stay until he entered the chaplaincy. He was followed by Frederick May Holland, a Harvard Divinity School product with Theodore Parker's vision of "a universal church; as lofty as the love of God, as ample as the wants of Man." But the Rockford liberals were not as liberal as all that! In his letter of resignation (1863), Holland complained of the intolerance of many members toward Parkerites, Spiritualists, and Roman Catholics – especially of that of the Universalist element, who wanted "open and consistent profession of Universalism."

His own statement of faith suggests by its non-doctrinal emphases and language what "Parkerism" meant in those days:

> I believe that God our Father loves all men and that all men are worthy of love and will finally become holy and happy in love to Him. I believe in the Order of Nature, the Power of Truth and the Spirit of Christ and in judging actions by their results.

The next minister, Rev. W. G. Nowell, seems to have done extremely well at first. Attendance at services increased, all the church organizations flourished, freedmen and women were welcomed to the congregation. Yet after a little more than a year of ministry he was dismissed. A very worthy and popular Universalist minister was called from Dubuque, Iowa – Rev. D. M. Reed. Yet the critics and malcontents kept a spirit of discord alive, prosperous and thriving though the institution outwardly seemed to be. When Reed resigned in 1870, the Rockford Unitarian Society disintegrated. The progressive Unitarian and Universalist elements joined with a group of progressive Baptists led by an enlightened Emersonian, Dr. Thomas Kerr, to form the Church of the Christian Union, which permitted "the exercise of the freedom of the individual conscience, independently of Traditional and Conventional interpretations of Divine Truth." The conservative Unitarians joined the Congregational church. The Church of the Christian Union, through Dr. Kerr's broad and vital ministry of thirty-four years, became a great religious and educational institution.

The First Christian Congregation of Geneva, Illinois (1842)

Closely connected with the fortunes of the Chicago and Rockford churches is the society which Rev. Augustus H. Conant organized in Geneva, Illinois, on the twelfth of June, 1842. Hopes of a liberal village church had inspired nine or ten families of Unitarian affiliation in Boston, Roxbury, and Maine who had migrated to Geneva to recoup their fortunes after the depression of 1837. They acquainted Rev. George W. Hosmer of Buffalo, then visiting in Chicago, with their dream. One of their number, Caleb Buckingham, a young lawyer from Harvard, had already started a Sunday school, the first in the village. Hosmer could only recommend to them Elder Walworth of

Belvidere, until there came to him one Sunday in Chicago a young farmer [A. H. Conant], who had stopped in the Clarkes' store there and picked up a copy of their brother's *Western Messenger.* Through it and tracts they loaned him, he became converted not only to Unitarianism but also to the idea of becoming an evangelist of a faith that united religious devotion with rational inquiry, and piety with philanthropy, particularly the anti-slavery movement. Hosmer sent him out to the Geneva group, who liked his earnestness but felt that he needed something of the Harvard Divinity School's polish in speaking, writing, and liberal Biblical understanding. With the financial help of Harm Jan Huidekoper, Conant spent a winter in Cambridge; was ordained a Unitarian evangelist in Boston by James Freeman Clarke, Henry Ware, Jr., and others; returned to Geneva; and was called to the ministry of the new church, which had prefaced a conventional statement of Unitarian Christian doctrine with the declaration: "The undersigned, being desirous of promoting practical godliness in the world and of aiding each other in moral and religious improvement, have associated themselves together, not as agreeing in opinion, not as having attained universal truth in belief or perfection in character, but as seekers after truth and goodness."

This declaration made it possible for the church, the only one in the settlement for some years, to include not only Unitarians and Christians but Episcopalians, Baptists, Friends, and even "Presbycongregationalists." The Geneva church thus became an interesting example of the feasibility of Channing's vision of a non-sectarian Unitarianism. Likewise it fulfilled the Christian Connection's principles in that respect – and also in the fact that Conant, who was also a licensed Christian preacher, supported himself and his family by farming and carpentry work quite as much as by ministerial stipend and missionary subventions from Boston. Thus he was enabled to travel extensively through central and northern Illinois, preaching and purveying Unitarian literature, with the result that not only Geneva but the Unitarian Society in Elgin (1846; merged with the First Universalist Church of Elgin in 1865) and that in Dixon (1854-62) owed their existence to his efforts. The sturdy neo-Doric stone church that, with the help of $800 from the Unitarians of Roxbury, and their own strength and skill, he and the men of his congregation built in 1843, is in a state of excellent preservation today and in regular use.

The First Unitarian Society of Chicago (continued)

The church in Chicago had no such luck as Geneva with its Conant or Buffalo with its Hosmer. Harrington left in 1844. Even with short pastorates and pulpit supplies, however, the church survived and made progress. In 1849 Hosmer persuaded a young Meadville School graduate, a grandnephew of its founder, Rush R. Shippen, to accept a call to Chicago. His eight years of service were "most felicitous."

Congregations at both services bulged out the walls and the church was enlarged twice. A daughter society was devised for the north side of the river. The non-sectarian social-service and relief work of the church was growing rapidly. A great-hearted, massively built, English-born ex-blacksmith, converted from the Methodists, Rev. Robert Collyer, came to inaugurate the Ministry at Large in Chicago, conducting a Sunday school for poor children, a day and evening school, together with prison visitation and general relief work.

In 1860 the new north-side Unity Church called Collyer to their ministry. It was fortunate for Chicago Unitarianism that he stood by and kept the flag flying through the war years. Shippen had resigned at the peak of his popularity, and his successor, George F. Noyes from Harvard, had followed suit a year after a very pretentious ordination because of objections to his Parkerite views on the plenary inspiration and veracity of the Bible. His radicalism caused such consternation that when a new church was built, gifts of land and money were made contingent on the adoption of a Statement of Faith affirming the members' belief in the divine inspiration of the Scriptures and the divinely appointed mediation of Jesus the Messiah. The new church building was give the name "Church of the Messiah" to avoid any misunderstanding! This conservatism was maintained during the seventies and eighties by two exceptionally scholarly, gracious, and eloquent British Unitarians – Rev. Robert Laird Collier (1866-1874) and Brooke Herford (1876-1881).

The First Congregational Unitarian Society of Detroit, Michigan (1850)

After steamboats came into operation between Buffalo and Detroit in 1831, that small, shabby French settlement began to attract emigrants from the East; and by 1837 the Association's Secretary Briggs underscored the opportunity there for Unitarian missionary work. None was undertaken, however, until his successor, Rev. F. W. Holland, came prospecting in November, 1849, and preached in a hall to a fair-sized group of New Englanders on the staff of the Michigan Central Railroad, then being extended to Chicago. Holland complained bitterly in his report that "nothing but a frowning refusal met every attempt to procure even a settee for a vacant room and getting a tolerable place to meet was as vexatious, wearisome and disgusting a task as I ever have known ... we have been bitterly denounced by the clergy." But his sermon was heard by "many hearty, intelligent, excellent friends of our cause [including] General Cass and some other prominent persons." Holland "felt free to say that after fourteen years' acquaintance with similar enterprises [he] never had seen a better, more needed opening for our views." However, he doubly stressed the precaution: "Rather than commence in a listless spirit or under a feeble preacher, *they had better wait another twelve years!*" Then, thinking perhaps of the record of disappointments in Chicago, Milwaukee, Quincy, and other places, he pleaded: "May we not depend on our eastern friends to save our hopes here from the untimely blight of an inefficient, incompetent laborer in our vineyard?"

When Holland got back to Boston, he extended himself to find such a minister as George W. Hosmer to volunteer for Detroit. None did. The group had to depend on sporadic supplies and lay efforts, and it was only through the grim determination of its leader, U. Tracy Howe, that it held together. It even got organized with seventy-five members on October 6, 1850, after Dr. Hosmer had preached a revivifying sermon. He later persuaded them to wait no longer for a gifted Messiah from Harvard but to consider Chicago's good luck with young R. R. Shippen and to call another Meadville graduate – Thomas J. Mumford, a protégé of Samuel J. May. But before they gave him a definite contract they required him to go East and beg for money for a church building – a cruel but customary imposition on young ministers in those days. When he returned with the bacon, they finished their handsome neo-Doric temple with its portico of six tall Ionic columns approached by curving staircases.

The nine years of Mumford's pastorate were blessed with progress and harmony. The Universalists, whose building had been sold, joined the Unitarians in worship. The Parkerites among the latter condoned his mild theological conservatism because of his forthright social prophecy and activity. Besides standing alone among the Detroit clergy on behalf of prison and penal reform, he upheld the Higher Law and escorted hundreds of fugitive slaves across the river to Canada. When he resigned in 1861, he left the church so well established that it survived the twelve ensuing years of short pastorates and theological tensions. The "Railroad Church," as it was locally known, stayed on the track and kept going!

Conclusion

With the exception of the Independent Congregational Church of Meadville, Pennsylvania – the circumstances of whose foundation in 1829 will be set forth in the following chapter – our axial surveys have covered all the churches that participated in the organization of the Western Unitarian Conference in 1852. The story of each church has been followed through to the threshold of the crucial period, 1870 to 1886, in which the Conference won its institutional and spiritual independence. Have we not, indeed, noticed in the annals of virtually every society minor incidents that portended the major conflict bound to come between static and dynamic Unitarianism?

Almost thirty years of traveling to the Mississippi and back to New England by hundred of ministers; of missionary preaching in schoolrooms and courthouses; of the delivery of thousands of sermons and the distribution of more thousands of tracts; of the contribution of large sums by Eastern Unitarians for the building and furnishing of churches – yet only seventeen societies, several of them none too robust, were represented at the inaugural meeting of the Western Unitarian Conference in 1852 at Cincinnati. Something was obviously wrong! Was it the

Unitarian message or the ministers who presented it to the people — or lack of ministers? Was it the lack of ministers who if they put their hands to the plow in a parish would stick to the work until the whole field was furrowed? Was it the lack of a medium of comity and mutual counsel? A permanent regional supervisor with a central office? A periodical of, for, and by the Western churches rather than dependence on publications like *The Christian Register* in Boston or *The Christian Inquirer* in New York? Our next two chapters will deal with diagnoses of the slow rate of growth of Western Unitarianism and proposals for reducing the appalling discrepancy between efforts and results.

CHAPTER FIVE

The Founding of the
Meadville Theological School

BY 1843 SIXTEEN YEARS HAD PASSED since Moses Thomas's tour of reconnaissance into the West. He had not ventured into northern Indiana, southern Michigan, or northern Illinois, not only because they were so sparsely settled but also because it was before the Black Hawk wars which later ensured the traveler's as well as the settler's safety. Of the places along the Ohio River he had reported as propitious for missionary work or ripe for organization, strong churches had been founded at Cincinnati, Louisville, and St. Louis. Thanks to W. G. Eliot's vision and enterprise, societies had come into being in Alton, Quincy, and Peoria, Illinois, though their survival depended largely on his oversight and aid. Little or nothing had been accomplished at Paris, Kentucky; Marietta and Steubenville, Ohio; St. Charles, Missouri; Indianapolis, Indiana – though all had been recommended for intensive work by Thomas.

[The Independent Congregational Church of Meadville, Pennsylvania]
The only bright spot in the upper Ohio Valley – if a town only thirty miles south of Lake Erie could be so allocated – was Meadville, Pennsylvania, where a Unitarian church had been formed in 1829 with no counsel or aid from outside. Harm Jan Huidekoper, the erstwhile clerk of the Holland Land Company in Barneveld, thereafter its Western agent, and a large land-owner in his own right, heeded the challenge given him by John Campbell in Pittsburgh to search the Scriptures for him-self, and by 1825 he had bidden his (Dutch Reformed) John Calvin "Goodnight." To provide the best of tutoring for his five children, he imported students from the Harvard Divinity School, who could also lead Unitarian services on Sunday and discuss theology with him in the evenings. Although a goodly

share of the endowment from the local Allegheny College, including its library, had been given by Boston liberals, the Presbyterian
president of the college and the Episcopal rector of the city
showed such intolerance that more and more of the substantial
folk of Meadville joined the Unitarian group; by 1829 it became
organized as the Independent Congregational Church, whose
Fundamental Principles, while requiring members to believe
in the existence of One God and the Divine mission of Jesus
of Nazareth, the Christ, the Son of God, exorcised any latent
dogmatism from its spirit by adding: "Every person possesses the
inalienable right of judging for himself in matters of opinion and
no one has the right to call another to account for any religious
opinions he may hold."

The opposition even such lenient liberalism encountered may
be estimated by the comment of Rev. Ephraim Peabody, minister
of the church in 1830-31, speaking of western Pennsylvania: "It
is a land crushed under the blind brutalizing, palsying doctrines
of Calvinism!" To counteract such tyranny, Peabody and Huidekoper published in 1831 the *Unitarian Essayist*, a remarkably
scholarly vehicle for liberal apologetics. Then, when the Unitarian
society could find nowhere to meet but the courthouse – sitting
for Communion around the weekday lawyers' table – they built
themselves a stately neo-classic brick temple with massive Doric
columns that has stood for over a century at the head of Meadville's
public square. As the scene of the graduation exercises of the
Meadville Theological School from 1846 to 1925, it is perhaps the
most venerable landmark of Unitarianism in the Midwest.

[The Need for Missionary Preachers]

Now that the School has been introduced into our story it is
proper that we should examine the circumstances of its founding,
particularly those of the selection of the rather remote and rural
town of Meadville for its seat.

A *crescendo* of appeals from Western liberals and of criticism
from New England Unitarians persuaded the new A.U.A. Secretary, Charles Briggs, to spend eight months in the West in 1836-
37. The report he rendered at the May meeting on his return
is full of suggestions for missionary work in liberal groups in
the rapidly growing communities. He must have dazzled – or
depressed – his hearers by his enthusiasm and optimism over

"the valley of the Mississippi, which at no distant period will contain many millions of souls and give laws to the whole country!" Not only does New York state in his opinion offer alluring opportunities for missionary preaching, "where with little effort societies may soon be gathered" (*viz.*, Albany, Troy, Syracuse, Oswego, Ogdensburg, Utica, Rome, Rochester), but Ohio is a fallow field. There are groups of nostalgic New England Unitarians and indigenous, wistful liberals at Erie, Cleveland, and Toledo in the north; at Marietta, Zanesville, Oxford, Columbus, and Dayton in the central and southern zones. But Illinois is the new Macedonia for Unitarianism: Galena, Atlas, Pittsfield, Juliet (*sic*), Pekin, Jacksonville, Hillsboro, Tremont call for help. Already at Hillsboro, [W. P.] Huntington is preaching, supported by Old Colony churches for the sake of their former members now settled there. Tremont is "emphatically a New England village," and James Thurston recently formed a society there – but left soon after. "The destiny of our country, the destiny of Unitarianism is to be decided in the West."

The decision would be favorable, thought Charles Briggs, if the supply of missionary preachers could be increased. In New England there were scarcely enough to supply its churches, and the Cambridge Divinity School was inadequate even for the East. That a theological institution should be established in the West was a "universal opinion." Also, he ventured, a "traveling secretary is needed there."

This was the view of W. G. Eliot also: "We need preachers – strong, thinking, fervent devoted men ... I do not speak of great talent; we can do without that; but without men of disinterested, persevering devotion we cannot do! It is not any peculiar powers of oratory that we need ... or a declamatory style but good sense, a devoted love of Christ and above all, a willingness to labor long and arduously in laying the foundation on which others may have the honor of building."

Eliot might have added that funds for missionary work were needed. From 1826 to 1835 inclusive, A.U.A. expenditures for Western missions had amounted to $1,364! Yet $11,604 had been spent in printing tracts (principally) and in subsidies to the *Christian Register*. The tracts, of course, circulated chiefly in New England and the Eastern seaboard. No wonder Eliot exploded:

"There is no sect of Christianity, I may almost say, which has not done more for the establishment of permanent religious institutions in the West than we have done."

As the result, in all probability, of Eliot's strictures and Briggs' optimism, contributions and appropriations for missionary work increased, while appeals were made for more ministerial students for the Harvard Divinity School, whose graduates were adjured to turn to the West for their ministry – if only for a trial missionary year. A similar plea was made to settled ministers. Even in the years of the great bank panic (1837-39) almost a quarter of A.U.A. receipts were allotted to their traveling expenses or to aid in church building. W. G. Eliot kept up his propaganda for the West by an impassioned plea at the annual A.U.A. banquet: "If the time ever comes when irreligion and licentious freedom prevail over that great region and hold their blighting rod over the whole nation, Oh, Lord! How will the men of that day mourn that their fathers did not send out a moiety of their wealth to aid in building up the churches of Christ!" This plea was so poignant that in 1838-39 over a dozen ministers of high degree – or medium – were sent forth across eleven Western and Southern states *for a month or so, or for only one Sabbath.*" Rev. J. P. B. Storer, however, stayed at Syracuse longer than that. George Ripley had drafted their church covenant, indeed; but his heart was in Boston and back he soon went. Storer stayed (1839-44), got a Church of the Messiah built and them, to the grief of the congregation and community, died of heart failure. After a trying year of supplies, Samuel J. May consented to come on a five-year contract; a rather rash undertaking it seemed at first, because of May's radical anti-war and anti-slavery views, as well as his support of the crepuscular Women's Rights movement. But the present name of the church – "May Memorial" – indicates that the society has never canceled its contract with their brave, wise, eloquent, warm-hearted prophet and pastor.

Otherwise, for all this traveling to and fro and preaching one or more Sundays or weekdays in the promising communities large and small that Briggs had suggested – and several more besides – there was by 1840 nothing to show of well-established churches except the one in Syracuse. The one in Quincy had been organized by W. G. Eliot (1839) himself. The one at Hillsboro, Illinois, *cum* Tremont, antedated Briggs' report. The society in process of formation at Rockford, Illinois, was, as we have seen, the outcome of missionary work done by Christian Elder Walworth of nearby Belvidere, and Rev. Joseph Harrington from the Chicago church.

Why such disappointing results? James Freeman Clarke, who knew and loved the West, gave one answer in a vehement address at the A.U.A. meeting of 1840:

> A man is not fit to be a missionary who cannot ride over all forms. He must be ready to preach in a church or a shed, or on a canal boat, without a hymnbook, an organ or a pulpit; not to crowds only but to a single man; and speak, too, as a clergyman or a layman, wherever he finds men starving for the bread of life … preachers should not constitute a caste!

This was one phase of the difficulty, and Clarke's viewpoint was quite in keeping with his conception of a "Church of the Disciples" such as he was even then organizing in Boston. Another was indicated in a letter in *The Christian World* from Augustus H. Conant, the young Unitarian-Christian evangelist-pastor of Geneva, Illinois:

> The transient character of past efforts has been a powerful cause of the comparatively small success that has attended them … they who have come West to labor as missionaries have left their hearts and hopes in New England. If clergymen would come as men do in other professions, legal and medical, with the determination to be Western men, planting themselves here, the work would make progress. Shall it be said that Unitarian clergymen cannot bear to live out of New England – that they have no manhood?

These were obviously the indignant thoughts of a "Man in Earnest," and it is time that we made his further acquaintance – for Conant ranks with Pierpont, Clarke, Eliot, Huidekoper, and Hosmer as one to whom early Western Unitarianism was indebted for its existence and character.

Conant was a Vermonter by birth, with only a smattering of education to begin with – though he later was host to Margaret Fuller and Emerson – and with such a warm heart that he thought himself into Universalism! In 1832 he made a tour of the West, was sickened by the sight of slavery in St. Louis, and decided that a farm near Chicago was better than Vermont's thin and rocky soil. On a business trip to Chicago he found an issue of *The Western Messenger* in the Clarke brothers' stationary shop on Lake Street. Enthralled by its liberal spirit and literary excellence, he went on to Channing's sermon in "Self-denial"; then he went to hear Hosmer preach to the Chicago Unitarians and confided to Hosmer his desire to be a preacher. Hosmer put him in the way of spending a year under Henry Ware, Jr., at Cambridge. The sale of his farm and a gift from Harm Jan Huidekoper made this possible. Having learned New Testament Greek ("thought to be of so much importance") and to speak *ex tempore* as grammatically as Bostonians did, he was ordained as an "Evangelist" and returned to the West. There, as we have already seen, Conant began the dual work of village pastor and Unitarian-Christian itinerant throughout the northern and central part of Illinois, northern Indiana, southern Wisconsin (Rochester), and over to Burlington, Iowa. In the first year of his ministry he traveled 1,844 miles, distributed 150 books and 1,000 tracts; carried on his own church work in Geneva satisfactorily; and aided Joseph Harrington of Chicago and Elder Walworth of Belvidere nearby to carry on the work in Rockford until a minister could be found who would *stay*. But where could such be found? Hosmer was in a similar predicament with eager groups in Erie, Cleveland, Detroit: "We must have ministers!"

At this juncture, Walworth called Conant's attention to an old academy building in Belvidere, Illinois, offered for sale. Perhaps a hint given by a *Christian Examiner* reviewer recurred to the latter:

> If the people of the West want a theological school let us see them moving in the matter ... taking measures [for] raising funds, erecting buildings, doing something, in short, themselves!

Taking up the challenge, Conant called the attention of William Clarke, whom he met at a large Christian Conference in Burlington, to the possibility of buying the old academy and using it for Unitarian-Christian co-operation in ministerial training. William Clarke was immediately enthusiastic. He wrote to his brother James in Boston, and James launched a campaign for funds in a letter to the *Register* of June 3, 1843, in which he sketched the grand strategy of such co-operation:

> Their cause is identical with ours [but] they are able to do more to advance it among certain classes of society. They are breaking the rough land and gradually preparing it for the higher cultivation we may give it.

Brother James combined this rather patronizing plan with the fact of the graduation of Arthur B. Fuller, Margaret's brother, from Harvard that very month and broached "An Opportunity to Do Good" in the *Register* of July 1, suggesting the following steps: (1) buy and repair the Belvidere Academy; (2) appoint Fuller as principal,

> ... to make it in part now and hereafter wholly a theological institution of liberal character [since] many Christian ministers are now ready and anxious to attend such a school [and] by making the building the center of the best kind of missionary operation, [thus] at a very slight expense we lay the foundation of a western divinity school, an object long desired and much needed. [Either] our western missions and societies must be abandoned or we must provide means of educating our ministers on the spot.

The moral and financial response to these proposals was so favorable that in July the A.U.A. sent an agent to investigate the Belvidere situation. He sent back a report approving the purchase of the building as a liberal *academy*; but the *Register* editors, though conceding that such an academy might afford some theological instruction and a suitable preparation for the *Christian* ministry (italics ours), declared flatly that "Belvidere is not a favorable location for a theological school!" It was evident that the *Register* editors could not conceive of educating Unitarian ministers and Christian elders together in one institution.

Having in mind Conant's success after but nine months of Harvard, and knowing the desperate nature of the missionary crisis in the West, Clarke corresponded with his father-in-law, Harm Jan Huidekoper in Meadville, who was so lacking in intellectual *hauteur* that he had welcomed a Christian elder, [E. G.] Holland, to the pastorate of the Unitarian church there. Either to Clarke or to his father-in-law it must have occurred that the latter's younger son, Frederic, at that time a special student at the Harvard Divinity School, after two years of study in

Europe, might offer a solution of the educational problem. Frederic was anxious to serve the liberal cause; but he was somewhat reserved in manner, a proficient scholar but a prosy preacher, with weak eyesight that worsened with nervous fatigue. His solicitous, astute father evolved a plan not only for Frederic's future but for that of the Unitarian cause in the West. Elders Holland and Church liked the idea of a joint educational undertaking in ministerial training; Clarke and Hosmer heartily approved it when they came to Meadville to ordain Frederic as an evangelist. Hence, when Harm Jan Huidekoper – a Vice-President of the A.U.A., a wise, a good man, and a very wealthy one as well – went to Boston to seek A.U.A. assistance in finding and paying another professor to serve with Frederic, the A.U.A. and the *Register* officials reached the conclusion that under *such* circumstances a joint Unitarian-Christian theological school in Meadville would be quite acceptable. It was also arranged that a vigorous, hearty, scholarly graduate of the Harvard Divinity School, Rufus Phineas Stebbins, should leave his pastorate at Leominster for that of the Meadville church, Elder Holland having gracefully retired to facilitate this thrifty but effective way of providing the new school with a president.

Mr. Huidekoper had also been responsible for the purchase and remodeling, for use as a Divinity Hall, of a small brick church once used by Cumberland Presbyterians. The School was opened in October, 1844, with five students and four teachers: Stebbins, Huidekoper, Hosmer (who came every June from Buffalo to teach pastoral and parish work), and Elder David Millard (who came occasionally to keep watch over the Christian students and lecture on Palestine). Nine students in all registered for 1844-45, one of them from the East. Thirty-two came in 1845-46, with sixteen from the East. The enrollment for 1847 consisted of thirty-two, about equally divided between Unitarian and Christian affiliations. Following the Harvard Divinity School precedent, the charter of 1847 stipulated that "no doctrinal test was ever to be made a condition of enjoying any of the opportunities of instruction in the School except a belief in the Divine origin of Christianity." Tuition was free, living was relatively cheap (not over seventy-five dollars a school year), "beneficiary" aid was generous. The first

Divinity Hall was located just off the "Diamond" square of the town, north of the courthouse and about a block from the Unitarian church. Chestnut Street at its door sloped gently upward half a mile to the hilltop campus that Frederic Huidekoper donated to the School in 1850 as a site for the new Divinity Hall given by New York and Brooklyn Unitarians (1853). From its steps one looked out across the valley of French Creek, the route of the stagecoaches from Pittsburgh and Erie until 1862, when the Erie Railroad displaced them.

The regular curriculum of the School for which a diploma was given required three years to complete; but students, married or otherwise mature, could come for a single year. About one fourth of their study was in the field of New Testament; one fourth in Theology; one eighth in Old Testament; one eighth in Church History; one fourth in Elocution, Rhetoric, Sacred Oratory, Pastoral Care. Training in *ex tempore* preaching was stressed as well as the composition of sermons to be read. Students and faculty held at least two discussions and prayer meetings a week to consider questions of personal piety and Christian conduct, of theological interest, of philanthropic duty and action. President Stebbins was singularly fitted to deal with the Christian students who were rather more pietistic than the Unitarians, for he was an earnest, vigilant pastor to them as well as instructor. He was affecting in discourse to the point of revivalist emotionalism, and fervent in prayer. Like theirs, his devotion to the Bible was sentimental and virtually uncritical, despite his greater erudition, and he would not "permit his faith to be shaken in its [New Testament] divinity ... even though our Greek texts are not wholly verbally inspired." With Professor Huidekoper, on the other hand, he did not admit the often fluent (and ungrammatical!) verbiage of a young, rural Christian evangelist as a substitute for scholarship. Huidekoper's critical scholarship, like that of his Harvard friend and teacher, Andrews Norton, was at least heedful of doubts coming over from Germany and England concerning the Mosaic authorship of the Pentateuch, the historicity of the Deluge, geology's challenge of the Creation stories, the primacy of the Fourth Gospel, the more prodigious miracles of Jesus. The Christian students, having been brought up to believe in the Bible as sufficient in its

plain meaning, without Calvinist, Lutheran, or Catholic interpretation, as a divine oracle of faith and life, began to be sensitive
to the Higher Criticism that they read about in the Unitarian
periodicals from Boston, especially the *Christian Examiner* – even
if the new views were not taught in their classrooms. Their
letters home to this effect strengthened the suspicions and the
opposition of many Christian leaders who had been dubious
from the first about the Meadville alliance between the well-
educated, well-off Unitarians and the Christian country folk.
Such suspicion on the part of a large segment of Christians
appear in letters published in their *Christian Palladium* as early
as 1845. The consequences of such hostility to the Meadville
experiment; the concessions that Stebbins, Millard, and the
instructor in New Testament appointed in 1849 (N. S. Folsom)
made to save the federation and keep Christian students coming
to the School; the refusal of Frederic Huidekoper to subjugate
Unitarian freedom of inquiry and progress to Christian Funda-
mentalism – this series of events had such important consequences, not only for the School, that they should not be passed
over hurriedly.

Parkerism at Meadville

The Higher Criticism of the Bible was not, however, the only
factor in creating the tension between the two allies. Since 1841
Parkerism had been agitating the Unitarians, especially in the
East. Theodore Parker was an offense to the Executive Committee of the A.U.A. headed by Dr. Samuel K. Lothrop, because
Parker (a) reduced the Christian revelation and religion to just
one passing phase of Absolute Truth; (b) Jesus he held to be
only one, though thus far the sublimest, of many divinely sent
teachers; (c) the essential and only permanent elements of his
teaching and of Christianity are love to God and love to man;
(d) the natural and moral truth in his teachings and in the Bible
as a whole are its best authentication; (e) the supranaturalism
of the Bible miracles are "evidences" of northing but error and
credulity. Even if most of the Unitarians rejected Parker, yet,
observed the Christian Fundamentalists, their intellectualism
produced him! Though Professor Huidekoper was emphatically
not a "Parkerite," he, too, criticized the Bible!

On the other hand, the phenomenon of William Miller and his Second Adventism, which devastated the ranks of the Eastern Christians, opened the eyes of Eastern Unitarians to the basic intellectual and cultural incompatibilities of the two allies and the superficiality of their federation.

All these latent dissidences came to a dramatic climax in two incidents. In 1849, to appraise the qualifications of the School for his support in its campaign for an endowment of fifty thousand dollars, Rev. Henry Whitney Bellows, New York's brilliant and dynamic Unitarian leader, attended the trustees' meeting in June at Meadville and on his return to New York published in his organ, *The Christian Inquirer*, his impressions and conclusions. They present a pontifical *motu proprio* of such intellectual snobbishness and sectarian self-consciousness that many Christians were deeply hurt and set about raising funds for a school of their own. The second incident came in 1864, when Stebbins, Folsom, and presumably Millard voted that any student who doubted the miracles denied "the divine origin of Christianity" (the charter prescription) was thereby excluded from its privileges. Professor Huidekoper, though still believing in some miracles of the New Testament, did not believe in such obscurantism and dogmatism as the faculty action implied, and, at the risk of the sacrifice of his beloved teaching, resigned. His father, who would never have become a Unitarian had his questioning mind been halted by such a veto, died shortly afterward – with what misgivings over the future of the school we can but surmise.

However, President Stebbins' position proved untenable, although some very conservative Unitarians rallied to his support and the Christians made him president of their General Conference meetings in Cincinnati in 1855. In 1856 he resigned, after twelve years of memorable achievement for the School, but of sorrowful failure in getting oil to mix with water. He was succeeded by Oliver Stearns, another Harvard College and Divinity School graduate, a scholarly and successful minister in Hingham. Immediately the exclusion rule was rescinded; for the new president, among other virtues, had that of sensitivity to the need for reconciling – for Unitarian thinkers, at least – Transcendentalist intuitionism with rational supranaturalism,

Biblical inspiration with Higher Criticism and geologic science, revealed religion with philosophic theories of evolution. Frederic Huidekoper was invited to return to the faculty and the teaching of Church History, a subject in which he had now attained eminence. By 1866, when Elder Millard resigned, the influx of Christian students was steadily diminishing. His successor, Austin Craig, a highly esteemed New Testament scholar who had worked with Unitarians on the Antioch College faculty, resigned in 1869 to preside over the Christian Biblical Institute at Eddytown, New York.

There can be no doubt that the connection with the Christians assured a student body sufficiently numerous to get the School started and to justify the raising of funds for its worthy continuance. But the fact that most of the money came from Unitarians did, we know, hurt the Christians' pride, though with fine considerateness the names of the Christian elders were for years placed first in the list of trustees.

A negative but immensely valuable result of the basically incongruous federation was the principle vindicated in the controversy between Stebbins and Huidekoper. The latter's stand for the open mind and honest doubt proved through the replacement of Stebbins by a more progressive theologian to be a most influential factor in strengthening the naturally liberal spirit of the Western Conference to resist the efforts of conservatives to narrow its spiritual boundaries by doctrinal formulae.

Yet, though Huidekoper's firm stand was a victory for free and high standards of scholarship, it eventually had the effect, by extruding the Christian emphasis on the training of preachers *of* the common people and *for* the common people, of imposing on its students – many of whom were to pass to Western pulpits – the patterns of New England Unitarianism's upper- and middle-class ministry.

PART II

ORGANIZATION IMPERILS FREEDOM
(1844-1875)

CHAPTER SIX

Western Unitarianism Organizes

THE FOUNDING OF THE MEADVILLE SCHOOL seemed at first to give a marked stimulus to the morale of Western missionary work. Yankee immigration was again increasing and the canal-side and water-power towns were booming in population and industrial prosperity. Eliot and his assistants in the Ministry at Large in St. Louis went about preaching and urging organization of churches among the expatriate New Englanders of central Illinois; while Conant covered northern Illinois and even invaded Wisconsin Territory and crossed over into Iowa, sending to the Unitarian periodicals in the East frequent reports and persistent appeals for more money for literature to distribute and more ministers to come west and consolidate his gains. For, encouraging though the growing enrollment appeared, the Meadville graduates who chose the West for their field of labor were, until 1849-50, disappointingly few. Only three men from the classes of '46, '47, '48 – together with a one-year student, the Jew converted by Eliot in St. Louis, Mordecai DeLange – came west looking for settlement. Of this number [J. C.] Learned ('48) served Tremont and Peoria, Illinois, for two years and then went east, as did Stillman Barber, his classmate who served Como, Illinois. As Conant wrote plaintively, the West must have ministers who would stick to their posts and surmount discouragement. He was also convinced that these isolated ministers and churches must have nearer support and fellowship and more systematic supervision than far-off Boston, by tedious correspondence and intermittent emissaries, could provide. He felt that the Unitarians might do well to copy the Christians' method of holding regional quarterly and annual Conferences, such as he himself regularly attended with great edification. He corresponded to this effect with the new General Secretary of the Association (appointed in January, 1848, to succeed Charles Briggs), Frederick W. Holland, with whom he had co-operated in organizing the Rockford church in 1840-41.

Probably with Holland's approval, certainly on his own characteristic initiative, Conant with William Adams (at that time minister in Chicago) and Mordecai DeLange (then minister in Quincy) undertook to summon a "Conference of Unitarian Ministers" in Chicago on May 10, 1849. Eliot was prevented from coming by the cholera epidemic raging in St. Louis. Heywood telegraphed his regrets, as did Huntington of Hillsboro and [G. W.] Woodward of Galena. Hosmer confidently expected to come but at the last moment changed his plans. Elder Nicholson of Jackson Grove, Illinois, came and participated – as a Unitarian *and* as a Christian. Whether they met in the Unitarian church is uncertain.

First and foremost, perhaps to forestall any possible reproach of Parkerism, this little Conference adopted a touchingly simple and practical, but definitely Christian profession of faith. Next it recommended to the churches a certain trustworthy person to conduct, for the West, a "General Repository of Unitarian Literature." Then it proceeded to pass resolutions or remarkable prescience and practicality:

That this Conference invites the students of Meadville School to regard the West with special consideration.

That destitute societies in the West must look chiefly to Meadville for a supply of ministers;

That this Conference address a Letter to all the Western Unitarian ministers not present inviting them to consider the propriety of the formation of a Western Unitarian Association with a view to a discussion of the subject at a future Conference, to be held at such a time and place as shall be agreed on by the Chairman (Wm. Adams) and the secretary of this Conference, Mordecai DeLange; the objects of this Association to be:

(1) A closer union between our several churches;

(2) To supply the spiritual wants of the various small groups of Unitarians now scattered in the West and unable to supply themselves;

(3) To establish connection with other denominations of Christians whose views and positions assimilate them to us;

(4) To add to the prosperity of our cause generally by the efficiency of united action in the distribution of books, tracts, etc., and the support of missionaries.

Another resolution, passed with Conant in the chair, concerned a proposal made to him in correspondence with "Brother Holland who is desirous of visiting the West provided his visit is pleasing to the Western brethren and likely to be profitable to the churches":

That we cordially invite Brother Holland and all others of our Eastern clerical brethren so disposed to receive our hospitality, preach in our churches; and we believe their labors will be beneficial to our cause.

The "Letter to the Western Ministers" was drawn up and approved before the group adjourned. Whether or not it was circulated, it is sure that the minutes of the meeting were published in *The Christian Inquirer*, though without editorial comment; and a commendatory mention of the enterprise was made in Secretary Holland's annual report to the May Meeting of the A.U.A. What response to the Letter came from the regional ministers? We can only surmise – though with some basis of fact to support the surmise – that Eliot, whose conspicuous success in St. Louis gave him leadership prestige in the West as well as in Boston, with Hosmer and Huidekoper also, may have felt the time for a Conference was not ripe; or that its organization should not be initiated or its character determined by the little group of earnest and eminently practical – but intellectually and ecclesiastically lowly – brethren in Chicago.

The possibility that considerations of this general nature were responsible for the pigeonholing of the Chicago group's proposals for two years and a half is strengthened by the circumstances of Holland's visit to the West in the winter of 1849-50 and its sensational *dénouement* at the A.U.A. meeting in May, 1850.

Holland was no stranger to the West, as we have seen, and he had further proved his zeal and capacity at Rochester, New York, which he twice rescued from demise; and in the Ministry at Large in Brooklyn. His sympathies were always with the lowly in fortune, and this trait drew him to disparage ministers who shunned hardships and sought the "cosy stove" of New England parishes. Conversely, as we shall see, he admired and preferred the rugged, self-supporting, democratic Christian evangelists and elders of the West. He did not realize that by virtue of their Gospel ideal of itinerancy and their lack of literary and urbane graces, they usually did not and would not suit the role of a settled parish minister of an educated liberal group in a growing railroad city of the West.

The serial reports from "Our Western Correspondent" that Bellows published in his *Christian Inquirer* in eleven numbers, commencing with Holland's departure from Albany in early November and ending with his return to Boston in January, 1850, are singularly vivid, percipient, astute, affording a remarkable conspectus not only of the status of Unitarianism and the Christian Connection in the West but of Western travel, scenery, cultural and economic conditions and prospects. He sent back encouraging estimates of Unitarian strength in Buffalo ("a second church is needed there"); of Conant's hard work and rich harvests in Geneva, Elgin, Rockford; of Woodward's gallant struggle in Galena; of DeLange's similar fight in Quincy; of Eliot's triumphs in St. Louis ("the New York of the West"); of Heywood's steady tenure and gains in Louisville; of Perkins' noble service in Cincinnati ("which ought to have four churches"). He lamented that the Chicago and Milwaukie (*sic*) churches were leaderless and that the latter's handsome church had been sold. In Cleaveland (*sic*); Detroit; Janesville, Wisconsin – "the finest opportunity in all this territory"; Pekin, Illinois; Burlington and Davenport, Iowa; Wheeling, Virginia, where he himself organized a church – he found wistful groups of liberals who wanted regular services but could at first pay very little to a minister.

A solution of this salient problem he claimed to have found in Meadville – as the little Chicago group had done. "The School of the prophets is a *missionary* institution. It educates no one to expect a high salary, aspire after literary fame or claim the honors of theological science. It is not intended to propagate an 'ism.'" He eulogized a recent graduate of the School who had turned colporteur and traveled about selling Channing's works, sleeping in the woods if necessary beside his donkey cart, and preaching at crossroads. The trouble with the Chicago and Milwaukee churches was, he insisted, that they had been "started on an intellectual basis, in a fastidious spirit." For a better start, Holland got Rush R. Shippen, a recent Meadville graduate, ordained by President Stebbins with an anti-intellectualist sermon (Colossians 11:8) and dispatched to Chicago (where he virtually saved the church) with no previous agreement to salary. He induced another graduate to continue the work at Wheeling and secured the appointment of Mordecai DeLange as kind of supervisory missionary-at-large in the West.

Holland's first official report of his journey was given at a mass meeting in Boston in January, called to further Meadville's campaign for a fifty-thousand-dollar endowment fund. It is a masterly analysis and prognosis of the Western missionary situation, without railing accusations and sarcasm. But in his official report at the A.U.A. business meeting in May, he used scathing and denunciatory language:

> It has been our misfortune from the beginning to do much of our hardest work by men fresh from the theological cloister and inexperienced in the ministry … our clamorous want now is Western laborers – men of nerve, will, common sense, self-devotion, prayer … What a record of cowardice, indulgence, selfishness, faithlessness! How unenterprising, unadapted, unwise, unsystematized our efforts have been! We have done so little with so much truth, wealth and power!

Barring its severe but fairly well-founded aspersions on the capacity and dedication of some of his fellow ministers, Holland's indictment of the denomination for the inadequacy of its Western missionary work was thought, by many of the members present at this upsetting meeting, to be justified. But Holland was not continued in office! Since he was no Parkerite, but pietistic and conservative in his theology, our general conclusion must be that his dismissal was due not only to distaste for his ("Parkerish") censures of his colleagues but also to his praise and commendation of the Christian-Unitarian type of minister, in contradistinction to the conventional New England, Harvard Divinity School type and product. Are there not premonitions here of the tension of similar purport that came to a crisis, as we have seen, in Meadville in 1854? In Holland's fate we may also find a parallel to the disinterest and neglect with which the proposals of the Chicago group were treated.

Nevertheless, Mordecai DeLange, its secretary *pro tem*, did not propose to let them be forgotten, for as Western missionary-at-large he saw more clearly than ever the advisability of Western organization and collaboration. On a visit to St. Louis in 1850, he called the project to the attention of Eliot and his

Minister at Large, young Robert Hassall (Meadville '49). Again it got put into cold storage until there was a gathering of Unitarian ministers *only* (Conant was not present) at St. Louis, on the occasion of the dedication of Eliot's majestic and costly new Church of the Messiah in January, 1852. At a post-Communion tea in Eliot's home, the gathering

… took into consideration the expedience of forming a Western Unitarian Association. It was now thought the time had arrived for something to be done. It was decided that on the first day of May next, all the ministers and churches of the West should meet at St. Louis to form an association which should unite them more closely and enable them to act more effectively in the spread of the truth. The movement is regarded as an important one.

Hassall's letter in the *Inquirer*, from which these sentences are taken, was followed by hearty editorial endorsement and more letters, one of March 17 announcing the substitution of Cincinnati for St. Louis in language worthy of a modern convention bureau: "Nothing could be pleasanter than a visit at the flowery city, the Queen City of the West, the pivotal spot, where convenience is the main object to be considered." Another editorial notice written by "J. F. C.", then in Meadville, is militant in tone: "I am going to propose to my Western brethren to do something for ourselves and stop depending on the East."

The publicity was effective! How pleased DeLange and Conant must have been to see their project materializing, as they stood at the door of the rather somber "Gothic" church on the corner of Fourth and Race Streets and greeted the ministers and lay delegates gathering on Friday morning, the seventh of May. Every Western minister save [C. M.] Taggart of Nashville came, as well as Elder Millard of the School and Elder Silsbee of Cincinnati. There were also several prominent laymen among the delegates (no laywomen, of course, in those days), one of whom, William Greene, a patriarch of the Cincinnati church and an able lawyer, was chosen chairman. The President of the American Unitarian Association, Dr. Samuel K. Lothrop, and three other denominational officials attended. Four Harvard Doctors of Divinity, who were also eastern Unitarian clergymen, sent letters "expressing regrets at being unable to attend and sympathizing with the design of the meeting."

Getting down to business, after reports from the individual churches as to their history, condition and prospects, the meeting passed a definitive resolution:

(1) It is desirable to form a permanent Association Annual Conference [*sic*] composed of delegates from each of our Western churches, to meet once a year, by their delegates in different parts of the West.

(2) The name of this Association shall be "The Annual Conference of Western Unitarian Churches."

(3) The objects of this Conference shall be to advance the interests of vital, rational and practical Christianity.

The rest of the series of resolutions deals with delegate representation; permanent committees (on missions and churches, on books and tracts, on arrangements and correspondence); contributions assessed by the churches on themselves for missionary purposes, to be disbursed by the Treasurer of the Conference.

Perhaps the discussion of the name of the Conference, which was very animated, has more interest for us today. Clarke argued for "Lake and River Conference" so as not to exclude by a narrow sectarianism such men as Henry Ward Beecher or Horace Bushnell, whose catholic Christianity might incline them to join such an Association if not deterred by a name committing them to peculiar and non-essential doctrines. Conant, who declared himself "a decided Unitarian," doubted, however, the advisability of that name for the Conference, since in the West, at least, it had been confounded with skepticism and inoperative Christianity. Huidekoper seemed to prefer "Association of Liberal Christians." But Eliot stood out for "Unitarian," and in the end it was accepted.

Lawyer Greene, the chairman, drew the attention of the Conference to the necessity for adopting specific articles for a constitution, which was done in the afternoon session. Since several are repetitions of the preliminary resolutions, it may be well to single out for special mention only the following:

Article III – Any other Christian churches may join this Conference who desire to cooperate with it in the objects for which it is formed.

Article IV – The objects proposed by this Conference are: (1) the promotion of the Christian spirit in the several churches that compose it and the increase of vitality – practical religion; (2) the diffusion of Gospel truths and the accomplishment of such works of Christian benevolence as may be agreed upon.

The other articles are of the conventional sort, regulating the number and names of officers, the method of their election, (voluntary) financial contributions, means of amendment of the constitution. Article V expands the objects of action as "the support of home missionaries, the distribution of religious books and tracts, the promotion of theological education and the aid of feeble societies."

Every word, perhaps every punctuation mark, was given, we may be sure, the most meticulous and loquacious consideration, for the Conference extended over four days. Its business sessions closed with the appointment of a regional missionary for the ensuing year, Whitney of Hennepin, Illinois; the selection of St. Louis as the meeting place for 1853; the election of Eliot of St. Louis as President; as Vice-Presidents, Greene of Cincinnati and Nahum Ward of Marietta (who later was to give over twenty thousand dollars to build the Marietta church) — both of them loyal and substantial laymen. As Corresponding Secretary, Rev. A. A. Livermore of Cincinnati was a logical choice, for to his careful planning, in collaboration with Eliot, the success of the Conference was mostly due.

It is doubtful if a modern publicity expert could have made shrewder arrangements in order to put the denomination's best foot forward — its Boston foot, of course. The strategy provided for *five* sermons — none from the Christian elders, however. Their role, like Conant's, was to lead the not-too-well-attended morning prayer meetings (at eight o'clock!) and Conant was assigned to assist Heywood of Louisville with the Communion service on Monday evening. The Sunday-morning sermon was preached by Dr. Lothrop on Christianity as the great instrument for developing the Divine image in man and preparing him for immortal life (with 1 Corinthians 15:49 as the text). Dr. Lothrop, it will be remembered, was Theodore Parker's chief critic in Boston. It is significant, too, that in his Autobiography he confesses that "for fifteen years I stayed [on the Executive Committee of the A.U.A.] to exert such influence as I could in favor of conservative Unitarian theology and conservative action on the part of the Association ... I am a very decided Liberal Congregationalist ... I have always disliked the Unitarian name." However, Livermore reported to the *Inquirer* that

Lothrop's "remarkably powerful discourse ... was pronounced by some who heard it as the ablest sermon ever preached in this city." Next in merit, according to Livermore, came "the beautiful and impressive discourse of brother Clarke on 'Christian Union' on Sunday evening [which] did much to spread in this community the sentiments of Unitarians on this subject, and to teach us that the unity of the Spirit was not a unity in the bond of form, or a unity in the bond of dogma, but a unity of Spirit in the bond of peace." A significant forecast of the future development of the Conference and its present inclusive position!

Altogether, in spite of the fact that rain precluded the picnic for the Sunday-school workers, Livermore felt that

... we have had a well-attended, harmonious, spirited and delightful Conference – not one unkind remark nor one discordant incident. It is a serious reflection that we have, in this Conference, planted an institution which will endure for many years ... will probably measure its twenty, one hundred, one thousand years – perhaps as long as the Ohio River itself shall run!

CHAPTER SEVEN

Progress and Tension

TO THE PEACE-LOVING REV. A. A. LIVERMORE, the amicable inauguration of the Western Unitarian Conference seemed to presage "a church and a denomination in which there is diversity and discussion but perfect love and harmony among all the members. In the insane attempt after intellectual identity of doctrinal statement will we be forever breaking the supreme law of love and good will?"

As we shall see, however, few of his fellow Unitarians were prepared to purchase harmony at the sacrifice of what seemed to them to be truth, and righteousness, and freedom for the human spirit from any form of bondage. All these values were involved in the theological strife within Unitarian ranks over Parkerism and in the nation at large over slavery, whose efforts during the fifties to extend its domain into Kansas, Cuba, northern Mexico, and California went on *crescendo*. To these stimuli of excitement in this decade were added the fever of railroad-building, the Gold Rush and vigilante dramas in California, and the avalanche of immigration from Great Britain, Ireland, and Germany. By 1860, 50 per cent of the population of the Republic lived between the Alleghenies and the Rockies.

In its first year (1852-53) the Conference did not exhibit the vitality hoped for. Little more than $1,000 was received from the churches for missionary work; only two part-time missionaries had been kept in the field. The only new church formed during the year was that at Wheeling, West Virginia, where a graduate of Meadville had been transforming into a Unitarian society and a church building the inspiration given by Rev. F. W. Holland in 1849. For the instruction of its missionaries, the Executive Committee, headed by Livermore, prepared the following rather broad-gauge document:

78

The grand object which the Conference proposes is the promotion of vital, practical religion … Christian, not sectarian. Therefore it does not require of its missionaries the wearing of any sectarian name, the doing of any sectarian work. All it requires of them is that they should believe in the Lord Jesus Christ as one who spake with authority and whose religion is the divinely appointed means of the regeneration of men, individually and collectively.

These instructions, which were obviously made broad enough to include liberals of all denominations, had no sooner been adopted by the Conference at its meeting in 1853 than, with perfect incongruity, one of the Louisville church's patriarchs, Judge Henry Pirtle, offered a Unitarian *creed*:

Whereas there is a misunderstanding of the views of Unitarians on important subjects, it is deemed proper to make some declaration in reference thereto:

Resolved that we regard Jesus Christ not as a mere inspired man but as the Son of God – the Messenger of the Father to men, miraculously sent – the Mediator between God and Man – the Redeemer of the world; and that we regard the miracles of the New Testament as facts on which the Gospel is built.

The Lothrop-Eliot-Pirtle Attack on Parkerism

Whatever could have moved Judge Pirtle to try to commit the Conference against Parkerism? The explanation is probably to be found in the fact that in 1852 Theodore Parker had published three volumes of *Speeches, Addresses and Occasional Sermons*, the first volume of which contained one of his most radical utterances, "The Relation of Jesus to His Age and the Ages," as well as a number of upsetting social preachments – notably "A Sermon of the Dangerous Classes in Society." Then, after his savage obituary on Daniel Webster, which rocked Boston, the increasing size of its congregations constrained his Society to move to the new Music Hall, which seated 2,700 persons. Yet Parker had never withdrawn from the Unitarian ministry, and the orthodox took mischievous delight in holding the Unitarians responsible for his iconoclasms! To counteract them, the Executive Committee of the Association, of which Rev. Samuel K. Lothrop was President, devoted most of its annual report in 1853 to making a General Proclamation of the true Unitarian views – though they assured the membership that "we do not propose the presentation of anything like a creed [yet] we desire openly to declare and record our belief as a denomination as far as it can be officially represented by the American Unitarian Association."

Lothrop – whose Brattle Street Church, like King's Chapel, had never contributed a cent to Western missionary work – was in all probability the chief motor force in this attempt to exorcise Parker; and not only Parker but the whole *échelon* of Transcendentalism, German metaphysics, and Biblical Criticism, "as having offensively assailed and denied all traces of the supernatural in the history of Christianity and the life of its August Founder, shocking many pious hearts and alarming many sensitive minds," and "providing a chief clog to our numerical advance as well as one of the chief sources of the odium with which we are regarded." Lothrop's rotund style reached its height in the famous passage that Parker later held up to ridicule:

God, moved by His own love, did raise up Jesus to aid in our redemption from sin, did by Him pour a fresh flood of life through the withered veins of humanity and along the corrupted channels of the world; and is, by His religion, forever sweeping the nations with regenerating gales from heaven and the hearts of men with celestial solicitations.

Even some members of the Executive Committee demurred at such surreptitious creedalism, but they were outvoted, and the members of the Association adopted the "Proclamation." Did Rev. E. B. Hall, the Vice-President of the Association, bring news of the forthcoming Proclamation to Mr. Lothrop's Western friends, Heywood, Livermore, and Eliot – thence to Judge Pirtle? At any rate, the Conference did not straightway adopt the Pirtle resolution but referred it to a committee – consisting of Messrs. Eliot, Heywood, and Pirtle – for revision and resubmission in 1854.

Over the twelve months, Eliot applied himself assiduously to elaborating the resolution into a pamphlet later published as [Henry Pirtle's] *Unitarian Views*, which he submitted to the well-attended third Annual Meeting at Louisville, 1854. Judge Pirtle presented, and Eliot seconded, the following to serve as a preamble to a forth-coming constitution:

We regard Jesus Christ not as a mere inspired man but as the Son of God, the Messenger of the Father to men, the Mediator between God and Man, the Redeemer of the World. We regard the miracles of the New Testament as *facts* on which the Gospel is based.

Virtually the wording of 1853! Yet a very similar resolution had been rejected by the Autumnal Convention of Unitarian Ministers of the entire country that met in Baltimore in 1852. Thereupon *The Christian Register*, the Association organ, had bitterly complained:

> What is Unitarianism? The world has a right to know this. What is there in which we all agree? Let it not be one thing in Boston, another in New York, another in Philadelphia and another in St. Louis! It is, if it is anything, *quod ubique et ab omnibus creditur*. We want a *Church*, we want a Book of our Church, not authoritative but declaratory. We must have more thorough and efficient organization!

This was of course camouflaged creedalism. No wonder an animated discussion ensued! For some reason, the Association delegates were not permitted to take part in it, as President Lothrop, who was also present, complained with considerable pique when he was at last recognized. Rev. T. J. Mumford, Detroit, was not impressed by the resolution: "While I am willing to admit that my religious sensibilities have been somewhat wounded by some words of Mr. Parker, I am unwilling to have it appear that we consider *his* the most dangerous infidelity. The worst is, Christian ministers demanding obedience to the Fugitive Slave Law!"

The upshot of the discussion was that the Report was accepted and *Unitarian Views* ordered to be printed; but that a Preface to the Report, drawn up by Noah P. Sprague of Buffalo, should be printed *first*:

> Under our organization as the Conference of Western Unitarian Churches we have no right to adopt any statement of belief as authoritative or as a definition of Unitarian faith other than the New Testament itself, which is the divinely authorized rule of both faith and practice.

Not for decades to come would the missionary collections from the churches reach the 1854 figure – $3,424.28; but it could scarcely be claimed that results were commensurate. The Independent Christian Church had been organized at Cleveland, Ohio, by Rev. A. D. Mayo; a society and a church building were imminent in Dixon, Illinois; the First Unitarian Society of

Keokuk, Iowa, had come into being through the exertions of a New Englander, Dr. Freeman Knowles, and a Pennsylvanian of Dutch stock, Samuel Freeman Miller (who had been converted to liberal Christianity by President Horace Holley in Transylvania University at Lexington, Kentucky, and whose eminent career of public service culminated in his appointment to the Supreme Court by Lincoln).

Adventures in Higher Education

The 1854 Conference was marked by the first trip west of Rev. Henry W. Bellows of New York City, with his millionaire parishioner, Peter Cooper, to solicit the interest of the Western Unitarians for Antioch College, the new Christian Connection foundation in Yellow Springs, Ohio. With its inception the Unitarians had nothing to do; indeed, a major reason for its creation was that the Christians felt they were "being swallowed up" at Meadville by the Unitarians. When, however, Antioch's board, in the face of Fundamentalist objections, called the country's most famous educator, Horace Mann, the Boston Unitarian, to its presidency, the latter sought the advice of his friends in the East before accepting. Their hearty endorsement of the unique principles of the new institution (non-sectarianism and co-education), and their counsel that he should embrace the opportunity of adding the reform of higher education to his achievements in the elementary and secondary school fields, began the involvement of the Unitarians in the fortunes of Antioch for the ensuing seven decades.

Transylvania University

Horace Mann's experience at Antioch was in some respects regrettably similar to that of Rev. Horace Holley, minister of the Brattle Street Church in Boston, who accepted the presidency of Transylvania University at Lexington, Kentucky, in 1818. Holley was a man of deep interest in mental philosophy, of rich knowledge of classic letters, and of exceptional oratorical abilities; but his theological liberalism, though congenial with the Deism of the more influential trustees, some of whom were friends of Thomas Jefferson, was from the first suspected by the Presbyterians, a small but exceedingly compact and aggressive group. In spite of their open and covert attacks, he made steady progress in gaining for Transylvania the status of a Western Harvard or Yale, with law and medical schools of higher standards than any in the West at that time. By 1823 the success of his administration in terms of student enrollment, increase of endowment, national reputation, was undeniable. But Holley made no concealment of his dislike of bigoted and obscurant-ist Christianity. Various forthright utterances, such as that in a funeral tribute to a friend's Deistic convictions ("a life of virtue is the most suitable homage to the Deity"), were turned against him. The Presbyterians clamored that for an allegedly Christian minister to quote with approval such principles was plain proof that his influence on students was pernicious. The ensuing cam-paign of petty slander, gross falsehood, accusations of financial irregularities, is well-nigh incredible; but the combined effect was the stirring up of such suspicion and distrust that, in con-junction with political squabbles among the Republicans – his supporters – Holley felt constrained to resign in 1827. Shortly thereafter the student enrollment dropped from 419 to 184, and the law school had to be suspended. Under four succeeding orthodox presidents, the University gradually expired of sect-arian narrowness and dryness. The episode ended in personal tragedy as well, for Holley died of typhus fever in the South a year after his resignation.

Antioch College

Horace Mann had no such unscrupulous enemies to contend with at Antioch, but from the first the conservative Christians deterred their churches from giving him the full support he had depended on. Yet with radiant enthusiasm he entered upon the planning of the curriculum and outlining the moral and religious instruction to be given the students, insisting that every diploma should be a testimonial of character as well as knowledge. From the first, the handicaps under which he labored were forbidding: naïve and shady methods of financing the College; insolvency even before the opening; a faculty chosen for Christian piety rather than educational competence. Nevertheless his intellectual and spiritual leadership was so inspiring that the registration of students soared and the appreciation of both students and faculty was deep and affectionate. His theological critics became proportionately hostile. He was accused of craftily seeking to convert good Christian youth into Unitarians through such devices as Unitarian literature set out in the library, and lectures by his close friend, Theodore Parker, at the College. By 1854 he was forced to appeal to his friends in the East, particularly Henry W. Bellows, for financial aid to rescue Antioch from bankruptcy, since his Christian trustees were powerless to do so. Hence Bellows' journey west to appraise the situation and his appearance at the Conference of 1854.

Substantial assistance from either the Conference or Peter Cooper was not forthcoming; but Bellows persuaded certain New York friends to buy the College property in June, 1859, to prevent foreclosure. Just after this auspicious turn, Horace Mann died, worn out with worry and overwork, leaving as his last message to Antioch students the famous challenge: "Be ashamed to die before you have won some victory for Humanity."

Since there was no Christian minister or layman of scholarly ability equal to that of Horace Mann, the Christian trustees perforce chose a Unitarian minister, Thomas H. Hill, though he was already slated for the presidency of Harvard, which claimed him in 1862. The Civil War and the total lack of an endowment had reduced Antioch almost to the point of no return when in 1865 Rev. Henry W. Bellows (now a trustee) and Rev. Edward Everett Hale (henceforward to be Antioch's guardian angel) raised an endowment of $100,000, which was given with the express understanding that thereafter election to the board should be on an absolutely non-sectarian basis. Thereupon the trustees, a majority of whom were Christians, elected George W. Hosmer president. In reaction to a Unitarian president, the Fundamentalist Christians, who — as in the closely analogous situation at Meadville School a decade before — ranked pietistic and evangelical work before intellectual disciplines, did all they could to keep their young people from Antioch. When the College was forced to close in 1881 because of this policy, they agreed to undertake its reopening if they were given the right to appoint the president and faculty — to which the now largely Unitarian board consented, retaining, however, their charter responsibility for approving the appointments. These, however, proved so inadequate and even injurious that in 1891 the Unitarians re-assumed their right to appoint the College staff, and the Christians gave up the struggle.

Though the Unitarians had poured hundreds of thousands of dollars into Antioch, and had contributed able and self-sacrificing professors and trustees, as well as a fair number of students, yet the relationship with the Christians and the relative inaccessibility of Yellow Springs prevented the College from receiving enthusiastic and generous support from Western Unitarians. When its demise again seemed imminent in 1920, no resuscitation through Unitarian beneficence was foreseen, as had been the case in 1858, 1865, and 1890. It came, however, through the daring vision and executive efficiency of Arthur E. Morgan.

The fact that the Unitarians had carried on Antioch's life and ideals by faithful working and giving through six decades of struggle with poverty and opposition, so as to make possible its present prosperity and distinction, would seem to justify the inclusion of this narrative of its fortunes in a denominational history.

First Unitarian Church of Marietta, Ohio (1855)

Delegates from twenty churches gathered at Buffalo in 1855, and there were letters and reports from six or seven more. The best news of all came from Marietta, Ohio. Ever since 1826, when Moses G. Thomas had visited the beautiful city on the bluffs overlooking "*la belle rivière*," Nahum Ward, a native of Shrewsbury, Massachusetts, had been cherishing the dream of a Unitarian church in the Calvinist Congregational stronghold, meanwhile building up a fortune – like Harm Jan Huidekoper in Meadville – by selling farm land on lenient terms. On January 20, 1855, he inserted in the local paper a notice: "The day has arrived when I think an attempt should be made to form a Unitarian, rational, liberal religious society in this place for the worship of God in Unity." To the resultant gathering of liberals, Ward suggested a preliminary statement which was accepted as the basis of organization for the "First Unitarian Church":

> Overlooking all minor differences, sinking all alienating controversies, in the generous and conciliatory spirit that becomes us best; that we

may go forth and live the Christian life with a warmer philanthropy, a holier consecration, a united front; in the fear and affection of God and in the faith and love of Christ, we do form ourselves ...

In accordance with the New England custom, a doctrinal church covenant followed this basis of union for the larger Society. It affirmed the paternal character and merciful government of God; his Unity; Man's natural capacity of virtue but liability to sin; the supernatural authority of Jesus as teacher, redeemer, perfect moral exemplar; and then – "the soul's immediate ascension on release from the body to its accounts and rewards." No "Ballou nonsense" here!

These bases of union having been ratified, Ward set about building, at his own expense, the imposing neo-Gothic church that still stands as an architectural landmark of Marietta. In 1858, Ward brought Rev. Rushton D. Burr from the Cambridge school as "instructor in divine truth." Though he stayed but a year – and later pastorates were not much longer – the Wards kept the church alive and solvent until the blessed era of less transient ministries began with that of Rev. James T. Lusk, 1876-90.

The Chicago Conference (1856)

Returning to the Conference from our detour to Marietta, we find its delegates excitedly discussing an apparently innocuous but, as later events will prove, a very significant resolution, offered by the peace-loving Livermore: "That, avoiding all side issues and secondary points, we regard the religious life as the leading object of all our religious efforts." It seemed to the delegates, as it does to us, that its author desired to forestall debates and motions concerning slavery! Bellows, S. J. May, and Conant protested to such good effect that the references to "side issues" and "secondary points" were eliminated before the resolution was passed. How important it would prove to be in the heat of Abolitionist anger we shall see at the Alton Conference in 1857.

One might make the mistake of supposing that the dozens of guests from the East at the Conference in Chicago in 1856 came out of pure enthusiasm for Western Unitarianism. Partly, perhaps; but the provision of free passes and cut-rate hotel prices offered Easterners by the Chicago and Rock Island Railroad and the Chicago and Galena Railroad in celebration of their penetration to the Mississippi was also an inducement. Then, from the river ports, free rides with berths, meals, and band music, to St. Paul and Minneapolis, were to be had at company expense. So it was a well-attended Conference, and the Secretary proudly reported that the churches now had 1,285 families, 904 communicants, 1,302 Sunday school teachers and pupils, and $225,000 worth of property.

Conant seemed to have forgotten the Livermore resolution of 1855 about "the religious life as the leading object of all our religious efforts." He presented a resolution condemning the attack of slavery men on Free Soil colonists in Kansas, and coupled with it the assault of [Rep. Preston] Brooks on Senator Sumner in Congress. Eliot and other immediately protested. The resolution was amended from expressing condemnation of the slavers to "heartfelt sympathy" with Senator Sumner, "our Christian brother." Eliot still protested. Conant withdrew his motion. In closing, the Conference voted its thanks to the railroads, the Tremont House – and the *Chicago Daily Tribune* for its courteous reporting of the proceedings of the Conference!

The Schism at Alton (1857)

At the threshold of this disastrous meeting it should be said, in justice to W. G. Eliot, Jr., of St. Louis, that he was as much opposed to slavery as his old comrade in the mission field, Conant, or even the new minister at Cincinnati, Moncure D. Conway. But Eliot was a Christian humanitarian and abhorred violence. He disliked, as did many of his older colleagues, the harsh language and drastic policies of the Immediate Abolitionists, whom he regarded as utterly impractical. His own practicality of judgment was highly esteemed by the many lawyers, bankers, and businessmen in his congregation. Never in twenty-six years had he brought a political sermon to the pulpit, although he freely sought and gave counsel on such secular matters on weekdays. In his border state of Missouri, the balance between the slavery and the anti-slavery forces was very delicate.

Eliot came to Alton, to the church he had but recently rehabilitated, with two dozen delegates, including Judge Samuel Treat. With a goodly number of others they listened, doubtless with pleasure, to optimistic reports from the field: from Toledo, where Rev. Charles Ritter from the Meadville School had revived a former movement; from Peoria, where a new chapel had been built; from Milwaukee, where Eliot had so decisively created a new society the year before and had personally pledged five hundred dollars toward the Church of the Redeemer. Eliot's delegates at least probably applauded the diatribe of Rev. W. R. Alger, the A.U.A. representative, against Parkerism, and his assurance that the great body of Unitarians in New England remained faithful to the theology of Channing.

But the next item on the agenda started the fireworks! The young Parkerite and Abolitionist who had take Livermore's place in Cincinnati, Rev. Moncure D. Conway, "on the basis of the Fatherhood of God and the Brotherhood of Man," submitted a scathing resolution anent the Dred Scott decision, "which fastens slavery on every man, woman and child in America … these open designs on our liberties demand a firm, united effort of the free States to emancipate our country at any cost whatsoever and enthrone justice though the heavens fall!"

Judge Treat of St. Louis jumped up to protest that the Conference was a religious body, not the Supreme Court or Congress – and not a Synod, either. Judge Headley of Cincinnati differed with Judge Treat as to the competence of the Conference to deal with such subjects. Judge Treat retorted that "great injury is done the Church and Humanity by the agitation of such topics in and out of the pulpit. Ministers should be scrupulous to render unto Caesar the things that are Caesar's." James Freeman Clarke replied that in the case of Negro slavery, "Caesar has got hold of something that belongs to God and ought to give it up."

The following day Eliot offered a resolution "that delegates have no right or authority to prescribe principles and modes of action or articles of faith for the churches they represent." The resolution was declared not germane by the chair. Hosmer recalled that it was the original intention of the Conference to pass no such resolutions as that of Conway. U. Tracy Howe of Detroit observed that as one of the drafters of the original constitution he dissented from this interpretation. To calm ruffled tempers and to find a compromise, it was voted to have a committee which included W. G. Eliot, Jr., and Judge Treat reconsider the whole matter overnight. Eliot and Treat declined to serve on such a committee. Skipping the observance of the Lord's Supper, they departed for St. Louis with most of their delegates. Eliot never returned to the Conference he had done so much to create; the Church of the Messiah, as long as he was its minister, had officially withdrawn; its missionary contributions were suspended. From time to time his assistants reported for the St. Louis church; but he himself stood aloof. No one knew better than Eliot what a heavy loss to the Conference was the withdrawal of its largest and wealthiest constituent.

Eliot explained his action by the argument that it was understood at the outset there should be no binding resolutions made or passed. Yet he had been insistent in 1854 that the delegates commit the churches to the theological positions of his conservative *Unitarian Views*. Unless we explain his action as due to personal pique against Conway, the conclusion in inescapable that Eliot, who had heretofore been so successful in making and keeping the Conference theologically and socially conservative, feared that Conway's victory on the slavery issue might encourage him to try to commit the Conference to Parkerism as well. Thus Eliot's act of secession was both a threat and a precaution. Had the Conference capitulated, it would have forfeited any claim to being a democratic Unitarian body. We shall presently encounter other instances of such domineering tactics on the part of the conservatives – 1870 and 1886, specifically. With what constancy for freedom they were defeated and the spirit and method of genuine democratic co-operation firmly established is a central theme of succeeding chapters.

Although Rev. Samuel Longfellow, brother of the great poet, came from his church in Brooklyn, New York, to preach the Conference sermon at Quincy, Illinois, in 1858 and heartily supported its condemnation of slavery the preceding year, a shadow of regret at its first division obviously hung over all the proceedings. From Cincinnati came news of a rift in the church there and the withdrawal of a large number of its members to form the Church of the Redeemer. For Conway had denied "in the pulpit" the miracles of the New Testament, especially Christ's resurrection from the dead. To offset this disaster, however, reports came of the organization of new societies in Kalamazoo, Michigan, and Lawrence, Kansas.

The First Unitarian Society of Lawrence, Kansas

That the first church building in Kansas should have been that of a Unitarian congregation was not strange, in view of the fact that many of the Free Soil immigrants had been brought up in that faith in New England. Scarcely had the first contingent arrived in Lawrence than E. B. Whitman, the agent for the Massachusetts Emigrants Aid Society, determined on the building of a large structure of palisaded stakes which could be used on weekdays to shelter newcomers and on Sundays for church services – that the words of the poet Whittier might be fulfilled:

> We go to plant the common school
> On distant prairie swells;
> And give the Sabbaths of the wilds
> The music of her bells.

Rev. Ephraim Nute, Jr., was sent out from Boston, and not only preached but taught school. When the makeshift church school burned, he enlisted the aid of New England friends and got another under way, school desks, library, clock, and bell coming from New England via New Orleans. Though they went into the mud of the Mississippi because of a shipwreck, clock and bell were fished out in time to be placed in the church tower, the cost of which was partly defrayed by the city of Lawrence. Meanwhile Nute had organized "The Unitarian Society." When he resigned to enter the chaplaincy of the First Kansas Volunteers, a former Brook Farmer, later a Free Soil immigrant, Rev. John Stillman Brown, took up the work for the love of it, editing the *Kansas Farmer* and helping with the public schools. The church building was used as a hospital after the terrible Quantrell sack of Lawrence in 1863, but church services went on nevertheless – on the slope of Mount Oread when necessary – and if seasonable! Mr. Brown carried on the church life and leadership to 1869, when Rev. W. C. Tenney arrived to relive him. *One* Brook Farmer, at least, proved to be a very practical visionary!

Free Congregational Society of Bloomington, Illinois (1859)

Similarly connected with the momentous events preceding the Civil War was the Free Congregational Society of Bloomington, Illinois, organized August 8, 1859, by fifty-seven liberal friends of Kersey W. Fell and of his brother, Jesse W. Fell – the power behind the throne. As in the case of Harm Jan Huidekoper and the Meadville church, it may justly be said that the Bloomington church is "the lengthened shadow of a great man." Jesse W. Fell, whose genial nature, keen mind, and high character had made him a man of substance, was also a community benefactor of amazing vision and enterprise. If he was not taking the lead in starting a public library, a charity aid society, a daily newspaper (Bloomington's famous *Pantagraph*), he was engaged in persuading the legislature to establish a normal school for high-school teachers (now Illinois State Normal University). Of primary historical significance, however, was his religious influence on Abraham Lincoln.

In the records of our Western churches one frequently finds evidence of the co-operation of Hicksite Quakers (or Progressive Friends) with the Unitarians in church and community work. Of such affinities and joint efforts, Jesse W. Fell was the very embodiment. He was born a Hicksite Quaker in Pennsylvania; the reading of Channing's works in later years gave his original mysticism and humanitarianism a rational basis and an activist urgency. Law business first drew Lincoln and Fell together, and a close friendship developed. In the course of it Fell brought Channing's though to Lincoln's attention, just as the latter's law partner in Springfield, William H. Herndon, a fervent Parkerite and Abolitionist, introduced him to Parker's sermons and addresses – from one of which Lincoln borrowed the immortal last sentence of the Gettysburg Address. Herndon's later statements on Lincoln's religious convictions fully support Fell's judicial testimony that "Mr. Lincoln did not believe in what are regarded as the orthodox or evangelical views of Christianity, [but] Theodore Parker most nearly represented Mr. Lincoln's views [which] were strictly practical and rationalistic." This estimate is verified by Lincoln's own summarization of his faith:

When any church will inscribe over its altar as its sole qualification of membership the Saviour's condensed statement of the substance of both Law and Gospel, "Thou shalt love the Lord thy God with all thy heart and with all thy soul and with all thy mind, and thy neighbor as thyself," that church will I join with all my heart and soul.

In the same law office where, in all probability, Lincoln and Fell had discussed these very questions and manifestly with the same reverent freedom of thought and conscience, the Preamble of the new Bloomington Church was drawn up and adopted. It declared the object of the Society to be simply "the study and practice of Christianity" and "recognized among its members and all men the right and duty of private judgment, [looking] for unity of feeling and opinion in the solemn matters of religion to come through freedom of inquiry conducted in an honest and reverent spirit rather than through fixed standards of belief." A more explicit Declaration of Views adopted in 1861 reiterates this spinal principle:

> The following Declaration ... is in no wise binding upon the members nor does it pledge to unchanging adhesion those who now adopt it; but it is adopted as a useful exponent of our present way of thinking.

The first minister of the church was Rev. Charles G. Ames, who, while a "grass roots" missionary of the Free Will Baptist faith in Wisconsin, had been converted to Unitarianism by Channing's works. He had also been a Republican party worker with one of Fell's brothers. The first president of the Society was C. P. Merriman, editor of the *Daily Pantagraph*, a vehemently Republican organ. No wonder the church was popularly known not only as "The Broad Gauge Church" but as "The Church of Lincoln's Friends."

Conclusion

The militant anti-slavery spirit of the two churches just introduced indicates both the fact and the explanation of the retreat of Channing Unitarianism which had been predominant in the first two decades of Western Unitarianism before the rising tide of Parker's theological and political ideas. The temper of the eighteen-fifties was increasingly uncompromising and belligerent; Channing's was reasonable, moderate, conciliatory; Parker's break with the old theology was radical and drastic, like his repudiation of the Whigs' placation of the slave power. The apocalyptic anxieties of the decade, the financial depression of 1857 reacted violently on the churches. Churches divided, ministers who preached too much or too little on the slavery issue were dismissed – Conant "resigned" from Geneva. Revivalism swept the orthodox denominations. The Conference received less than $300 for missionary work in 1859-60. Weak societies dependent upon such aid gave up – Peoria, Dixon, Hillsboro, Illinois; Cleveland and Austinburgh, Ohio. Many calls came to the Conference at Milwaukee in 1860 for ministers – "or else we perish!" The success of the orthodox revivals perplexed the Conference leaders. "What is needed in our preaching to give our views of Christianity greater power ... over the masses of men?" In the discussion, Conway and Bellows stressed extemporaneous preaching – not sermon reading! Young from Boston recommended a positive liberal theology. A newcomer to the Conference, Rev. Robert Collyer, ex-blacksmith, ex-Methodist, ex-Englishman, endorsed the proposal of Staples and Conant for a separate Missionary Society and Fund, which liberals of all denominations were to be invited to join. For a Basis of Fellowship, a prophetically simple and practical statement was adopted:

We welcome as fellow-laborers all who are seeking to learn and do the will of the Father and work righteousness; and we recommend that in all places, with or without preaching, they organize for religious worship and culture, the works of faith and the labors of love.

The progress this broad, fraternal Basis marks over the Pirtle-Eliot *Unitarian Views* is obvious. Its spirit was underscored by the "eloquent tributes" paid by Conway and Ames to Theodore Parker, who had died in Italy a month before. How great was the distance yet to go before the Conference reached spiritual maturity was indicated by Bellows' comment: "Though I would not certainly affirm that Parker was a lost soul yet he [Parker] did not accept the conditions of salvation."

CHAPTER EIGHT

The Struggle for Independence

IN 1870 THE CONFERENCE held its annual meeting in Cleveland, Ohio. Thirty-six churches were represented by either delegates or written reports. June co-operated with three of her rarest days. At the end of the rainbow glowed a pot of gold in the form of a reception in the palatial Euclid Avenue mansion of Jeptha H. Wade, vice-president of the Western Telegraph Company. But in the midst of the first session, after listening to the report of the Western Secretary of the A.U.A., Rev. Charles H. Brigham, the Unitarian minister of Detroit, Rev. W. R. G. Mellen, "felt much depressed, yet he did not feel like giving up the ship." To strike a positive note he offered a resolution:

The Conference has listened with profound and painful interest to the Report ... but feels that any abandonment of its work is not to be contemplated.

Before disclosing how the Conference finally voted on this resolution, it will be instructive to look back over the decade since 1860 to discover, if possible, the grounds for Brigham's pessimism. With the results of the survey before us we may then decide how we ourselves would have voted had we been present in 1870.

[The Western Unitarian Conference in 1870]

The four sessions in wartime (that in 1861 was omitted) were marked rather by reports and resolutions concerned with the great struggle than by announcements of new churches founded. The work of the two Sanitary Commissions was commended; President Lincoln was assured in 1863 that "we will continue cheerfully to share any and all sacrifices and burdens in the holy cause of our country." When the triumph of the cause was assured, Rev. Henry W. Bellows, president of the United States Sanitary Commission, transferred the executive ability he had so brilliantly demonstrated in that capacity to a project for co-ordinating under Unitarian leadership the liberal Christian forces of the nation. Accordingly, he engineered the formation of the National Conference of Unitarian Churches, which resulted in an extraordinary intensification of denominational consciousness, confidence, and generosity, as shown in the raising of hundreds of thousands of dollars for the two theological schools (Harvard and Meadville); for Antioch College; for the experiment of theater mission preaching to reach the unchurched multitudes; for the missionary work of the A.U.A., including the appointment of a Western Secretary, Rev. Carlton A. Staples, who had been serving efficiently as chairman of the Executive Committee of the Western Conference while minister in Milwaukee.

By 1869, with the greatly increased funds at his disposal for ministerial support and church building aid, Staples had piloted the organization of some twenty-eight societies – not including the Church of the Unity in St. Louis, a proliferation on the city's south side of William G. Eliot's Church of the Messiah. Working out of Milwaukee in the first period of his activity, he had stimulated the organization of churches (generally with the title of "Liberal Christian" or "Church of the Unity") in the Wisconsin cities of Janesville, Kenosha, Sheboygan, and Whitewater – and presided over the obsequies of the Madison society, which had died of Copperheadism. He had supervised the formation of churches in Winnetka, Princeton, Sheffield, Roscoe, Geneseo, Springfield, Evanston, Hinsdale – all in Illinois. To the "Apostle of Southern Illinois," Rev. Jasper L. Douthit, Staples, in alliance with Rev. Robert Collyer of Chicago, had given encouragement to an experiment of Unitarian "circuit riding" with its center in Shelbyville, and within its circumference Mode, Jordan, and Mattoon – where, after a lecture by Emerson on "Immortality" (of which no one understood anything much but the noble, benevolent face of the speaker), the Unity Church of Liberal Christians was organized (1868). In Ohio, churches had been gathered at Sandusky and Columbus; in Indiana, at Evansville and Indianapolis; in Missouri, at St. Joseph and Kansas City, the last church having the good fortune of the abiding loyalty of Major White, Alfred Pirtle, E. K. Rugg, and Henry

N. Smith, as well as the leadership of Rev. W. E. Copeland. To Rev. Stephen H. Camp's work with the First Unitarian Church in Toledo (1860), Staples had given hearty support. During his secretaryship, the First Unitarian Church of Davenport, Iowa, was organized (1868), although the credit for the seed planting should perhaps go to Rev. Thomas L. Eliot of St. Louis, Rev. Robert Laird Collier of Chicago, and Rev. S. S. Hunting of Quincy, in collaboration with such "pillars" as Mr. and Mrs. John L. Mason and others of equally tenacious and substantial loyalty. To Council Bluffs, Iowa, Rev. Charles H. Brigham had journeyed on the Burlington's new tracks to preach to a group of New England engineers; then he crossed the Missouri to Omaha and rallied similar liberals there, with the result that the First Unitarian Church was incorporated in 1869, with Thomas Davis as president of the trustees and Rev. Henry F. Bond called as first minister.

The policy adopted by the National Conference in 1866 and 1867 of organizing regional conferences throughout the country had been followed by Staples. The Wisconsin Conference of Unitarian and Other Independent Societies and the Ohio Valley Conference of Unitarian and Other Liberal Christian Churches had come into existence. Indeed, there were some who felt that, following the National Conference policy by which all missionary funding and planning should be turned over to the A.U.A., the Western Conference should do the same. This tendency had been resisted by many in the Conference on the ground that "we are so completely identified with the Western Conference that nothing can induce us to allow it to stand subordinate to any other organization. It is the natural outgrowth of the West; but we need and must have the assistance of our Eastern brethren." Nevertheless the pressure for centralization was so strong that in 1869 the conservatives succeeded in amending the Conference constitution to the effect that its churches' missionary contributions should be paid to Boston, there to be allocated back west as the Association's Executive Committee, in more or less sympathetic consultation with the Western Secretary, might see fit. Against this amendment [T. B.] Forbush had protested vehemently: "*We* understand best what we want. We ought to stand on our own feet ... though called by the same name, Unitarianism is not *just* the same West as East … Western Unitarianism has a different spirit, is broader and more liberal, looks more to the future and less to the past."

Evincing just such independence and initiative, the two Unitarian churches in Chicago formed the Chicago Conference and soon added to themselves a Third (1868) and a Fourth (1869) under the leadership of Rev. Carlton A. Staples and Rev. Charles W. Wendte – the Third Church meeting for its first three years in a hall on the west side, the Fourth in similar accommodations on the south side. All had participated in the Chicago Liberal Union, an organization that included the two Universalist churches in the city, and had as its rationale the refusal of the Young Men's Christian Association (whose president was then Dwight L. Moody) to allow the Unitarians any voice in its policies, though accepting Unitarian contributions of nearly $15,000 yearly. Moody, indeed, would not even reply to the Unitarian protest. To Moody's salvationist tenets, the president of the new Liberal Union answered that "a pure life abounding in good works is the only true test of religion; the Union's only doctrinal basis is: 'Do you believe that God is your Father and Man is your Brother?'"

With such proofs of the progress of Western Unitarianism before us, it is difficult to understand the pessimism of Secretary Brigham's report in 1870. But before casting our vote for or against Mellen's resolution, we might do well to consider the possibility that Brigham's forebodings as to the future of the Western movement rested on theological bias rather than on the facts in the case.

Undoubtedly there were indications that all too many of the younger ministers in the Conference, even those whose work was subsidized by the A.U.A., were showing strong sympathies with Parkerism – a drift that was displeasing to most of the Eastern leaders, especially Rev. Edmund H. Sears, author of the famous Christmas carol, "It Came Upon the Midnight Clear." Two of the new missionary churches had withdrawn from the Conference – those at Toledo and Salem, Ohio; the former had gone so far as to disavow all taint of Christian sectarianism in calling the arch-radical, Rev. Francis E. Abbot, to its pulpit (1869) and changing its name to "The Independent Religious Society." When Secretary Staples – who resigned in disgust in 1869 – complained that missionary contributions from the conservative churches in the West and grants in aid from the Association in the East were falling off, the reply was made: "If we only knew whom you are going to employ, we would do more for you." To which Staples had answered that he employed "any good and efficient minister ... no matter if he is radical, if he meets the needs of the people to whom he ministers ... so also if he is conservative."

To replace Staples, the Boston Association appointed Rev. Charles H. Brigham, a scholarly medievalist, minister of the University missionary church (1865) in Ann Arbor, professor in the Meadville School. Brigham had not cared for views expressed by Rev. T. B. Forbush at the Conference in 1869:

> Religion has no necessary connection with any man's or any church's scheme of doctrine or plan of salvation, however ancient, logical or well-authenticated; it is recognition and trust in God, joined to good will toward men; it is loving, humble worship and good hearty fellowship ... the Liberal church of the West is to preach a gospel of the new thought, the new science, the new civilization ... we present a theology not founded on ancient tradition nor upon the authority of any name, however sacred, but upon the actual facts of this mighty universe and upon the real relations of man and God as revealed in human life.

This, of course, was pure Parkerism, and Brigham had good reason to believe – as he reported to the Association in Boston – that it expressed the views of many of the younger Western ministers and their churches. To stem the tide Brigham arranged to have Rev. A. D. Mayo, minister of the schismatic Church of the Redeemer in Cincinnati, deliver the opening address to the Conference of 1870, taking as his subject "The True Vocation of Western Unitarianism." It was a long, earnest, eloquent plea for a return to Channing Unitarianism:

> I have come to believe that the vocation of the Western Unitarian Church is not essentially different in its central aspect from any other branch of the Christian Church. It is to be a Christian Church, founded upon a platform of faith and directed by a consistent polity held and administered in the spirit of Christian freedom with as much allowance

for individual independence as is consistent with a progressive and efficient Church.

Then came Brigham's dolorous report! Under the circumstances it seems clear that its pessimism had indeed a theological bias – and purpose. To him the main significance of the Conference was its preponderant doctrinal position in 1870. In its value as a comradeship in the age-long struggle for spiritual freedom, intellectual progress, and inclusive human brotherhood, he found no basis for confidence and hope. Lest any of us be equally shortsighted and through conservative theological predilections inclined to vote *against* Mellen's resolution, it will be profitable to look back over the record of Western Unitarianism since 1826 in larger fields than that of theology.

Literature

From the beginning of the pioneer days, observing travelers in the West noted that the settlers were omnivorous newspaper readers, to the exclusion in most cases of anything of higher literary quality. A fair judgment would explain this by the frontiersman's need of getting the latest business, legal, political, and transportation news. Here and there, indeed, one might find log cabins with volumes of Shakespeare, Pope, Milton, Fielding, Burns, Goldsmith, sometimes Paine and Volney, on shelves high enough to escape children, dogs, mice, and dampness. These books had, of course, been brought from the East; the West had neither bookstores, publishing houses, nor even authors of any consequence until after 1820. Then they appeared in Lexington, next in Louisville, Kentucky, then in Cincinnati – each city claiming in its turn to be "the Athens of the West"!

Doubtless desiring to reproduce in this most civilized portion of the West the literary culture and creativeness practically synonymous with New England Unitarianism, and assuming that the number of well-known writers in Cincinnati and Louisville would insure success, Rev. Ephraim Peabody, who came in Cincinnati in 1832 from Meadville, Pennsylvania, consulted with his friend Rev. James Freeman Clarke in Louisville, as well as with J. H. Perkins and William Gallagher of the Unitarian church; and in 1834 he formed a Western Unitarian Association for the publication of *The Western Messenger*. The first number, "devoted to Religion and Literature," appeared in June, 1835, in Louisville. For its first two years it was candidly propagandist: "This periodical is devoted to a rational and liberal religion ... no other form can prevail in the West. A primary object of this work is to set forth and define correct views of Christianity." It did this, however, not by a plethora of such heavy theological argument as H. J. Huidekoper's article on "The Unitarianism of the First Three Centuries of the Christian Era," but by an ingenious medley of moral poetry and tales, religious news, essays, and book reviews, all of a literary excellence approaching that of the *North American Review* and the *Christian Examiner* and in some cases surpassing both. Clarke, who was editor from 1836 to 1839, dropped the Unitarian name, stressed non-sectarianism, and cannily intercalated *gratis* contributions from his New England friends – Dr. Channing, Ralph Waldo Emerson, O. W. Holmes, J. S. Dwight, Jones Very, Margaret Fuller, Hawthorne – and even Carlyle and German authors, between articles by his Western friends, Perkins and Gallagher, and his parishioner, Mann Butler. He begged an unpublished poem of John Keats, "The Ode to Apollo," from the latter's brother, George Keats, then living in Louisville. It was from Emerson, however, that Clarke received his most notable assistance: four unpublished poems, "Each and All," "The Humble Bee," "Rhodora," "Goodbye, Proud World"; and gradually the periodical became a "Western *Transcendentalist* Messenger." From no other source did Emerson's Divinity School Address of 1838 receive a more appreciative, though discriminating, tribute. Mere rational and liberal Christians, unfortunately, were so transcendentalized that they did not renew their subscriptions! In 1840, after editors William Henry Channing and Christopher Cranch had volatilized the *Messenger* in their best style, this gallant and brilliant literary venture of Unitarianism in the West hailed *The Dial* of Boston as its heir, and expired.

Not until *Unity* was launched in 1878 did the movement have a worthy periodical composed, published, circulated in the West. *The Christian Repository*, published by the Meadville School faculty in 1852-53, was a scholarly but limited theological magazine. Moncure D. Conway's *Monthly Dial* (Cincinnati,

1860-61), was a one-man, one-year meteorite – in [W. H.] Venable's words, "the most original, peculiar, audacious publication that ever issued from the press – an avatar of the Boston *Dial*." Its most interesting features – besides dozens of Conway's own delightful contributions – were the early poems of William Dean Howells; a "Catholic Chapter" of passages from the classic and ethnic scriptures that presaged Conway's later *Sacred Anthology* (1874); and a capital review of Emerson's forthcoming *Conduct of Life*, for which the author obligingly sent the proof sheets out west! In conclusion, it is worth repeating that while all the other denominations in the West had their Western periodicals, however elementary and Fundamentalist, the literary Unitarians were without a regional organ until 1878 and had to depend upon *The Christian Register* and *The Christian World* from Boston, *The Christian Inquirer* from New York, for news of Unitarian activities in their neighboring cities and states. Though all these organs eagerly and accurately printed Western Unitarian news, correspondence, and appeals, their editorials and articles were Eastern in policy and temper. For instance, their attitude toward the Universalists was less friendly than the Western; their attitude toward alcoholism was far more lenient. (The *Register* regularly accepted wine advertisements.) Consequently, their subscription lists in the West were short and uncertain; their circulation depended mostly on friends' mailings or missionaries' gifts. The bearing of these facts upon the slow development of denominational consciousness, co-operation, and missionary giving is obvious.

With respect to books written and published in the West, the record is not so barren. Cincinnati's Unitarian authors included Timothy Flint, the most prolific, versatile, and popular of all in the pioneer days. His *Recollections ... of Journeyings in the Mississippi Valley* (1826); his *History and Geography of the Mississippi Valley* (1832); his fourteen-edition *Daniel Boone* (1833) – as well as three romantic, banal, prolix, but profitable novels of frontier life – were all written in the years of his prominence in the Unitarian church. The same is true of W. D. Gallagher's three books of poems (1835-37). James Handasyd Perkins' mystical, lyrical, sentimental poems, as well as his unique contributions to the *North Atlantic Review*, fall in the decades from 1830 to 1849, as does, parenthetically, his part in the founding of the Historical Society of Ohio. At least a third of the founders and officers of the famous Cincinnati Literary Club were Perkins' parishioners – notably Manning F. Force.

When Rev. A. A. Livermore came to the Cincinnati church in 1850, it acquired a minister who had already become nationally known for his thoroughly documented, scathingly critical *The War With Mexico Reviewed* (1850) – which closed with an appeal for a Congress of Nations and a World Court. Livermore's *Discourses*, a volume of which was published in 1854, are signally eloquent and yet practical. His lucid, scholarly commentary on Romans (1854) for lay as well as ministerial users, supplementing similar studies of the Gospels and Acts, prepared the way for his appointment to the presidency of the Meadville Theological School in 1863.

But the productions of his successor, Moncure D. Conway – whose sortie into Transcendentalist journalism (*The Monthly Dial*) has already been mentioned – were not so pietistic. His collection of sermons in *Tracts for Today* (1857) is a dynamic compound of Methodist fervor, Unitarian reason, and Emersonian originality, with each ingredient at its best – notably Sermon XII, "The Communicant." Sermon II, "The Skeptic," gave high praise to the very free thought that even Unitarian theologians had for decades been denouncing as synonymous with moral anarchism. It may well explain why the followers of Thomas Paine invited him to speak at their annual Paine Memorial meeting. There his mind was opened to the fact that the calumnies with which the orthodox and the Federalists had blackened Paine's character were of dubious veracity. Forty years of research in this country, Britain, and France culminated in the publication of the two-volume *Life of Thomas Paine* in 1892 and the four-volume *Writings of Thomas Paine* in 1894-96, by which the stereotyped slanders that Paine was a "filthy little atheist" – Theodore Roosevelt's compliment to him – were completely refuted. The rehabilitation of Paine's nobility, integrity, sacrificial patriotism, and reverent, ethical religious position, which has proceeded apace since Conway's work, has been a gratifying victory for truth and justice.

Next to Cincinnati, Meadville was the nodal point of Unitarian literary production before 1870, commencing with the collaboration of layman Harm Jan Huidekoper and his minister, Ephraim Peabody, in *The Unitarian Essayist* (1831-32), an arsenal of Unitarian Christian theological apologetic. Professor Frederic Huidekoper's curious work on *The Belief of the First Three Centuries concerning Christ's Mission to the Underworld* (1854) is a memorial both of Huidekoper's immense erudition and of his solicitude to establish the credibility of the Gospel narratives – a concern shared by virtually all Unitarian Christian theologians until the problem was rendered obsolete by Transcendentalism, the Higher Criticism, evolution, the comparative study of non-Christian religions, and other modern ways of thinking. Frederic Huidekoper's *Judaism at Rome* (1870) is equally impressive in its erudition and is today useful as a storehouse of data and reasons for the crucially tolerant policy of the Stoic Emperors toward the Christian Church.

After leaving Louisville and *The Western Messenger* in 1840, James Freeman Clarke spent some years in Meadville, finishing and publishing his translations from De Wette of the latter's religious novel *Theodore; or The Skeptic's Conversion* (1841). It is an acute, ingenious treatment of the critique of Christianity at the hands of later German Rationalism, with Clarke's (that is, De Wette's) Transcendental Christianity eventually winning Theodore over! During a later stay in Meadville, besides publishing two appealing but sentimental theological works, *The Christian Doctrine of Forgiveness of Sin* (1852) and *The Christian Doctrine of Prayer* (1854), Clarke collaborated with Emerson and W. H. Channing in the *Memoirs of Margaret Fuller Ossoli* (1852), a notable tribute of her close friends to one of America's great women leaders who had perished shortly before in a tragic ship disaster. In addition to these early productions of a literary career that grew in volume, scholarly value, and spiritual wisdom to its close in 1890, scores of ordination, installation, and church dedication sermons – and many appropriate hymns as well – printed in Unitarian periodicals from 1834 to 1880 attest to Clarke's unfaltering loyalty to the Western field where he began his ministerial service. But no such literary heritage was left by his lifelong friends and colleagues in the same work, George W. Hosmer of Buffalo and W. G. Eliot of St. Louis. From Hosmer's pen we have nothing but several A.U.A. tract sermons.

Eliot's prodigious pastoral and community labors for charity and education prevented him from publishing anything but his *Discourses on the Unity of God* (1852); his often reprinted *Lectures to Young Men* [1852]; his *Lectures to Young Women* (1854); *The Discipline of Sorrow* (1855), a tender book of consolation prompted by the death of his own daughter; *The Story of Archer Alexander* (1885), the story of a loyal Negro who sought refuge with Eliot in 1863 after terrible experiences at the hands of slavers. Eliot's extraordinary executive ability, manifested not only in the conduct of the Western Sanitary Commission during the Civil War, but later also in the chancellorship of Washington University, was his Nemesis so far as authorship was concerned. Duty held him a slave to the motto on the Eliot family crest, "Tace et fac!"

Treasures of thought and eloquence and of poetic beauty as well, in occasional hymns, lie hidden in the dusty files of the Unitarian periodicals of this period: the *Christian Register*, the *Christian Examiner*, the *Christian Inquirer*, after 1865 the *Liberal Christian*, the *Christian World*, the *Monthly Religious Magazine*, the *Monthly Miscellany*. Similar treasures lie in innumerable pamphlet sermons that may yet come to light in old church and home collections, in city, college, and historical society libraries. In all probability many worthwhile books were written by laymen and laywomen of the Conference, a specimen of which is the *Brief Sketch of the State of Ohio* (1822) by Nahum Ward of Marietta; another is the novel *Zoe, or the Quadroon's Triumph* (1853), from the pen of Mrs. A. A. Livermore, then in Cincinnati.

Paradoxically enough, it is Robert Collyer – the former Yorkshire blacksmith and Methodist preacher, with no formal education at all but with an inborn love of good books and a native genius for speaking and writing lucid, winsome, graphic English – who gives Chicago a place in this survey of Western Unitarian literature. Coming to Chicago in 1859 as the First Church's Minister at Large to care for its extensive public relief and religious education work, he was almost immediately pressed into service as pastor and preacher not only for the First Unitarian Church but also for the newly formed Unity Church on the north side, which wasted no time in securing him as their regular minister. In their enthusiasm they forgot to install him in the conventional manner; and when they undertook to draw up a constitution and a "platform of faith" – to use Mayo's term – they got nowhere theologically: "We once tried to work out some simple form of creed," wrote one of the founders, S. S. Greeley, "but our belief was too inclusive to be imprisoned in words and we gave it up. The one point on which all agreed was that all might differ." This entirely suited their minister, whose personal and pulpit faith was a warmhearted, non-doctrinal, practical Christianity.

During the Civil War, Collyer was a dynamo of strength and service, not only to Unity and the old First Church but to the work of the Sanitary Commissions as well, in the East, in Tennessee and Kansas. In Chicago he gradually became the leading prophet of Union, Emancipation, Lincoln, and victory. *Some Memories* vividly narrates his experiences during these years, climaxed by the disaster of the burning of Unity's stately and costly new church on Walton Square in 1871 and its rebuilding in 1873, aged William Clarke being the prime mover in the latter undertaking! On the great anvil of the smithy in the north of England where he had done his apprentice work, and which had been brought over in 1866 and installed in his church study, Collyer hammered out some of the sermons included in *Nature and Life* (1867) and the noble biography of Chaplain A. H. Conant, *A Man in Earnest* (1868).

Since James K. Hosmer, a son of the Buffalo manse, spent his mature years within the borders of the Western Conference as a member successively of the Antioch College, Washington University, and University of Minnesota faculties, it is suitable to mention here his two books of wartime actions and reflections – *The Color-Guard* (1864) and *The Thinking Bayonet* (1865). In the same category is *An Artilleryman's Diary* by Jenkin Lloyd Jones, written in the field but not published until 1914.

If this register of Unitarian contributions to Western literature seems meager, an explanation offered by a writer in *The Western Messenger* is worth pondering: "Our people have as yet no literature because they are busy *living, doing, growing*."

Education

Among many things they had been doing was the fostering of educational institutions of all kind, particularly free, non-sectarian public schools. Any community in which a Unitarian church had been founded before 1850 was the beneficiary of the latter's pressure for a non-denominational and efficient school system – an interest which the Congregationalists and Presbyterians of the Great Lakes and Prairie States shared and in the furtherance of which in that area they often preceded the Unitarians. But in the lower Ohio Valley cities, in Cincinnati, where Nathan Guilford, Albert Picket, and Manning F. Force pioneered in the cause; in Louisville, where Mann Butler was a prime mover for the high schools and the public library; in St. Louis, where W. G. Eliot headed the successful campaign in the city's darkest year (1849) for a school tax, then for public evening schools for working people (1850), then for the O'Fallon Polytechnic Institute (1855) – the Unitarians were conspicuously active and influential.

In St. Louis in the field of higher education this was even more obvious. The Eliot Seminary of 1853 had become the Washington Institute of 1857, then university of thoroughly non-sectarian character with an ambition to become the "Harvard of the Mississippi Valley." From 1853 to his death in 1887, Eliot was (gratuitously) president, then chancellor of a university four-fifths of whose endowment of a million and a half dollars in 1878 had been given by members of his own church. W. G. Eliot's son, Rev. Thomas Lamb Eliot, first Unitarian minister in Portland, Oregon, continued his father's interest in higher education, becoming a co-founder of Reed College there and for many years its president (1904-20).

Of Unitarian participation in the founding and continuance of Antioch College in Ohio an account has already been given. The collaboration of the Unitarian Andrew D. White with the Quaker Ezra Cornell in the founding of non-sectarian Cornell University in 1865 – whereof Rev. Samuel J. May of Syracuse and Rev. Rufus P. Stebbins of Ithaca were counselors and trustees – is another instance of the value of inclusive religious principles. On the same basis the municipal University of

Cincinnati, endowed in 1858 by Charles M'Micken, opened in 1873 with substantial Unitarian support. To insure its non-sectarian character, to tide it over financial and political difficulties, and to enlist the co-operation of the large German and Jewish population of Cincinnati, Rev. Thomas Vickers, who had left the ministry of the First Unitarian Church in 1874 to become chief city librarian, assumed the duties of rector and president of the new university, as well as the professorship of German, from 1877 to 1884.

Because of this willingness to work and to give generously on behalf of non-sectarian education, there is no institution of learning within the boundaries of the Western Unitarian Conference at the present time which is under Unitarian auspices or control.

The Ministry at Large

As with education, so with practical philanthropies – the Western Unitarians followed closely the ideals and methods of their co-religionists in New England. There the liberal movement had long since been committed to institutional and legislative work for the humane and intelligent care of the blind, deaf, and dumb; to the advocacy of international peace, which manifested itself in a uniform disapproval of the Mexican War; to the temperance movement in its various phases; to humane and constructive treatment of mental patients and of criminals; to the crusade against slavery. This earlier form of the "Social Gospel" received more nearly unanimous agreement and co-operation among Unitarian ministers both east and west than any set of theological views. Both the Harvard and the Meadville ministerial schools had professors who wrote and spoke unreservedly in favor of these reforms; the students and teachers held prayer meetings and discussions devoted to their advancement.

Wherever the new Unitarian churches grew strong enough and their ministers remained long enough to have and to use influence, the humane application of Christianity was frequently advocated and committees were formed to exert persuasion and pressure on city councils or state legislatures. Such work by W. G. Eliot in Missouri succeeded in getting appropriations from that state for the education and aid of the blind as early as 1853. A decade earlier a group of laymen of the Cincinnati church had won over the state legislature of Ohio to the cause of the blind. Across the Ohio, the Unitarian minister, Rev. Benjamin B. Huntoon, did memorable work in the Kentucky Institution for the Education of the Blind, which expanded into the wider service of the American Printing House for the Blind. The effective appearances of Dorothea Dix before the legislatures of the three states in question were supported by Eliot, Perkins, and Heywood – the latter the Unitarian minister of Louisville. His church in that city was responsible for starting and maintaining a half dozen or more institutions for the weak and helpless, notably the Benevolent Institute for Old Ladies and the Louisville Charity Organization.

The latter, like similar bodies in Cincinnati and Chicago, was the outcome of the work of the Ministry at Large. This office and its plan of duties had its inception in the vision of a young Unitarian layman of Boston, Frederick T. Gray. Commencing in 1826, Rev. Joseph Tuckerman actualized the vision as a form of non-sectarian religious social work among the poor of the North End, 18,000 of whom in a population of about 55,000 had no connection with the churches, and hence did not qualify for assistance in terms of pastoral care, or of relief of destitution, unemployment, poor housing, juvenile and adult illiteracy and delinquency. To bring not only a religious message of spiritual hope and moral reform, but wise counsel, personal interest, and practical aid to all who are today cared for in civic programs of social work was Tuckerman's aim: "It is the first object of the Ministry at Large never to be lost sight of and to which no other is to be preferred, to extend its offices to the poor and to the poorest, to the low and to the lowest, to the most friendless and the most uncared for, the most miserable." Of course one notices a resemblance here to the projects of Thomas Chalmers in Scotland and of William Booth during the "Black Forties" in England. But it was Tuckerman's unique contribution to the idea that he added to his fifteen annual reports and included in his summary of *The Principles and Results of the Ministry at Large* (1838) masterly sociological analyses and suggestions for the physical and moral amelioration of the plight of the submerged classes.

In helping them, Tuckerman and the many associate ministers he gathered into the work as the years passed (he died in 1840, but the Ministry continued after him) paid no attention to sectarian boundaries, as practically all charity work of the early period did, and presented Christianity without any sectarian flavor.

Four Western Unitarian churches supported, from about 1835 to about 1860, Ministers at Large: St. Louis, Cincinnati, Louisville, and Chicago. In this role James Handasyd Perkins labored so well in Cincinnati that he became co-founder and president of the city's Relief Union; while, in Chicago, Robert Collyer won the confidence of the city officials and the Board of Trade by his tireless, intelligent performance of such duties as the conduct of day and evening schools, as well as Sunday schools, for the underprivileged; the administration of food, clothing, and medical aid to hapless families; the procurement of work, decent housing, legal advice for Irish and Polish immigrants. Any and all of these services were rendered without regard to the denominational status of the recipients. It is easy to understand why the Ministry blazed the trail from the skimpy, sentimental, unsystematic, and – through duplication of bounties – demoralizing parish charities of 1826 to the great structure of sociologically scientific public relief and rehabilitation work we have today in city, state, and nation.

The United States Sanitary Commission

Such essentially religious and Christian yet scrupulously non-sectarian humanitarianism, associated in the mind of the nation over many decades with Unitarianism, explains in large part the success of Rev. William G. Eliot in the West, as well as that of Rev. Henry W. Bellows in the East, in the conception and development of those two indispensable and invaluable services to the soldiers' well-being in the Civil War, the Western Sanitary Commission and the United States Sanitary Commission. When President Lincoln in April, 1861, called for volunteers to put down the rebellion, and hundreds of thousands of young men

rushed to the hastily prepared camps, the stodgy Medical Department of the Regular Army was totally unprepared to cope with
the problems of hygiene, camp sanitation, transport of wounded
soldiers, hospitalization, drug and dressing supplies, convalescent
soldiers, and crippled soldiers that crashed down upon it.
Washington and St. Louis were focal points of rebel attack
within four months; the *débâcle* of Bull Run (July, 1861) worsened
conditions in the camps and hospitals around Washington; the
costly Union victory of Wilson's Mills in Missouri (August, 1861)
brought a flood of wounded soldiers to St. Louis.

Well aware of the success of Florence Nightingale in the
Crimean War in reducing wounded soldiers' mortality from 60
per cent to 12, Bellows in New York led in the organization of
the women of the city. Then, when this Women's Central Association of Relief was enlarged to include eminent physicians and
lay executives, becoming the United States Sanitary Commission,
President Lincoln and War Secretary Cameron gave it official
status as the non-military auxiliary of the Medical Department
of the Army – whose obstructionist anger at civilian criticism
of its shocking inadequacy was only ended by an Act of
Congress! Meanwhile Dorothea Dix had been appointed General
Superintendent of Female Nurses, and Bellows undertook to
recruit over two thousand volunteer male nurses. The organization of Ladies Union Aid Societies mounted to over fifteen
thousand units. Depots for supplies were established in all
the large cities of the loyal states, from Milwaukee to Boston.
Hospital ships and hospital trains were fitted up for transport of
the wounded. Hundreds of thousands of cases and barrels of
hospital dressings, warm clothing, drug supplies, food delicacies,
books and tracts were forwarded to the camps and the Army
hospitals and Commission convalescent homes, all of which
underwent rigid sanitary inspection by the Commission experts.
The threat of a winter epidemic of scurvy in the camps was
countered by the dispatch of tens of thousands of bushels of
potatoes, onions, turnips, cabbages – and lemons! Five million
dollars of cash, yet more millions in the value of supplies,
flowed through the hands of the Commission, which virtually
forced the President to appoint a Surgeon General who would
efficiently and cheerfully co-operate with it. Wrote Bellows: "The

one point which controls the Commission is just this: a simple desire and a resolute determination to secure for the men who have enlisted in this war that care which it is the will and the duty of the nation to give them. That care is their right and in the government or out of it let who will stand in our way!"

The Western Sanitary Commission

Meanwhile, in embattled St. Louis, William G. Eliot had led in the organization of an independent *Western* Sanitary Commission, very astutely adapted to the political situation there, where four fifths of the wealthy were pro-rebel and half the cannon in the city forts were trained on the city itself! A Southerner, but a Union man, James Yeatman, was made president of the Commission; Eliot kept his Yankee – and Unitarian – stigma out of sight in a co-chairmanship. Nevertheless, when the larger eastern Commission denounced the Missouri Commission as a kind of secessionism, Eliot packed his bag and hurried to Washington. He took with him a letter of high commendation for the Western work from General Halleck, and he returned with War Secretary Cameron's decision: "Let the Western gentlemen be as independent as they please, so long as they work well with the Medical Department" – as they always did, even when their field was extended to cover the campaigns on the east bank of the Mississippi under Generals Grant and Sherman. This meant chartering a dozen and more steamboats and fitting them as hospitals to bring the wounded from Fort Donelson and Vicksburg to St. Louis; it meant leasing and furnishing four great buildings as hospitals, with thousands of beds. It meant forwarding over fifty thousand cases and barrels of clothing, comforts, food delicacies, reading matter to the camps in the South and maintaining five large Soldiers' Homes (recreation centers and hospices) where everything was free.

Eliot's name signed to articles in the *Boston Transcript* had the magic to bring over $500,000 from Massachusetts, $200,000 from Boston alone; and $35,000 from James Roosevelt's committee in New York. Fifty thousand dollars came from California through Thomas Starr King to the Western Commission. In the winter of 1863-64, mammoth Sanitary Fairs were held by the U.S. Sanitary Commission in the largest Northern cities. The Northwestern Sanitary Fair in

Chicago opened with a procession three miles long of farmers' wagons loaded with food and clothing; it lasted fourteen days; its star exhibit was the manuscript of the Emancipation Proclamation. Two remarkable Universalist women, Mary A. Livermore and Jane Hoge, were largely responsible for its success. In St. Louis, the Mississippi Valley Fair lasted longer, and netted $500,000! – chiefly due to the management of the Ladies Union Aid Society, a third of the executive board of which were members of the Unitarian church. Apparently Eliot was right: "Independence and individuality of action should always be kept if possible; when lost, no amount of system can take their place."

The Western Sanitary Commission had more than enough funds to extend their services to the fugitive, forlorn freedmen and to the equally forlorn whites made homeless by the ravages of war. Confederate wounded and prisoners were always accorded, by Commission officials, consideration and service equal to that given the Union soldiers. It is worth noting that had the Fundamentalist South, whose churchmen quoted the Bible so freely in support of slavery, organized a Sanitary Commission with a policy of Christian charity to foe as to friend, there might be no National Cemetery today at Andersonville, Georgia, with its thousands of Union graves! Eliot made no effort to staff the Western Commission with Unitarians, although several ministers served in important ways: Rev. J. G. Forman as the Commission's secretary, Rev. Newton M. Mann of Alton as Superintendent of the Soldiers' Home at Vicksburg. Eliot himself shrank from prominence or gratitude for his work, though, in Yeatman's words: "To you more than to anyone else is the success of our Commission to be attributed. It was your head that conceived, planned, guided the work. [You] were the soul and embodiment of the Commission." In this, as indeed in all his benefactions, Eliot displayed the sure sign of spiritual maturity: "Amabat nesciri."

In retrospect the political significance of the work of the Western Sanitary Commission is seen to have been as great, perhaps, as its humanitarian services to the soldiers. The headquarters of the Sanitary Commission in St. Louis was an electric center of Union activity, enthusiasm, solidarity – amid a sullen secessionist atmosphere that gradually changed as the Union strength became manifest. Moreover, the work done by the Commission in safeguarding the health and sustaining the morale of the soldiers in Missouri was of incalculable value in keeping that state, and therefore Kentucky, in the Union. What would have been the fate of the Union if the Confederacy had advanced to the Ohio River?

Since for the most part the soldiers from the loyal states west of Ohio were in action in Tennessee, Georgia, and the Gulf area, most of the contributions of the Western Conference churches went to the Western Sanitary Commission. Hence, from 1861 to the summer of 1863, church life centered in the rooms, often the sanctuary itself, where young and old, male as well as female, members and friends were sewing and packing with an occasional prayer and hymn service. Services of worship and sermons could be dispensed with, but the soldiers' aid work went on day and evening. The Unitarian churches, virtually without exception, were outspokenly and wholeheartedly loyal and gave unstintedly of men, money, and service to put down the rebellion and secure freedom (and equality of citizenship rights) to the Negroes. Unlike some of the Boston ministers – Rev. Samuel K. Lothrop, for example – their recognition of Lincoln's greatness was immediate and fervent. Because of a sermon criticizing him after his martyrdom, Rev. Charles E. Ellis, a Meadville School fledgling, was persuaded to make a very hurried exit from both the Bloomington pulpit and the city itself. The church in Louisville, and to a less extent that in St. Louis, were weakened by their ministers' valiant stand for Union and Emancipation, but pulled through – and the disaffected often returned! "Copperheadism" split the Madison church wide open and killed it – temporarily. How profound was the devotion of Western Unitarianism to the great cause is indicated by the fact that sixteen out of twenty-nine Unitarian ministers in the West went into the Army, four as soldiers, twelve as chaplains; seven served as Sanitary Commission agents with the armies or the Hospitals and Soldiers' Homes. Why the churches did not record similar facts about their laymen is a mystery; but one chronicler assures us that "all their names are written in the Lamb's Book of Life" – a comforting thought, though the document is not at present available to this historian.

Since the war was obviously not one of conquest, on the part of the North at least, the scruples of the anti-war Unitarians of the Channing tradition were so far abrogated that in 1862 the Conference adopted as its battle cry "Mercy to the South – Death to Slavery!" Robert Collyer confessed that "before Sumter he would have found five hundred texts in the Bible in favor of peace for he had always been a peace man; but after Sumter he looked for a text for next Sunday's sermon and found only one: 'Go sell thy garment and buy a sword.'" (His trustees later persuaded him not to heed his own sermon!) After the sermon they "sang 'America' together amid a storm of sobs and cheers – then settled down to work for our country and her soldiers."

Conclusion

Now that we have a conspectus of what Western Unitarians had accomplished in the fields of literature and social action, spurred by the morale of Conference comradeship and by the profit of shared experience and wisdom, how would we have voted on Mellen's resolution of 1870 "that any abandonment of its work is not to be contemplated"? The Conference itself passed the motion unanimously as well as an accompanying stipulation for "the employment of a competent secretary who can devote his whole time to the duties of his office."

Did the young veteran sitting in the back row of the hall, who had just come up to the Conference from graduation exercises at Meadville, surmise that this resolution would vitally affect his whole life and ministry? His name was Jones.

PART III

INDEPENDENCE IS WON (1875-1894)

CHAPTER NINE

The Conference Elects
a Grass-Roots Secretary

Jenkin Lloyd Jones came of a long line of Welsh ministers and lay folk who adhered to that seventeenth- and eighteenth-century form of liberal Christianity known as Arminianism. His parents emigrated to this country in the early eighteen-forties and settled on the Wisconsin frontier. Their son's memories went back "to the Indian, the trapper, the itinerant preacher, the weekly mail, the stream of arriving immigrants, the gruesome battle with mosquitoes and malaria." His early schooling, like that of Robert Collyer, was meager, but the home was one of religious seriousness and literary culture. Jenkin read all the books he could come by and dreamed of college during chores on the farm. When the Civil War came, he enlisted in a Wisconsin artillery battery not only to help save the Union and end slavery but also to preclude a married brother's enlistment. The "blind push on thought lines," however, produced a percipient and reflective *Artilleryman's Diary*, published long after the war, in 1914. It is a remarkable chronicle, not only of a soldier's ordeals and feelings but of Jones' tenacity of purpose and ideals: "Cannot I, too, learn the much that is to be learned; is there not a niche somewhere in this free country that I may yet occupy with profit to myself and others? I'll never give up! No grim despair shall ever forge a chain for me!"

The first year after his discharge from the Army, Duty forged a chain for him, nevertheless; he returned to his home to help his aging father with the farm work. But the chain was of straw; a winter of school teaching frayed it, summer harvesting snapped it! He confided to his family that all through his boyhood he had wanted to be a Unitarian minister: "I must strive to attain to the highest good that lies in my power." With his parents' blessing but with little money in his purse, he left for the Theological School in Meadville in the autumn of 1866. The tale of his omnivorous reading in Army days and his transparent sincerity admitted him at once to the Preparatory Department, where he found himself obliged to study Greek and Latin in a class the majority of whose members had been in the war. Wrote a rather sophisticated visitor:

> What is very striking about these men is their earnestness; they have no dreams about oratorical success in the future, or ready-made parishes begging that they settle down and go to sleep, but they anticipate a hard struggle, a sacrifice of body and spirit ... they have the pioneer spirit of their fathers ... so here he is today [Jenkin Lloyd Jones], a genuine Western boy, unspoiled, uneducated, poor but earnest, persevering and as bright and keen as you could desire.

Jones' four years in the School fortunately coincided with the beginning of the presidency of Rev. A. A. Livermore (1863-90). The latter's predecessor, Rev. Oliver Stearns, had been an outspoken foe of Theodore Parker. "We must crush this Parkerism!" he had once exclaimed in the students' presence. In 1860 one of them had been expelled for maintaining that he did not regard the theory of biological evolution set forth in Darwin's *Origin of Species* (1859) as necessarily atheistic nor did he regard the Tübingen School's attack on the apostolicity of the Fourth Gospel as untenable.

President Livermore, however, though definitely in the tradition of Channing Unitarianism, was genially tolerant and open-minded, as is shown by his *Discourses* (1854) and their treatment of non-Christian religions. "I doubt not that Mahomet saved some [souls] as well as Moses and that China has not been a mere blank and desert of souls." In Jones' third year at the School (1869), President Livermore was giving a course on comparative religions that with many gracious bows to Buddha, Zardusht, and others adroitly led the student up the steps of Christ's dais to his throne. His instruction in theology stressed the minister's obligation to be concerned with the field now known as Social Ethics. The imprint of such teachings on Jones' mind becomes plainly discernible in later years, while his teacher's views on "The American Church" surely stirred Jones' imagination:

Free America must have a free church ... the old idea was, all for the glory of God. The new one is, all for the good of man and then all will be for the glory of God.

Jones and his fellow students must have spent many lengthy "bull sessions" grappling with the problem of reconciling [Herbert] Spencer's and Darwin's comprehensive evolutionary theories with the beliefs so dear to the hearts of their professors, Livermore, Huidekoper, [Brigham], Mayo: the ethical finality and infallibility of the Gospel, with Jesus Christ as the supreme Incarnation in history of prototypal Man. Both of these doctrines were absolute, yet both were dated. Even the Parkerites found their tenet of the absolute and plenary validity of the ethical intuitions gravely challenged by evolution. Hence they endeavored to reconcile Darwinian biology with religious faith long before Henry Ward Beecher or Lyman Abbott took up the subject. As early as 1860 a young Unitarian minister in Cincinnati, Newton M. Mann, preached a sermon accurately predicting the revolutionary effect of Darwin's *Origin of Species* (1859) in all provinces of thought, particularly Biblical theology and the psychology of religion and ethics. After 1865 articles and sermons on the subject multiplied in the religious press, primarily *The Christian Examiner* and *The Radical*, both of Boston. Evolution offered a solution to so many ancient problems – yet how it did upset the securities of faith! Probably for that very reason, Jones' commencement "piece" in 1870 dealt with the "Theological Bearings of the Development Theory." For one of his auditors, at least, a young lady named Susan C. Barber, his "Sura" settled everything.

[The National Conference and the Free Religious Association]

Of equal interest to Jones and his fellow students in Meadville from 1866 to 1870 must have been the tidings of theological conflict in the sessions of the new National Conference of Unitarian Churches, whose formation Henry W. Bellows, James Freeman Clarke, and Edward Everett Hale had instigated as soon as Union victory appeared certain in 1864. Their idea was to capitalize on Unitarian co-operation and success in the leadership of the United States Sanitary Commission by a grandiose program. They planned to gather all the Unitarian churches of the country – about 237 – into one National Conference, which would then seek to co-ordinate the other liberal Christians of the country, by virtue of the great precedents of wartime giving and doings, into equally generous support of Antioch College, the two ministerial schools, and the missionary work of the American Unitarian Association. At a preliminary meeting in Boston in December, 1864, Bellows – who had spent the summer in California and was indignant at the inability of the then poverty-stricken American Unitarian Association to subvene all the missionary opportunities he had recommended to them – declared that "he would not endure this thing and be quiet any longer – he would go out and organize and beat the A.U.A. all hollow!" Only large objectives, he insisted, would interest Unitarian laymen of large affairs – and means! Thereupon a committee was appointed, including A. A. Low of Brooklyn, Henry P. Kidder of Boston, Enoch Pratt of Baltimore, Artemus Carter of Chicago, to plan a Unitarian mass meeting in New York City the next spring. To forfend any theological controversy between the Old Unitarians, such as Samuel K. Lothrop, and the Parkerites, such as Octavius B. Frothingham, a very irenic Preamble was agreed upon unanimously; and it was arranged that it should be presented by Rev. E. E. Hale, while Rev. James Freeman Clarke should preach a correspondingly conciliatory opening sermon. This he did to about 500 delegates from 195 churches, gathered in New York City in April, 1865. Clarke stressed the point that the convention did not meet to make a creed but to get work done. Hale then offered the committee's Preamble which had scarcely a trace, as he believed, of supranatural, creedal Christianity in it:

Whereas the great opportunities and demands for Christian labor and consecration at this time increase our sense of the obligations of all disciples of the Lord Jesus Christ to prove their faith by self-denial and by devotion of their lives and possessions to the service of God and the building up of the Kingdom of His Son ...

Then the fireworks began! A well-known Abolitionist, C. C. Burleigh, leader of an independent religious society in Florence, Massachusetts, a rough Parkerite diamond in a flannel shirt, objected to the phrase "the Lord Jesus Christ" and insisted that Jesus should only be called "Master," or, in modern parlance, "Mister." He was gaveled down by Chairman S. K. Lothrop, who declared that Burleigh was not a proper delegate, his church not being in the Unitarian list. A Brooklyn magnate, E. E. Mills, stated that he objected to uniting with "rag-tag and bob-tail" radicals, and seconded a Preamble offered by another wealthy Brooklynite, A. A. Low, which limited participation in the Conference to those believing in "one Lord, Jesus Christ our Savior, the Son of God and his specially appointed messenger to our race, gifted with supernatural power, approved by God with miracles, signs …" Protests against this as resembling a creed, made by Rev. E. C. Towne, were brusquely cut short by the Chair. But Robert Collyer of Chicago also demurred and expressed the wish that "he could regard this Conference as free and broad as the Western Conference, where they did not act on a policy of repression of opinion but gave each and all a free utterance and therefore they had no divisions, but acted with spiritual unison and harmony." Lothrop taunted in reply: "And what was the result of the free and broad basis in the West?" Whereupon Robert Collyer "challenged anyone to find a body of Christian ministers or men more entirely united and of one heart than the Western Conference." Bellows angrily denounced the intolerance of the radicals – who had been given little opportunity to say anything – and said "he would rather go with orthodoxy in any form in which it could be stated than with those who would throw Jesus Christ into comparative contempt!"

In the end the Hale-Clarke Preamble was adopted by an overwhelming vote and the delegates, confident that neither the theological nor the social radicalism of Theodore Parker would characterize the Conference, proceeded to raise about $60,000 for the denominational advance. How could the group of Meadville students discussing the meeting *pro* and *con* up in Jones' room in Divinity Hall have failed to conjecture that, had the Parker elements in the Conference been represented by the patrician Octavius B. Frothingham, minister of the great Independent Religious Society of New York City, or the equally aristocratic and distinguished Col. Thomas Wentworth Higginson of the *North American Review* – instead of by "rag-tag and bob-tail" Burleigh – they would not have been treated so discourteously or silenced so unfairly! Indeed, the obvious intention of the "disciples of the Lord Jesus Christ" to suppress, even to extrude, the followers of the "Great Friend to all the sons of men" received such unfavorable comment, not only from the secular press in New York, and in Boston and Springfield, Massachusetts, but even from many of the conservatives within the denomination, that a whole session was set apart for consideration of the Preamble in the meeting of the National Conference of Syracuse in 1866.

On that occasion, on behalf of the "young men" in the denomination, Rev. Francis E. Abbot, a Meadville alumnus of the class of 1863, spoke for a faith stripped of theology, urging that since "perfect freedom of thought which is the right and duty of every human being always leads to diversity of opinion, the only reconciliation of the duties of collective Christian activity [with] individual freedom of thought lies in an effectual organization for practical Christian work, based rather on unity of spirit than on uniformity of belief." As a substitute, therefore, for the Preamble of 1865 he proposed:

> The churches here assembled, disregarding all sectarian and theological differences and offering a cordial fellowship to all who will join them in Christian work, unlike themselves in a common body to be known as the National Conference of Unitarian and Independent Churches.

Further on, Christian work was defined as "the universal diffusion of Love, Righteousness, and Truth."

But to Rev. A. D. Mayo and others, the way to demonstrate "unity of spirit" appeared to be to accept the phrase of 1865, "disciples of the Lord Jesus Christ." Bellows showed no enthusiasm of being led by "young men" and again threatened secession "sooner than lower the standard of faith." Robert Collyer earnestly urged "the young men" to yield on "minor points." Clarke deplored the effect on public opinion of newspaper reports that the Conference had gone back on "Jesus Christ the Lord." And Rev. Rufus Ellis, minister of the First Church in Boston, frankly tendered the young men much the same counsel given Theodore Parker in 1843 by a member of the Boston Association of Ministers: "Let the young men who do not believe in the Preamble [of 1865] go their own way and work in their own way but not join a body and a platform they cannot believe in."

So likewise Edmund Burke, in 1773, counseled the clerical

signers of the Feathers Tavern Petition against the Athanasian Creed to "hire a hall" – and Theophilus Lindsey did!

So did Abbot, W. J. Potter, O. B. Frothingham, and other radicals. They withdrew from the National Conference and formed a kind of "spiritual anti-slavery society," as Potter put it – the Free Religious Association, whose organizational meeting was held at Horticultural Hall in Boston on May 30, 1867, "to promote the interests of pure religion, to increase interest in the scientific study of theology and to increase fellowship in the spirit." For the seal of the association, the motto "Freedom and Fellowship in Religion" was adopted.

Student wits in "bull sessions" are unusually swift and keen. Surely Jones and his friends did not overlook the fact that the Free Religionists had done just what Bellows had threatened to do in 1866: They had seceded – by invitation! Alarmed, indeed, by the impressive attendance at the F.R.A. meetings, Clarke tried, at the National Conference meeting in 1868, to bring the radicals back into the fold by an amendment of the 1865 Preamble:

> To secure the largest unity of the Spirit and the utmost possible practical cooperation, it is hereby declared that all expressions in this Preamble are expressions only of the majority of the Conference, committing in no degree those who object to them. We hereby welcome to our fellowship all who desire to work with us in advancing the kingdom of God.

The Westerners – Rev. J. H. Heywood of Louisville, Daniel L. Shorey of Chicago, and both Collyer and Collier – spoke in favor of this proposal. Rev. O. B. Frothingham, president of the F.R.A., surmised that if it were adopted the young men of the F.R.A. might return to the National Conference. But Lothrop wanted the words "and of our Lord Jesus Christ" to follow "the kingdom of God" and frankly stated that he desired the F.R.A. radicals to stay out of the National Conference anyway. Bellows vigorously objected to the amendment. The phrase "kingdom of God" would undermine the idea of the personal authority of Jesus Christ, and the amendment would open the flood gates of infidelity. "Moreover, if it were adopted, he and his church would withdraw from the Conference!"

A delegate from Chicago's First Church, D. L. Shorey, com-

mented that he "cared nothing for preambles" and urged that
the Conference get on with its business. Apparently he voiced
the sentiments of the large majority, for they finally passed an
amendment, offered by Rev. E. E. Hale, that omitted even the
"kingdom of God":

> To secure the largest unity of the spirit and the widest practical
> cooperation it is hereby understood that all the declarations of the
> Conference, including the preamble and the constitution, are expressions
> only of its majority and dependent wholly for their effect upon the
> consent they obtain from the churches here represented or belonging
> within the circle of our Conference.

If the junior senators of the "bull sessions" in Meadville in the
autumn of 1868 deemed the issue settled, they showed themselves
naïvely ignorant of the tenacity of the *odium theologicum*, and
they sadly miscalculated the determination of the conservatives
to keep the Conference, and the Unitarian Association as
well, explicitly "Christian." The contributions of the monied
churches in the East began to fall off. The ancient Society for the
Promotion of Theological Education in Harvard University, in
which Lothrop was influential, instituted a kind of Inquisition at
the Divinity School and declined to give two of the students their
promised beneficiary stipends; whereupon the whole student
body refused to accept anything at all, the School was on the
verge of closing, and the S.P.T.E.H.U. had to surrender. Then
the faculty at Meadville attempted to apply similar coercion to
its student body, and the Harvard victory was repeated.

By 1870, however, the effects of what was virtually a financial boycott of the A.U.A. treasury had become serious. Nevertheless, its Secretary, Charles Lowe, refused to agree to the
conservatives' desire, as suggested by Rev. Edmund H. Sears, that
every missionary and aided minister of the association should
submit to an examination for Parkerite or F.R.A. symptoms. In
collusion with Sears, Rev. George H. Hepworth of Boston, with
fifteen ministers and fifteen laymen, circulated a letter projecting
an Evangelical Unitarian Association and demanding that every
church in the National Conference should be of unquestioned
Christian character. Hepworth also demanded that the forthcoming
National Conference should adopt an explicit Statement of
Faith – a proposal that Bellows was supporting in *The Liberal*

Christian with *ipse dixit* expositions of "Unitarian Belief." The Old Guard, through Rev. A. P. Putman of Brooklyn, millionaire Low's minister, was urging the definite separation of conservative and radical Unitarians so that the former would no longer be responsible for the latter, either morally or financially. Things looked dark for liberty until, in a dramatic moment at the annual meeting of the Association in 1870, Bellows turned against the Hepworth group's demand for a creed and a creedal test and adjured the members to stand fast "as the only body in Christendom that occupies the position of entire and perfect liberty with some measure of Christian faith." He was upheld by a large majority; but Hepworth did not give up until the National Conference in the autumn compromised the issue by a new Preamble that twice used the contentious name "Christ" but without the title "Lord" or any other supranatural connotations:

Reaffirming our allegiance to the Gospel of Jesus Christ and desiring to secure the largest unity of the spirit and the widest practical cooperation we invite to our fellowship all who wish to be followers of Christ.

The sympathy of the majority of Jones' fellow students at Meadville was with the radicals. Army experience inclined them to associate dogmatic Christianity with Army chaplains who messed with the officers and preached asceticism or hell-fire to poor devils in muddy trenches facing death. In the South the veterans had encountered preachers who were still sanctifying slavery and secession by Bible texts. They heard Wendell Phillips remind the nation that the Union was saved chiefly by the lower middle classes, especially the farmers and the immigrants; the upper classes had been willing all along to compromise on the slavery issue, at least. On the other hand, the leaders of the Free Religious Association had mostly been well-known, unpopular, but steadfast Abolitionists. Moreover they were "young for liberty" not only with respect to Biblical criticism, the sympathetic study of non-Christian religions, and evolution, but social reforms as well.

Such was the briefing in contemporary Unitarianism that his four years in Meadville had given Jones.

Immediately after his graduation in 1870, he hurried to near-by

Cleveland to attend the Western Conference sessions. He arrived in time for the pessimistic report of Charles H. Brigham and the discussion of Mayo's plea for an explicit doctrinal basis. He must have listened with amazement to Mayo's description of Western Unitarianism as a "New England plant, a Boston flower and not a forest growth." For in every respect save place of birth Jones himself embodied the major traits of the West – yet he was a convinced Unitarian! He was an immigrant, inured to hard work and thrift; self-reliant, hard-muscled, thoroughly at home with humble folk, yet avid of the graces of intellectual culture beyond the farm's horizon. Though he knew and loved books, he loved folk more: little folk, young folk, average folk, different folk, too, like Negroes and Orientals and Scandinavians. As a typical frontiersman, he was prone to drive his dreams on into action with energy and persistence. Jenkin Lloyd Jones, at least, was decidedly *not* "a Boston flower"!

Many other features on a Conference program must have interested him. He heard the allusion of A. D. Mayo to the "spiritual vagrancy" of those who praised Mohammedanism or Brahmanism rebuked by Robert Collyer, who pleaded that "where there is a good heart in heathendom, let us give credit for it." He heard Mayo's plea for an "authorized statement of faith" – the Hepworth propaganda – stoutly opposed by the young Chicago lawyer, D. L. Shorey. He must have given special attention to the address of the Conference president, Artemus Carter of Chicago, on "The Want of Ministers in the West and How to Supply It," wherein Carter declared that "the case has become desperate; the ministerial schools [Harvard and Meadville] are totally inadequate in numbers of graduates and the methods of their educations; the students should have opportunity all along in their course to practice the art of preaching and of pastoral duty." Mr. Carter ended by urging the Conference to endorse an offer of $50,000 from a group of Chicago Unitarian laymen for the purpose of moving the Meadville School to Chicago. The endorsement was heartily given – Shorey, the constitutional lawyer, assuring the delegates and the dubious James Freeman Clarke that the Court would permit the move.

The subtle, perhaps strategic, pessimism of the conservatives, Mayo and Brigham, had had such a dispiriting effect – the polite words of the recording secretary and the *Register* notwithstanding – that no Conference at all was held in 1871. For Jones, however, pessimism spelled opportunity: a field to be cleared of orthodox brush and liberal truths to be planted – with a handsome farmhouse in the distant future! In July, in Meadville, he was married to Miss Susan C. Barber, whose interest in his work, self-reliant competence, and infinite capacity for cheerful self-sacrifice proved to be invaluable in the crucial years of parsonage thrift and an absentee missionary husband.

Together they went to Jones' first charge, Artemus Carter's nursling, the Liberal Christian Church in Winnetka, Illinois, where Jones was ordained. But even Carter's prestige and wealth could not give Jones the support he needed for his large plans, and he moved on to the First Independent Society of Liberal Christians in Janesville, Wisconsin, the headwater port of the Rock River, where, after innumerable missionary efforts as early as Conant's time, a Society had been in existence since 1864, with a church built and paid for since the war.

[The Early Career of Jenkin Lloyd Jones]

At the very outset Jones' initiative and energy asserted themselves. His interest in the character development of children – his own were now arriving – combined with the feeling that the Sunday school material of the Unitarian Sunday School Society in the East was too formal and doctrinal, led him to begin, in February, 1872, the publication of *The Sunday School*, dedicated "to all those who seek to work for practical Christianity, liberated from creeds and dogmas, based on Love, Service and Devotion." Everything about the little monthly was original and surprisingly modern: theory, method, lesson material. Jones abandoned the catechetical question-answer memorizations, as well as the "preachy" story lessons, and recommended class discussions and investigations under the guidance of teachers who had read and thought into their subjects. For mutual inspiration and counsel he insisted on weekly teachers' meetings; simpler and less funereal songs; the subordination of Biblical and sectarian doctrines to practical moral duties – the latter to be integrated in

… faith in the Infinite Goodness, in the eternity of Law, the omnipotence of Right, in man as the rising child of God, in reason as his divine endowment, in worship as the gesture of the soul upward, in prayer as the wings on which a soul would soar to its ideals, in the church as the commonwealth of all noble hearts, in a Bible inclusive of all the sweet distillations of literature.

Corresponding with these principles, the first course over four Sundays dealt with Micah 8. "To do justly" is given practical application as truthfulness, honesty, kindness to man and beast; "to love mercy" is interpreted as considerateness in the home, politeness as an expression of love; "to walk humbly with thy God" headed lessons on Reverence, Prayer – and the evil of profanity!

The Sunday School was so enthusiastically welcomed, particularly in the West, that the Conference, meeting at Meadville in 1872, recommended the new Sunday school lessons as "Christian in spirit and doctrine, clear in statement, happy in illustration, adapted to the minds of children and youth by their emphasis on practical aims ... they will help greatly to develop sincerity of heart and mind and a noble type of Christian character." So *The Sunday School* went on to more original study under the title *Leaves from God's Book of Revelation*. A uniform topic series of lessons on the world of nature was outlined not according to Genesis but as modern science described the universe. Under the "Uniform Topic" method (i.e., the same theme for all classes each Sunday) of "Our Own Nature," excellent counsel as to physical and mental hygiene was imparted. The topic "Great Teachers" introduced Zoroaster, Buddha, Confucius, Socrates, Mohammed, Abraham, Moses, Samuel, all leading up to Jesus, to whom eight lessons were devoted. The course for 1874 offered a systematic, critical, and appreciative study of the Bible, including the interesting, revealing, yet seldom studied Apocrypha of the Old Testament. In addition, responsive readings, songs, and poetical selections accompanied the lessons, and in 1877 these elements were collected in a *Service of Song* for youth and adults. Jones was very fond of poetry.

With the Christmas number in 1874, *The Sunday School* was merged into *The Liberal Helper*, edited by George Cooke, which carried on Jones' ideas but had none of his refreshing creativity. It ceased publication in 1877. Straightway the newly founded *Unity* began the publication of new Sunday school courses (September, 1878) and service material. Mrs. Kate Gannett Wells contributed a series of twelve lessons on "Corner Stones of Character"

– the ethical polarity as before. Then appeared *The Little Unity* (1881-83), a monthly publication combining Sunday school lessons with children's story material. After two years, the big *Unity* resumed the work, and its weekly Sunday School Department was continued from 1883 to April, 1919. During these years the Seven Year Course was developed by a committee of the Western Unitarian Sunday School Society, with Jones as secretary and editor. The course furnishes a broad survey of religion, commencing with a study of the differentiations of legend, myth, the scientific method, and fact. Then the formation of the planet, the rise of man, civilization, religion, morality, the Hebrew religion, the Bible, Christianity, the early Church, finally the flowering of Christianity into Universal Religion – the Unitarian story. Continuing this preparatory course, Jones provided a syllabus with ancillary literature for his confirmation classes at All Souls Church in Chicago; this introduced the young people to the classic questions in theology, with a *finale* of affirmations from great poets – Pope, Tennyson, the Longfellows, Whittier, Emerson. Then in *Love and Loyalty* are collected the best-liked of his confirmation-service sermons.

Jones' emphasis on the importance of the religious education program for the youth of the liberal churches was fundamental and insistent. Its rationale has never been better stated than in an early article in *Unity*:

> We Liberals who are working so hard to secularize our public schools; who insist so loudly that religion is the result of slow growth and not of sudden conversion; we who believe that Character is the ultimate end of all living and of all study; we who believe in intellectual freedom and know that the air is full of bigotry and error – we, of all people, have most need of Sunday Schools.

In the pioneering nature of this work, its revitalized methods, its cultural modernization and enrichment of the curriculum, its polarity in integrated and socialized Character, Jones was decades ahead of his time. The Western Conference not only formally endorsed his work, as we have seen; it fostered the organization in 1873 of the Western Unitarian Sunday School Society, of which Jones became secretary and which proceeded to sponsor the publication of a song book, *The Sunny Side*, edited by Rev. C. W. Wendte. This was enlarged and enriched as *Unity*

Services and Songs, edited by Rev. James Vila Blake in 1878; and *Unity Festivals,* for festival occasions, in 1884. The stimulating effect of such original and practical work in religious education was felt in some circles of Eastern Unitarianism; but the tension between Christocentric and Theocentric conceptions delayed for a decade and more the introduction of the new spirit and ways into the Sunday school activities of the Unitarian Association in Boston.

Another innovation during Jones' Janesville ministry was the Mutual Improvement Club (1874) whose object was "to encourage home study [and] to establish social fellowship around the lasting and cosmopolitan verities of letters, art and life … character is the final word." Jones sought to lift the conventional social life of the church, especially of the women, to a higher level than sewing, gossiping, and church-dinner cooking. The Club was virtually a combination of post-graduate Sunday school study, adult education, and social service and reform work. It was organized in nine committees: current events, current literature, biography, classical literature, art, dramatics, current periodicals, lectures – and a Saturday afternoon section for busy homemakers on modern poetry. We must leave the content of the various committee programs, which reflect the broad, eager range of Jones' own reading and interests, to the reader's imagination. It must suffice to note that the art committee in 1878 crowned its season of study with a "Loan Art Exhibition" of oil paintings, statuary, engravings of old masters, and even local wood-carvings, pottery, and needlework. Since Janesville was a uniformly prosperous community, with practically none of the indigence or slum problems of larger cities, the social-action activities of the Club were limited to promoting lectures and discussions on women's rights, temperance, civil service reform, and international peace.

Of kindred nature was the Starr King Fraternity, started by Rev. C. W. Wendte at the Fourth Unitarian Church in Chicago in 1871, but owing to the great Chicago fire its work was indefinitely suspended. In Boston, William H. Baldwin promoted a Unity Club for young men; he later developed it into the work of the Young Men's Christian Union in Boston, then transferred it to Chicago after the fire of 1871. The direct provenance of the Unity Clubs of the Western Unitarian churches seems, how-ever, to be the more comprehensive family and community program of the Janesville Club, replicas of which were rapidly multiplied in the Western churches, commencing with St. Paul. Their public lectures courses continued the old Lyceum tradition, and they anticipated the church-forum movement by many years. Their group discussions of masterpieces of ancient and modern literature foreshadowed the current Great Books study classes. Their programs were attended by many, especially young people who belonged to other churches or to none at all. For over twenty years the columns of *Unity* contained copious reports on the activities of the Unity Clubs, together with grate-ful testimonials from persons whose early education had been limited, and whose first introductions to the El Dorado of intel-lectual and aesthetic culture had been given them in local Unity Clubs. Was not this Jones' own story, and was not the Janesville enterprise a way of sharing his self-reliant solution of his own spiritual hunger? Moreover, such a correlation of the best of universal secular culture with religious ideals, which had also characterized Jones' program of religious education, presages the strong Humanist trend of Western Unitarianism in later decades.

In the Conference the forth-putting enthusiasm and compe-tence of the minister from Janesville were soon recognized, and to his less activist and optimistic colleagues he became "Incarnate Cheer." After the year of doldrums, 1871, a group of the younger men, who were determined not to allow the Eastern conservatives to demoralize the work in the West, got the annual meetings resumed at Meadville in 1872. None of the officers elected in 1870 was present; none of the larger, older churches was among the twelve whose ministers and delegates were present. The report on the state of the churches by Rev. S. S. Hunting, acting Western Secretary of the A.U.A., was moder-ately encouraging. He gave special praise to the persevering, self-denying labors of Rev. Nathaniel Seaver, Jr., at Davenport, Iowa; of W. E. Copeland at Emporia, Kansas; of Jasper L. Douthit in southern Illinois; and of J. L. Jones in Wisconsin. But the number of societies without ministers was dismaying. He complained of the decrease of aid from the A.U.A., arising from "a want of confidence that cripples all that is undertaken ... he had hoped to help worthy men and promising movements, and they had reason to think he could help them – but he was powerless." Secretary Shippen of the A.U.A. replied that the East had given over $60,000 toward the reconstruction of Unity Church, Chicago, after the great fire, as well as other thousands in relief; that Boston had had its great fire, too, and was suffering severely from the prevailing depression; that the contributions to the A.U.A. from the West were very meager, though the West, too, had its wealthy churches; that the Executive Committee would not trust the allocations for Western missionary work to the judgment of Hunting and the Conference's Executive Committee, on the ground that they failed "to cooperate with us to learn the record and antecedents of men who come to Western pulpits."

Then spoke up Jones of Janesville: "It would be much better for the West if the Association dropped it entirely and we were obliged to raise our missionary funds ourselves!"

Had Jones the suspicion, when he made this really audacious suggestion, that the insistence of the A.U.A. that it give its approval to all subsidized ministers and missionaries in the West was prompted by a design to exclude radicals? That the A.U.A. wished to reduce the Western Conference to a mere debating society?

In spite of one timorous brother who pleaded that the Conference would do well "to keep on good terms with the A.U.A.," the resolution was passed that "the existence and prosperity of the Western Unitarian Conference depend on its taking charge of Western missionary work and the disbursement of funds – in cooperation with the A.U.A." What is more, D. L. Shorey of Chicago was elected president, Carter having resigned; and the new Executive Committee included Rev. Frederick Frothingham of Buffalo, T. B. Forbush of Cleveland, and C. W. Wendte of Chicago – all of them moderate radicals, whose position was in general that of Wendte's: "I have little or nothing to say concerning radicalism or conservatism in religion ... I endeavor to preach a gospel of good sense, kindliness, mutual helpfulness and spiritual truth."

So satisfying was such a gospel to the members of the Fourth

Unitarian Church in Chicago (under Wendte's ministry) that in spite of the great fire of 1871 they managed to build a neat chapel of red and buff brick with cast-iron trimmings, toward which the A.U.A. gave $3,000 and which Secretary Shippen and Rev. S. K. Lothrop came out to help dedicate at the time of the Conference session in 1873. Though Professor C. H. Brigham read another conservative essay, "Theological Education," and Shippen and Lothrop expressed their convictions that "they had confidence only in the Christian basis, broadly interpreted," Secretary Hunting's report showed more gains than losses in the Conference – and most of the gaining ministers were radicals, such as M. J. Miller at Geneseo, F. L. Hosmer at Quincy, J. R. Effinger at St. Paul, J. L. Jones at Janesville. But Shippen would not give any assurance that the A.U.A. would publish Theodore Parker's *Discourse of Matters Pertaining to Religion* or continue Hunting as its Western Secretary – for he was a member of the Free Religious Association – so the Conference made him its corresponding secretary, that he might continue his oversight of the Western churches, though without salary or funds for grants-in-aid. Of all who had heard Lothrop preach the first of the long and honorable series of Conference Sermons in 1852, only John Heywood of Louisville was present in 1873 – and even he showed signs of sympathy with the radicals! Lothrop never came to the Western Conference again!

Fortunately for his feelings, perhaps, W. G. Eliot did not attend the Conference of 1874, though it was held in St. Louis, in the Church of the Unity, daughter of his own church and blessed with his blessing. For the spirit of 1872 and 1873 continued to grow more bright and steady. Hunting reported signal gains at the Third Church in Chicago, under the leadership of Rev. Minot J. Savage, a recent convert from orthodoxy; at Denver, under Rev. W. M. G. Stone; at Kenosha, Wisconsin, under Rev. Henry M. Simmons; at Toledo, where Rev. Charles Craven had reunited the remnants of the Independent Religious Society that Abbot had abandoned with the conservatives he had alienated – and at Janesville, where Rev. J. L. Jones not only had invigorated the local church life by his new Sunday school curriculum and a Mutual Improvement Club, but also in his capacity as state missionary had rallied movements at Racine,

Madison, Baraboo, and Whitewater. But Secretary Shippen was so resentful of the small contributions made by the Western churches to the A.U.A. treasury that he "thought it might be well for the Western Unitarian Conference to take money-raising under its immediate supervision." Jones needed only such a provocation to speak with "enthusiasm and confidence of the religious prospects of the West" and to move that the Conference assume responsibility for its own missionary work, organize along state lines, employ a supervising missionary – in co-operation with the A.U.A. The resolution was passed with scarcely a negative vote. Did Jones feel the hand of Destiny on his shoulder – or was it the other way around?

In any case, it was the Unitarian Association itself that decided the question. For in 1874 its Secretary had dropped the name of Rev. William J. Potter, minister of the strong and loyal church in New Bedford, Massachusetts, from the Association's Year Book list of Unitarian ministers on the ground that he did not call himself a Christian – just a Unitarian. Moreover, he was the Secretary of the Free Religious Association! But he was an exemplary and able minister, and the New Bedford church objected vigorously to the Association's action. Similar protests – one from W. G. Eliot, indeed – against what was regarded as high-handed ecclesiasticism were smothered or overruled by the Association; while the National Conference of 1874 tabled a resolution offered by Henry W. Bellows that "this Conference heartily endorses the action of its officers in inviting to be present with us the church at New Bedford by its pastor and lay delegates and wishes its general spirit to be interpreted by this particular action."

The Western Conference of 1875 took far different action on the matter. To Secretary Shippen's cordial letter of greeting from the Executive Committee of the A.U.A., the Conference, as befitted the Association's fiftieth birthday, replied graciously: "We recognize the generous and impartial manner in which the American Unitarian Association has promoted the cause of Liberal Christianity [and] we pledge cooperation in all its efforts to promote our common cause of truth and religious liberty." But the Conference balanced this greeting by expressing to the Free Religious Association its "hearty sympathy with its

endeavors to promote the cause of truth and religious liberty."
Then the Conference decided it would do something itself for
"truth and religious liberty"! First it passed a stern rebuke of
the Association for its action in the Potter case:

Whereas: "Fidelity in duty, not accuracy in belief" has been from the
first among us the essential test of Christian character; and

Whereas: We seem in danger of losing sight of this fundamental principle through the influence of ecclesiastical agencies,

Resolved: That we deprecate and deplore the action of the American
Unitarian Association in its effort to limit the fellowship of the Unitarian
body by practically defining the word "Christian" so as to make it a dogmatic shibboleth instead of a symbol of righteousness;

Resolved: That we protest against this erasure of names from the accred-
ited list of Unitarian ministers until (1) the minister himself shall request
such action or (2) shall have left the profession, or (3) shall have joined
some sect or fellowship which denies us ecclesiastical fellowship.

Resolved: That the removal of the name of Rev. W. J. Potter from the
Year Book of the Association was in our judgment a departure from
Congregational and Unitarian principles which can only be rectified by
its restoration.

The motion was made by Robert Collyer and seconded by
Rev. John Snyder of the Church of the Messiah in St. Louis,
with the full approval of his senior colleague, W. G. Eliot. It
was unanimously adopted.

Then the Conference went on to define its own liberty:

The Western Unitarian Conference conditions its fellowship on no
dogmatic tests but welcomes all thereto who wish to work with it in
advancing the Kingdom of God.

Finally, Learned of St. Louis reverted to the suggestion Jones
had made in 1872 and expanded it: "Let us take the missionary
work into our own hands and pay for it!" To implement this
policy, the action of 1869 directing all churches to send their
missionary contributions to the A.U.A. was canceled; the monies
were to be sent directly to the Conference Treasurer. But by
whom was this missionary work to be done? By whom but
the young man who had all along believed in "a strong, straight-
forward, aggressive course for Liberal movements" and had been
pleading for years that the Conference should stand on its own
feet and conduct its missionary work through the agents of the

state conferences, under the supervision of the General Secretary!

Everyone seemed to be of this mind though some wondered about the financial response of the churches. In the end it was agreed that for three months of the year, with the permission of the Janesville church, Jones was to be employed as Missionary Secretary at a salary of $750 and expenses. The Janesville church consented, and Jones entered upon his work that very June.

Jones as Missionary Secretary

Never before in the history of the Unitarian movement in this country – not even in the days of Priestley, Sparks, and Ware in the East, of Starr King in the Far West, or of Conant, Eliot, Clarke, and Hosmer in the Midwest – had anyone worked so intensively on propaganda and organization as did Jones between 1875 and 1880. He was constantly on the road; the three-months clause in his contract was honored more in the breach than the observance. He visited distressed churches, dormant churches, isolated groups of radicals, liberals that aspired to become church societies, gatherings of delegates to form state conferences. The Conference treasury was usually empty. To pay for the 9,988 miles he traveled by train or team the first year, he drew upon his own slender salary. He begged congregations for collections to cover his expenses, after the manner of a primitive, frontier preacher. He sold his watch, he pawned his wife's watch, he borrowed money from the children's penny savings banks – but go he would, when and where an appointment had been announced. To economize time he always took the last train, were it a passenger, a freight, or a cattle train. On the occasions when trains were late he would likely as not spend the night on the floor of the waiting room. The Conference office from 1875 to 1879 was in his portmanteau, and in the front parlor of the Janesville parsonage, which was piled high with "papa's truck" – hundreds of letters, tracts, books such as J. W. Chadwick's *Essential Piety of Modern Science*. Jones' annual reports were so filled with activity and optimism – even in depression years with grasshopper plagues that ruined whole areas in Kansas and Nebraska – that reading them gives one the feeling of marching in a triumphal procession.

When he began the work in 1875, there was but one state

conference (Wisconsin); there was no headquarters, no periodical. There were only 43 active societies, and they were in debt
for over $100,000. In 1880 there were 61 active societies; church
indebtedness had been reduced almost $50,000; the Women's
Liberal Union of the Conference was maintaining a Chicago
office and book room (75 Madison Street), with a full-time
office secretary. *The Pamphlet Mission*, commencing in 1878, had
become the semi-monthly *Unity* after three months, and *Unity*
was a cheerful, widely welcomed courier of Conference news,
liberal morale, and advanced theological and social opinion.
And there were now six state conferences – the Wisconsin
and Minnesota Conference, 1866; the Michigan Conference of
Unitarian and Other Christian Churches, 1875; the Fraternity of
Illinois Liberal Christian Societies, 1875; the Iowa Association of
Unitarian and Other Independent Churches, 1877; the Indiana
Conference of Unitarian and Independent Religious Societies,
1878; the Ohio State Conference of Unitarian and Other
Liberal Societies, 1879 – besides the Chicago Conference of
Unitarian Churches organized in 1868. Moreover, the Western
Conference was represented on the National Committee on
Ministerial Fellowship – since relations with the A.U.A. were
now so cordial than in 1879-80 it had allocated $11,500 for the
Midwestern and Pacific Coast field. Jones' theological breadth
and efficient supervision had inspired Secretary Shippen with
such confidence that he could assure the Conference: "Our
policy is one of impartiality; we aim to put earnest and able men
in pulpits without inquiring as to so-called radical or conservative opinions!"

Though Jones had told the Conference in 1877 that he
found his strenuous life "a perfect joy, an intoxicating delight,"
yet by 1880 when in one year he had traveled 14,676 miles,
visited 41 places, given 78 sermons and addresses – exclusive
of his Janesville duties – he had come to the verge of "physical
bankruptcy" and felt entitled to a release. The Conference thought
otherwise. It came to the unanimous conclusion, voiced by Rev.
J. H. Crooker, that "the rising tide of enthusiasm which, if it
continues, marks an era in the progress of Liberal religion in the
West" justified a motion that "Rev. Jenkin Lloyd Jones be invited
to take the Missionary Secretaryship of the Western Conference,

JAMES FREEMAN CLARKE

GEORGE WASHINGTON HOSMER

PLATE II

JOHN HEALEY HEYWOOD

WILLIAM GREENLEAF ELIOT

PLATE III

AUGUSTUS HAMMOND CONANT

HARM JAN HUIDEKOPER

PLATE IV

UNITARIAN CHURCH, MEADVILLE, PENNSYLVANIA
Erected 1835; still in use

UNITARIAN CHURCH, GENVA, ILLINOIS
Erected 1843; still in use

PLATE V

DIVINITY HALL, MEADVILLE, PENNSYLVANIA
President A. A. Livermore in left center, seated

ACADEMIC BUILDING, MEADVILLE SCHOOL, CHICAGO
Dedicated 1931

PLATE VI

JASPER L. DOUTHIT

JESSE W. FELL

PLATE VII

ABRAHAM LINCOLN

HORACE MANN

PLATE VIII

ROBERT COLLYER

JENKIN LLOYD JONES

PLATE IX

UNITY CHURCH, CHICAGO
The first building, dedicated 1869

ABRAHAM LINCOLN CENTRE, CHICAGO
Dedicated 1905

PLATE X

FREDERICK LUCIAN HOSMER

WILLIAM CHANNING GANNETT

PLATE XI

HENRY MARTYN SIMMONS

JAMES VILA BLAKE

PLATE XII

ARTHUR M. JUDY

MARY A. SAFFORD

FLORENCE BUCK

MARION MURDOCH

PLATE XIII

MORTON D. HULL

DANIEL L. SHOREY

PLATE XIV

CURTIS W. REESE

FRANKLIN C. SOUTHWORTH

PLATE XV

FIRST UNITARIAN CHURCH, CHICAGO
Dedicated 1931

PLATE XVI

PEOPLES CHURCH, CHICAGO
Dedicated 1926

The inscription on the proscenium is from Channing: "Live a life of Faith and Hope; believe in the mighty power of Truth and Love." The busts are of Lincoln and Emerson.

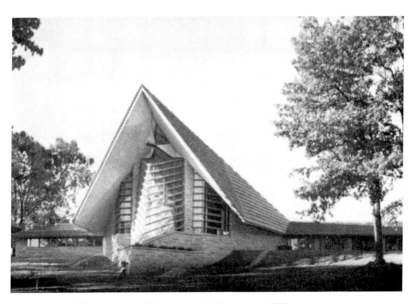

UNITARIAN CHURCH, MADISON, WISCONSIN
Dedicated 1951

CHAPTER TEN

The Growing Conference
and the Gathering Storm

We must march – we must bear the brunt of danger;
We debouch upon a newer, mightier world;
Fresh and strong this world we seize, world of labor and the march,
Pioneers, O Pioneers!

Walt Whitman

[*A Cloud on the Horizon in Southern Illinois*]

SCARCELY A MONTH after Jenkin Lloyd Jones' election as full-time Missionary Secretary, he received a letter from Rev. Jasper L. Douthit of Shelbyville, Illinois, formally withdrawing from the Conference on the ground that he "did not regard the non-Christian position of the Conference as calculated to enlarge our fellowship ... The name Christian has a charm and carries a great truth to tens of thousands of needy souls who must starve to death for all the good that such fellowship as the Conference is likely to afford them." Douthit added that his establishment of a monthly, *Church and Home*, changed after five months to *Our Best Words*, had been motivated by a desire to offset the radical tendencies of *Unity* – at least within the perimeter of his own mission field in southern Illinois.

To Douthit's letter, Secretary Jones returned a "kind, expostulatory note," warning the former not to yield to a "Monday morning spell." As Douthit's classmate in Meadville School fifteen years before, Jones was fully aware of a propensity for emotional evangelism in "the sickly, sorrowful looking man." In the pulpit, Jones had noted, "his eyes flame, his voice, though often strident and sometimes shrieking, always carries conviction and oftentimes enthusiasm" – after the fashion of his Baptist and Methodist antecedents. Hoping, doubtless, that Douthit would experience a Tuesday-morning reaction, Jones neither

139

published his letter of withdrawal in *Unity* nor read it to the next Conference session in 1881, although the secession of so zealous a worker, with four churches under his pastoral care, was as unprecedented as their founder's career had been heroic. Salient incidents of this career may serve to illustrate the nature and value of Douthit's work for Unitarian Christianity in southern Illinois.

Born of pioneer parents in a log cabin on the banks of the Okaw River, Douthit spent his youth in a community brutalized by corn whiskey and addicted to profanity, irreligion, and ignorance – "Hard Shell" Baptist preachers were seldom literate or salaried. An early visit to Texas set the youth indignantly against slavery; an incorrigible craving for book learning led him to Wabash College – near-by Antioch was shunned as "infidel." Through a correspondence with the authoress of poems published in the *Phrenological Journal,* he was drawn to the New England home of Emily Lovell, where he married her. There he heard and knew Parker, Clarke, H. W. Beecher, Starr King; he became an Abolitionist. In 1859 he brought his wife back to a shack on his father's farm and went about preaching in schoolhouses and courthouses since, without a license, he could not preach in Methodist churches – though he had been baptized into that communion when about twenty-one. Then he contrived to get a log meetinghouse built in the woods, called it "Liberty Church," and preached there so eloquently, as a "Linkum" man, for "Union, Liberty for the slaves, Temperance and Righteousness of life," that for this and for aiding the draft enrollment his life was threatened by Vallandingham Democrats. Loyalty to the Union and the rejection of orthodox doctrines brought him into contact in Chicago with Robert Collyer, who took him to the Western Conference session of 1862, where he was given ordination, "the Unitarians being the only body of Christian believers who would give me perfect liberty to preach the Gospel as God gave me to see it." Then Collyer got him admitted to the Meadville School, where he "spent the happiest and most helpful period of my life."

After graduating in 1867, Douthit returned to preaching in the "Log Church" and in nearby Mattoon where, after Emerson had lectured for him as a "labor of love" in 1868, he got the

Unity Church of Liberal Christians organized. With the manual help of his brothers and money contributions from all the country around, he built Oak Grove Chapel, which Robert Collyer and a Lutheran minister dedicated in 1870, the former writing to *The Liberal Christian* in New York City:

I cannot tell you how much good Mr. Douthit has done in that region ... it is to me simply wonderful. Religious men and women of other persuasions join with him and help in the singing and prayers ... his brothers, splendid, stalwart fellows are at his side [but] his best helper and friend is his wife, a poet and a thinker.

Collyer might have added that if she had not also been a capable chicken and turkey farmer, the family might have starved!

By 1873 Douthit had another such Union Church built at near-by Mode; in 1874 he started services in Shelbyville, with such good results that the next year the First Congregational Unitarian Church was organized, mostly by poor people of the town, many of whom had once been hard drinkers, even saloon keepers. By another year, with generous help from W. G. Eliot in St. Louis, a large brick church was built and dedicated by a galaxy of Douthit's friends – Clarke, Eliot, Heywood, Elder John Ellis, and Rabbi Sonnenschein of St. Louis. Thereafter Shelbyville became the center of the Douthit circuit, which expanded in time to include Jacksonville, Pana, Champaign, and Urbana.

Our Best Words, therefore, with its circulation of a thousand copies, served not only to counteract *Unity*, but as the semi-monthly bulletin of these rural churches. Notices of national and local liberal activities, or of the Swing, Thomas, and Briggs heresy trials, were juxtaposed with advice as to hatching chickens in a steam incubator, or a caution to young men: "Don't Marry a Doll!" An advertisement of the great new Hydropathic Sanitorium at Battle Creek, or of *The Phrenological Journal,* would be sandwiched in with announcements of a lecture on Women's Rights by Mary A. Livermore or one on Temperance by Frances E. Willard.

To a man of such Messianic earnestness, living literally from hand to mouth on the frugal offerings of poor farmers and his own garden produce, forever embroiled with vindictive saloon keepers, "whiskey politicians," and derisive revivalists, it seemed vitally necessary that Unitarianism should be conceived and presented in emotional, pietistic, authoritarian terms: "Jesus Christ is more to me than all other beings that ever trod the earth ... Unitarianism signifies to me Christian discipleship and Christian character."

No one could have more justly and sympathetically appreciated Douthit's consecration and service than did Secretary Jones, who had done his best to get Douthit subventions from the A.U.A., in spite of the fact that the latter had not caught the fancy of Boston Unitarians as had his prototype, Conant of Geneva, three decades before. We can only conjecture why Douthit risked chilling Jones' enthusiasm at the outset of his full-time program of advance by the letter of withdrawal. Sundry items in *Unity* from 1878 to 1880 may have been responsible. Jones had advertised in 1878 that, as Missionary of the Conference, he sought "the acquaintance and fellowship of all friends of Liberal thought of any or no name in the West ... he will accept invitations to speak in the interest of that Religion which is found in the Fatherhood of God and the Brotherhood of Man." Later on, there was a notice that the

... Eclectic Society of Liberals at Greeley, Colorado, is progressing finely ... There is need for organization among thinking radicals ... Let them drop their special names and *unite* in the common purpose of promoting morality, rational thought and a deeper understanding of our relations to the universe and its laws ... All believe as much as this and this is enough for solid and successful work!

Such work, reported *Unity*, was being done by Rev. W. E. Copeland in grasshopper-stricken Nebraska, at Omaha, Fremont, Lincoln, and Hastings, for "the Liberals of Nebraska are as a whole very radical, having cut loose entirely from the moorings of the old theology and they can be reached by no form of religious faith but our own." How inclusive that fellowship might be is hinted by *Unity's* pleasant comments on the convention of the Michigan Association of Spiritualists and Liberals in Grand Rapids, which was addressed by Rev. George Willis Cooke, Unitarian minister in Grand Haven; or on the National Convention of Freethinkers at Watkins, New York, attended by, among others, representatives of the Comtist Society of Humanity in New York City! In fact, *Unity* was so inclusive in its sympathies that its editors nodded cordially even to Voltaire, a capital essay on whom, as a paladin of religious tolerance, was contributed by Rev. J. W. Chadwick of Brooklyn, New York; to his modern counterpart, Robert G. Ingersoll, whose lectures on *Some Mistakes of Moses* (published in 1879) were jamming the largest halls in the cities and raising the pulpit temperature even of Unitarian ministers to the boiling point. *Unity* smiled on Felix Adler, whose new Society for Ethical Culture (1876) seemed veritably to fulfill those essays of Emerson on "Worship" and "The Sovereignty of Ethics" from which Jones and his co-editor, William Channing Gannett, so frequently quoted. And did they not fly the motto of the Free Religious Association, "Freedom and Fellowship," at *Unity's* masthead, with merely "Character" added! If they had put "Christ" instead of "Character," Douthit might have pardoned their radical vagaries and stayed in the Conference!

Did Secretary Jones have a premonition that Douthit's withdrawal was as a small cloud on the horizon portending a coming storm? In any case he went briskly to work, harder than ever. The headquarters office at 75 Madison Street, presided over by Miss F. L. Roberts – whose salary was paid by the Women's Western Unitarian Conference (1877) – throbbed with activity. Not only *Unity* but the Sunday School Society had a desk and closet there, whence were distributed the Seven Year Course Lesson leaflets; the Tool Chest aids for teachers; *The Way of Life*, a small book of Sunday-school services by F. L. Hosmer; *The Sunny Side*, a collection of simple, cheery, practical Sunday-school songs, edited by Rev. C. W. Wendte. *Unity Festivals*, prepared by Rev. J. V. Blake, and *Unity Hymns and Chorals*, edited by W. C. Gannett, J. V. Blake, and F. L. Hosmer, were meant for the adult congregations. After 1881 the work of the Post Office Mission, originating with Miss Sallie Ellis of the Cincinnati church, brought groups of women to headquarters for the purpose of mailing out to inquirers all over the nation "Unity Short Tracts," A.U.A. tracts, Unitarian and other liberal books and periodicals.

In the field, the founding of new churches and the reinvigoration of old ones went on at an accelerated pace, owing not only to the work of tireless Secretary Jones, but also to that of the state-conference missionaries.

[The Midwest]

In Wisconsin, the reorganization of the First Unitarian Church of Madison was effected in 1879 by liberals "desiring a religious organization in the spirit of Jesus of Nazareth which shall make integrity of life its first aim and leave thought free, [accepting into membership] all of whatever theological opinion who wish to unite with us in the promotion of Truth, Righteousness, Reverence and Charity among men." Three years of the ministry of Rev. Henry W. Simmons gave the new venture invincible momentum, and under Rev. Joseph H. Crooker a church building was erected, a Channing Club for University students was formed; and for the adults a Unity Club program, furnished largely by the faculty of the University, provided a rich intellectual feast. The Unitarian Church in Milwaukee, after two decades of vicissitudes under its misleading name "Church of the Redeemer," had the good fortune to secure Rev. G. E. Gordon, whose long pastorate (1875-85) assured it a prosperity and prestige it has never since lost.

In the Michigan conference, after Rev. J. T. Sunderland had assumed not only the ministry of the church at Ann Arbor (1878-98) but also the office of state missionary, churches came into being at Mount Pleasant, Muskegon, Osceola, Saginaw, Jackson, Grand Haven, Charlevoix, and Charlotte. In a new "Bond of Union" adopted in 1883, the Unitarian Church of Kalamazoo recognized "the right of private judgment and the sacredness of individual convictions" and required "no assent to any doctrinal statement as a basis of fellowship," but welcomed "all who desire to cooperate with us in advancing the Kingdom of God [and] promoting Truth and Righteousness in the world through the study, practice and diffusion of pure religion as taught and lived by Jesus of Nazareth in love to God and love to man." Such inclusiveness of spirit combined with the hard work of Rev. Clark G. Howland (1865-80) to plant the church deeply and sturdily in the rich soil of the Kalamazoo River valley. Work at Saginaw by Rev. Rowland Connor (1880-90), and at Midland and Big Rapids by equally able and faithful leaders, was eventually brought to nought by the decline of the lumber trade and the resultant removal of so many of the intellectuals of the professions that highly trained ministers could no longer be supported.

To the Society in Cleveland, Ohio, Secretary Jones recommended Rev. Frederick L. Hosmer just in time to save this long-struggling group from giving up. Very soon they were able to build a commodious neo-Gothic stone church – "Unity Church," they called it – and it was dedicated in 1881 by Rev. Henry W. Bellows with one of his last great sermons. The ensuing decade of substantial growth in Sunday school, Unity Club activities, and community service – a free kindergarten and a domestic training school in particular – gave the Cleveland congregation abundant cause for gratitude for Hosmer's ministry (1878-92), on which the later prosperity of the whole Unitarian movement in Cleveland was founded.

The recovery of the church in Toledo from the unfortunate divisions of the Abbot-Craven period was assured by the healing ministry of Rev. A. G. Jennings; and in Cincinnati the right-wing Church of the Redeemer and the left-wing First Unitarian Church – whose minister, Rev. Thomas Vickers, had resigned in 1879 after a pastorate of five years – were successfully reunited by Rev. Charles W. Wendte in 1876. Wendte halted a reviving theological dispute in the Committee on Reunion by wiring them from Chicago: "Confine your Articles to the practical administration of the Society. Don't have any Preamble – let your minister be your Preamble!" So they did, and he proved entirely satisfactory to both conservatives and radicals – for he followed the counsel given him by Professor David Swing of Chicago, who had recently been dismissed from the Presbytery and had founded the Central Church: "Only two doctrines are needed – God and Righteousness. Christ, faith, hope and love are helps toward these two large ideas." Wendte's cordial personality, positive preaching, and administrative gifts restored Cincinnati Unitarianism to its old vigor. His skill in music and youth work attracted to his new Unity Club a recent graduate of Yale, William Howard Taft. Taft so ably filled the role of the Sleeping Beauty in a burlesque given by the Club, as well as the part of the Captain – whose sailor suit proved too small for him – in a production of *Pinafore*, that he was elected president of the Drama Section, the first step on his ladder of fame.

Wendte's birthright proficiency in the German language brought him into close association with the Protestantische Verein of free churches, whose leaders were Pastors Carl A. Voss of

Pittsburgh and Hugo G. Eisenlohr of St. John's Church in Cincinnati. The very loose-knit Union comprised about fifty German-speaking congregations who accepted no creed save the Gospels as interpreted by reason, scholarship, and the Christian conscience. Not only were their members theologically far in advance of most other German bodies in this country, but their independence and progressiveness in social questions, both political and economic, created affinities which their pastors frequently proclaimed at the sessions of the Western Conference. During Eisenlohr's long and honored ministry (1885-1931), St. John's Church joined the American Unitarian Association (1923), though most of its sister congregations, from Pittsburgh to St. Louis, merged with the Congregationalists in 1924.

Over in St. Louis, Secretary Jones met with a warm welcome in the Church of the Unity, of which Rev. J. C. Learned had been minister since 1870. In contrast with the Church of the Messiah, which still retained "the study and practice of Christianity" as its basic purpose and bond, Unity Church had adopted the broader statement that "subscribing to no doctrines and imposing no creeds we cordially welcome to our fellowship all who desire to work with us in advancing the Kingdom of God."

[The Iowa Sisterhood]

Turning north to Iowa, Jones entered the territory of the Iowa Unitarian Conference, the most active and enthusiastic of all the state bodies. Here the "Iowa Sisterhood" of women ministers was fulfilling the hopes of the Women's Ministerial Conference, which Julia Ward Howe had organized in 1875 as an adjunct of the onsurging Women's Rights movement throughout the nation. Although the initiative in this reform had been taken in the late eighteen-forties by Unitarian women in central New York and in Boston – Susan B. Anthony, Elizabeth Cady Stanton, Lucy Stone, Maria Chapman – the denomination trailed behind its Friends, the Methodists, and the Universalists in opening its ministry to women. After the Meadville School in 1868 decided to admit women to its courses, the way was opened for the recruitment of educated and competent women at least for missionary service, where married clergymen found the stipends too meager. The opportunity for such service was given them partly through the efforts of the Women's

Western Unitarian Conference, which started in 1873 as an auxiliary of the main body, with Mrs. Jenkin Lloyd Jones as its president in the years under review. Her husband, as well as the Missionary Secretary in Iowa, Rev. J. R. Effinger, collaborated heartily in the women's insistence upon securing recognition as church trustees, Conference delegates and speakers – and as ministers. As a consequence, every church in Iowa was at some time served by a woman in the pulpit – save Davenport! We should not, however, attribute its exceptional status to a lecture that British-born Rev. Robert L. Collier delivered in the Davenport Opera House in 1871 on the "Follies of the Woman Movement"; for his Unitarian brother, Rev. S. S. Hunting, refuted Collier the very next Sunday in the newly dedicated Unity Church. Hunting's successor, Rev. Arthur M. Judy (1880-1906), though a graduate of the Harvard Divinity School – which, though petitioned and pleaded with for years, would never admit women – took a different position and welcomed them cordially. His ministry of twenty-six years was a turning point in the history of the Conference and of the church. To accommodate the thronged Unity Club lectures, concerts, and dramas, a large and attractive building was erected in 1898. During these years of progress many freethinkers of German stock joined the church in agreement with its comprehensive and friendly Bond of Union: "This church shall never adopt any articles of faith or a creed as a test of fellowship nor require its members to acknowledge any authority in matters of doctrine subversive of personal conviction and the light of conscience."

The other churches in Iowa were deeply indebted to the devoted labors of the "Iowa Sisterhood" during their crucial early years. Unity Church in Sioux City (founded in 1885) adapted an abandoned skating rink to its needs and then called Rev. Mary A. Safford (1885-89); with the assistance of Rev. Eleanor E. Gordon, she introduced progressive methods in religious education as well as a rich and vital Unity Club program, including a popular lecture and forum series on international peace, civil service reform and women's rights – so that the church was obliged to secure a larger edifice in 1889. Not until the ministry of Rev. Charles E. Snyder (1917-31) was such effectiveness resumed. From Sioux City, Miss Safford went to Des Moines where, with the aid of Rev. Ida C. Hultin and Rev. Marie Jenney, a gasping mission was revived, a church built, and the typical pattern of strong preaching, Unity Club programs, and community activities marked her long pastorate (1889-1910) with influence and honor. During these years, moreover, Miss Safford and Miss Gordon – who was a minister at Sioux City from 1889 to 1896 – raised funds for a building to house the First Unitarian Church in Iowa City, to which Miss Gordon was called in 1896. By her thoughtful sermons and sympathetic work with students, it acquired a worthy place in the university-city community. During a vacation in Florida in 1912, Miss Gordon took the initiative in organizing the First Unitarian Church of Orlando, which she then served as minister from 1912 to 1918.

The zeal of the "Iowa Sisterhood," most of whose members were given their field-work training under Miss Safford and Miss Gordon, led them to missionize across Iowa's boundaries. Rev. Caroline Bartlett started a movement at Sioux Falls, South Dakota. Rev. Anna J. Norris did pioneer work in North Platte, Nebraska (1882-84), and Fort Collins, Colorado (1883-87). Rev. Eliza T. Wilkes preached at points west from Rock Rapids, Iowa, to Luverne, South Dakota, developing in the latter city a large, well-housed Society, to which she ministered from 1887 to 1905. Rev. Mary L. Leggett preached in Beatrice, Nebraska, from 1887 to 1890. Crossing Iowa's eastern borders, Rev. Caroline Bartlett went from Sioux Falls to Kalamazoo, Michigan, where her reorganization of the Unitarian Society into "The People's Church," and her utilization of the institutional church features that had been adopted by the new All Souls Church in Chicago under Jones' leadership, won national attention (1889-99). Rev. Marion Murdoch's devoted service in Humboldt, Iowa (1885-90), was continued in association with Miss Bartlett in Kalamazoo (1890-92) and with Rev. Florence Buck in a memorable joint pastorate of six years in Cleveland, Ohio (1893-99). Miss Murdoch later served in Geneva, Illinois, Miss Buck in Kenosha, Wisconsin (1901-11). Rev. Rowena Mann, who was the first woman to receive a Ph.D. degree from a German university (Jena, 1904) and who had been ordained in the Geneva church in 1906, gave a ministry of four years to the Unitarian church in Keokuk, Iowa, then served the Third Church from 1910 to 1923 with marked success.

Owing largely to the tireless, unselfish work of the "Iowa Sisterhood" – so heartily supported by the State Missionaries Effinger, Hunting, and Judy, as well as by Conference Secretary Jones – the Iowa Unitarian Association attained not only a degree of spiritual integration but of financial independence, based on a substantial endowment, that was equaled by no other regional body in the denomination. This strength, which bore clear witness against the argument that radicalism cannot be efficiently organized, was loyally rallied to the support of the Western Unitarian Conference during the strain of the "Western Issue" decade to be dealt with in the following chapter. Such loyal support was implicit in the Resolution of Purpose adopted by the Iowa Conference at its start in 1877:

> *Whereas*, entire freedom is necessary to the growth of religion in the souls of men; and *Whereas* creed-bound organizations are an obstacle to human progress and happiness; *Resolved* that we freely unite ourselves into a permanent society for the purpose of building up free churches, based on practical righteousness, in the State of Iowa.

[Minnesota and the Norwegian Unitarian Mission]

Not only the Iowa field but that in Minnesota also was the object of Jones' vigilant care. The church in St. Paul had slackened the rate of progress it had reached during the ministry of Rev. J. R. Effinger (1872-76), when it acquired the Universalist building, to which it gave the name "Unity Church." A well-meaning minister named Parrott lasted only a year. In 1877 a tall, handsome young Brahmin of Boston and Harvard, who had been christened "William Channing Gannett" by the great Dr. Channing himself, was sent up to St. Paul as a candidate for the vacant perch, and the Society lost no time in calling him to its ministry. What a ministry it was – though of only seven years! The Sunday school burgeoned, the Unity Club offered a feast in art, literature, music, and the drama, a new church was built, and memorable sermons, poems, and hymn poems were written. Like his close friend Jones, Gannett was so assured that a momentous new development of religion was in progress in the Conference that nothing but a thoroughgoing rewording of old forms would do. The Covenant of 1872 stated that, "recognizing the Fatherhood of God and the Brotherhood of Man; and seeking the Spirit of Truth as the guide of our lives, in the hope of immortal life, we associate ourselves to maintain the public worship of God and promote the welfare of humanity." But Gannett found herein vestiges of monarchism in the phrase "the public worship of God," and of selfish salvationism in "the hope of immortal life." Moreover, there was no emphasis at all on religion's part in forming character through the inspiring fellowship of the Church. His new Covenant of 1879 was intensely, earnestly ethical:

As those who believe in Religion,
As those who believe in Freedom, Fellowship and Character in Religion,
As those who believe that the religious life means the thankful, trustful, loyal and helpful life,
And as those who believe that a church is a brotherhood of helpers wherein it is made easier to lead such a life,
We join ourselves together, name, hand and heart, as members of Unity Church.

On a similarly broad basis, Secretary Jones succeeded in persuading the Liberal League of freethinkers in Minneapolis, headed by Samuel C. Gale and Orlando C. Meriam, to transform itself into the First Unitarian Society, "an association where people without regard to theological differences unite for mutual helpfulness in intellectual, moral and religious culture and humane work [making] integrity of life the first aim and [second] the promotion of Truth, Righteousness, Reverence and Charity among men." To assure the coherence and continuity of this "congeries of individualists," Jones persuaded Rev. Henry M. Simmons – whom we have recently met at Madison, Wisconsin – to candidate at Minneapolis. Their choice of him was most fortunate, for Simmons' sermonic ability and scientific competence interpreted evolution as a summons to "upward living" and social self-realization to rapidly increasing congregations. Having outgrown any available theater, in 1887 they built a church, which Simmons' masterly preaching and sterling personality kept filled until his death in 1905.

The visits of Judge O. P. Stearns of Duluth to St. Paul and Minneapolis acquainted him with Unitarianism and with

Simmons. With the assistance of the State Missionary, Rev. Oscar Clute, a group was called together in a hall in Duluth in April, 1887, to hear Simmons. The response to his message was so encouraging that on May 18, 1887, the First Unitarian Church was incorporated with a statement of purpose very similar to that of the Minneapolis Society: "To form an association where people without regard to theological differences may unite for mutual helpfulness, intellectual, moral and religious culture and humane work." Rev. J. H. West was called from Geneva, Illinois, to start things off auspiciously; a Ladies Aid and a Unity Club came into being. The severe climate was too much for West; but in his short year, aided by Simmons' occasional visits, he had so conditioned the group against doctrinalism that when the next minister, Rev. T. J. Volentine, an A.U.A. missionary, tried to inject a conservative Unitarian Christian tone into the worship service and the Sunday school lessons, he created tensions that were not eased until the pacific yet energetic ministry of Rev. Franklin C. Southworth (1892-98). Unity Club lectures and forums got Duluth folk to thinking earnestly about the war with Spain, military training in the public schools, organized charities, and Mrs. Humphry Ward's sensational story of an Anglican priest whose orthodoxy capitulated to the revelations of the Higher Criticism – *Robert Elsmere*, published in 1888. In spite of the depression of the late nineties, Rev. Harry White (1898-1906), whose ordination sermon was preached by Rev. S. M. Crothers of St. Paul, increased the membership of the church, raised money for the purchase of a lot for its small wooden building; and with the aid of faithful Captain Triggs, one of the founders, and of the A.U.A., all debts were paid and enough left to turn the carpet, repaper the interior, and paint the outside of the modest structure.

Another enterprise within the Minnesota Conference in which Secretary Jones was deeply interested was the Norwegian Unitarian Mission of Rev. Kristofer Janson. This liberal of Viking vision and courage began his career in Norway as one of the young aristocrats who became religious and social radicals under the influence of Bjørnson and Ibsen. He deliberately sacrificed family support and social prestige when he applied his literary talent to interpreting modern thought to the peasants in their own language. During the eighteen-seventies he became interested in the impact of American liberal, democratic thought on the increasing numbers of Norwegians immigrating to our Northwest. In 1879 he came over to study the English language and American culture – particularly religious liberalism – at Harvard, where Jones met him and persuaded him to essay a lecture and preaching tour of Norwegian communities in the West as an A.U.A. missionary. In spite of bitter Lutheran hostility, he succeeded in organizing the Nazareth Free Christian Society in Minneapolis (1882), which served as a mission center for group work in Hudson, Underwood, Madelia, and Hanska, Minnesota, with ramifications into Dakota Territory. In the last three of the towns mentioned, buildings were erected; but only the Free Christian Church in Underwood (1890) and the Nora Free Christian Church in Hanska (1882) survive as living memorials to Janson. His religious periodical, *Saamanden,* and his novels of the problems of spiritual adjustment faced by his countrymen in the new home were pioneer works of their kind. Of special merit are [*Amerikanske forholde* (1881), *Præriens saga* (1885), *Vildrose* (1887), *Et arbeidsdyr* (1889). To this list may be added the novels of his wife, Drude Krog Janson – *En ung pige* (1887), *En salonkeepers datter* (1889), *Tore: Fortælling fra prærien* (1894).] Vivid and trenchant recollections of these years of conflict with his countrymen's conservatism and its stubborn resistance to democratic idealism are contained in Janson's autobiography *Ensom,* published in Christiania [now Oslo] in 1903.

Ten years before this, Janson had returned to Norway, where he founded a Unitarian [church] in Christiania, leaving his work in the United States in the hands of Rev. Amandus H. Norman. With unquenchable optimism, Janson, whose views were generally Christian Socialist in nature, summoned the younger generation of Norwegian Americans to the support of the rights of labor and of women, co-operation, international peace. The Lutheran clergy, whose social views may be judged by their general pro-slavery attitude in 1861, were successful in turning the first generation of Norwegian immigrants – hard-headed, tight-fisted individualists – against Janson. When a tornado struck Minneapolis in 1886 and demolished the new church of this congregation, Janson was taunted by the Lutheran clergy to the effect that this calamity was a judgment of God on his heresy – though in St.

Cloud this same tornado had killed a Lutheran pastor and his wife! But the time spirit has brought it about that many of the political and social progressives of Scandinavian stock in Minnesota since 1900 acknowledge Janson's prophethood of their broader social vision.

[The West]

There was no such opposition to liberal views among the Nebraska pioneers of New England lineage who settled in Omaha: the Davises, Longs, Kimballs, Russells, Smiths, Joslyns, and a bit later the Kilpatricks, most of whom were on hand to welcome Rev. C. H. Brigham in 1866 and to organize the First Unitarian Church in 1869 – the year of the building of the Union Pacific bridge across the swift and deep Missouri River. Scarcely had Rev. Henry F. Bond, their first minister, succeeded in getting a chapel built than Grant's depression and Pharaoh's grasshoppers conspired to force it to close. At Jones' solicitations the A.U.A. stepped in with funds to stave off foreclosure, and in 1878 Rev. W. E. Copeland began a ministry of eleven years. To the credit of the trustees, several of whom were officials of the Burlington and the Union Pacific Railroads, freedom was never denied Copeland to plead for justice for the trainmen and later for the farmers. The forward steps of the eighties became long strides during the nineties under the ministry of Rev. Newton M. Mann (1889-1910). By dint of innumerable oyster suppers and strawberry festivals, a spacious church was built, a Unity Club program of rich cultural content and wide popularity inaugurated. Of its initiation of a young woman's mind in the love of art and music, the magnificent Joslyn Memorial of modern Omaha is a permanent memorial. Such an alliance of culture with religion was both effect and cause of the adoption of a new Bond of Union in 1890:

> Basing our union ... on moral and religious purpose rather than upon any dogmatic statement of belief, and emphasizing the religion of character and daily life above all creedal confessions, we invite to our membership all who are seriously drawn to us in spirit and aims.

Somewhat more doctrinal in wording was the Statement of Belief of the First Unitarian Society of Denver, incorporated in 1871; for its sponsors (George Beckwith, H. P. Bennett, Alfred Sayre) took pains to affirm "the Unity of God, the immortality of the soul, the spiritual element in humanity, the necessity of its development and cultivation." Acting on these convictions the members "would seek the Truth wherever we find it, whether in the principles that God has expressed in the universe of matter, in the inspired words of all the great and good of all ages and climes, in the law of conscience which the Creator has written on the tablets of our own hearts." The source of this manifest Parkerism may be found in the sermons of a young graduate of the Harvard Divinity School who had just returned to Denver, Rev. L. E. Beckwith. Relying upon the sympathy of his parents and their friends, he immediately took steps for the organization of the church whose first minister he became and continued until his health failed in 1872. Since Denver, like Omaha, was then virtually a frontier city, the Unitarians could find only a basement room of the Methodist church for their meetings. After two Sundays, however, they were asked to leave. They moved to the basement of the Baptist church, but its minister very shortly came to the conclusion that the Lord would not give his blessing to his people if the Unitarians defiled his sanctuary. So the little group of refugees took shelter in a law office, where a Sunday school was organized. They barely got through the depression years of the eighteen-seventies. In desperation the trustees cast their burdens on the Ladies Aid, who presently had raised enough money to justify the calling of a minister. One came, did well, then died within the year. Another came, did well – and died in a year! Undaunted by such omens, Rev. T. J. Van Ness took the helm in 1884 and the ship got safely through its Sargasso Sea. In their new building, Denver's first free kindergarten was started, and a Charity Organization Society foreshadowed the Associated Charities that Rev. Samuel A. Eliot (1889-93) pushed through to general civic acceptance and support. Samuel Eliot lacked the pertinacious Westernism of his elder kinsman, W. G. Eliot of St. Louis; but the younger Eliot did not go back to "the neighborhood of Boston" until he had demonstrated his possession of the famous Midas-like aptitudes of the Eliot clan by getting an endowment fund for the Denver church well begun.

A struggle for survival as severe as those of the Omaha and Denver churches fell to the lot of that at Kansas City, Missouri.

Rev. W. E. Copeland, who – as we have seen – saved the cause in Omaha, had started the Unitarian Society off well in 1868, with a constitutional Preamble that pledged the founders as "trusting in God as the Source of all Wisdom and Power, [taking] the Bible as a sufficient rule of faith and practice [but asserting] no right to exclude any one from our Society on account of difference of doctrinal opinions." A church was built in 1871; but again the depression of the seventies jeopardized the Society, which in any case was none too strong because of frictions between the Unitarian and Universalist segments. To conciliate the latter, on whose behalf the church was given the name "All Souls," and to proclaim its character as a Unitarian Christian body, a new Covenant was adopted – written by Rev. R. L. Collier and Judge G. W. McCrary in 1887 – which committed members to

… the public worship of God and the practice of the precepts of Christianity … [the establishment of] all agencies calculated to promote true Christian life and thereby the highest good of society … without requiring of each other any creed of confession or faith and [claiming] no right to exclude anyone from this church on account of difference in doctrinal opinion.

Collier's ministry in the new brick church of 1887 was followed by that of a Universalist, Rev. J. E. Roberts (1887-97), whose views became increasingly Emersonian. In 1897 Roberts resigned from All Souls to found the "Church of This World." A reunified church was effected on the basis of the irenic National Conference Preamble of 1894. As time went on, however, even this seemed too narrow, and eventually the members adopted the very Ethical Basis that Judge McCrary had worked strenuously to defeat:

Avowing as the sole bond of our union a serious purpose to lead pure, reverent and useful lives, we seek together Love which quickeneth Service and Truth which maketh free … Good will is the Spirit of this church. Service is its law. This is our great covenant: to dwell together in peace, to seek the truth in love and to help one another.

Did ever a denominational official in the history of the American church have so vast a region under his care as did Jones, traveling from Cleveland to Denver, from Duluth to Kansas

City, reconciling, exhorting, warning – but always encouraging the brethren, lay and clerical? Yet to these Midwest burdens was added a considerable responsibility for the missions and churches beyond the Rocky Mountains. Commencing with the First Unitarian Church of San Francisco (1850), societies had been organized at Portland, Oregon (1866); Sacramento, California (1867); San Diego, Santa Barbara, Los Angeles, in California (all in 1877). But only the church in San Francisco, under the ministry of Rev. Horatio Stebbins (1864-1900), and that at Portland, served by T. L. Eliot (1867-93), had attained strength and stability. Hence a stream of correspondence concerning vacant pulpits, despondent or divided congregations, suitable or unsuitable candidates, came to Jones' desk in Chicago – and often the going or returning candidates themselves! Not until Rev. C. W. Wendte went to the West Coast as Missionary Superintendent of the A.U.A. in 1886 was this extra burden on the Western Secretary removed.

[The Chicago Area]

Secretary Jones' labors in salvaging from the ravages of the depression of the eighteen-seventies the several churches we have visited and starting them off afresh with consecrated and able leaders were obviously of crucial importance. Equally notable were the gains made with his counsel and encouragement in the Chicago area. The Third Unitarian Church, after a series of brief pastorates, including a one-year stay of Rev. Minot J. Savage (1873-74) on his way out of orthodoxy, had called a tall, sallow ex-Methodist preacher, so absent-minded that when he could not locate his "sermon barrel" he accused the sexton of stealing it and demanded his dismissal. A horrified board complied; but after a candid discussion of the whole situation with the sexton's wife, they ended the minister's contract and reinstated the sexton – with apologies. To restore equilibrium, Jones stepped in with the suggestion that Rev. James Vila Blake be invited to candidate. Thus began the longest (1883-97) and most brilliant ministry in the church's history thus far, for Blake modernized the Sunday school and not only provided it with *Unity* lesson material and methods but also composed original and beautiful festival services and hymns for its hundreds of pupils. A variegated Unity Club program was developed, and many cultural and humanitarian projects carried on in the community.

If sermons ever were worth stealing, those of Blake would have been! In our next chapter we shall glance at the long list of his published works – not only sermons but poems and plays. He was not, however, merely a clerical litterateur; for
when, in 1887, a jury and a judge notoriously under the control of Cyrus McCormick, George Pullman, and other barons of the "gilded age," condemned seven of the Haymarket Square Anarchists to death, Blake, acting with Jenkin Lloyd Jones, William M. Salter of the Ethical Society, and Rabbi Emil Hirsch, asked his congregation for signatures on a petition to Governor Oglesby for commutation of the sentence until new evidence could be presented. Over a hundred person signed, but twelve members walked out of the church and never returned. Then Blake, with Judge Russell and J. W. Wanger of the congregation, took the petition down to Springfield. The loyalty of his parishioners in this instance and others similar to it was reciprocated by Blake during the depression of the eighteen-nineties, when he secured a position in the public-school system in order to be able to carry on his ministry without being a financial burden to the congregation.

Yet even in these years Blake's energy was such that when a group of liberals in Evanston, Illinois – led by Mr. and Mrs. Herbert W. Brough, Mrs. E. C. Sawyer, and Mr. George Richardson – founded the Church of All Souls (1891) and invited Blake to preach for them on Sunday afternoons, he did not refuse. After 1897, when he resigned from the pulpit of the Third Church, he moved to Evanston and continued as its minister until 1917. The Covenant he wrote for Evanston and the Third Church has commended itself, for its simple, practical beauty of thought and words, to many Societies of later foundation:

> Love is the Spirit of this church and Service is its Law. This is our Great Covenant; to dwell together in peace, to seek the truth in love and to help one another.

In harmony with such poetic yet vital idealism was the small Gothic chapel built in 1904, distinguished in architecture by having a shelf high over the pulpit for the Scriptures of the great religions of the world.

In Hinsdale, Illinois, efforts had been made since 1869 to draw Universalists and Unitarians together in Unity Church. It was unable to secure a building of its own and had to depend on supply preaching from Chicago. But in 1887 Rev. W. C. Gannett resigned at St. Paul and accepted a call to the reorganized Unitarian church of Hinsdale (1887-89). The present structure of unconventional and homelike design is the result of his ideas and careful supervision.

Parallel with these openings in Evanston and Hinsdale was that which Jones himself effected, at the very height of his secretarial visitations around the Conference: the gathering and founding of All Souls Church on Chicago's south side. Population shifts after the Great Fire of 1871, combined with the departure of its first and very effective minister, C. W. Wendte, in 1875, had forced the Fourth Unitarian Church (1869) to sell its building in 1880. A remnant of the membership kept hoping and praying for a better day which finally dawned on November 1, 1882, in a bare, shabby hall furnished with kitchen chairs and a long table. For on that All Souls Sunday, Jones delivered a sermon on his "Ideal Church" to about twenty-five adults and three children. He had neither lectern nor organ – but seven years of missionizing in the West had taught him what similar experience had taught Clarke in the eighteen-thirties: to ignore surroundings and to preach with not less but with more fire and inspiration. So he put his deepest convictions and most earnest delivery into this sermon, as Theodore Parker had done in his sermon on "The True Idea of a Christian Church," which in 1846, in a similarly dirty, dingy upstairs hall, had launched the Twenty-eighth Congregational Society of Boston. Jones' ideal church would be

... a free congress of independent souls. It is to lead in the campaign for more truth rather than to indolently stand guard over some petty fragment of acquired truth ... it will be the thinker's home. The student of science will handle no discoveries that it will not prize and indulge in no guesses that it will not respect. Oldest India and newest America will hold no gem of thought that will not be welcomed into its sacred Scriptures. The skeptics will be the cowards who dare not exercise the reason God has given them. Over its portals no dogmatic test is to be written to ward off an honest thinker or an earnest seeker.

This church must emphasize the Universal Brotherhood; it will stand upon a grand emphasis of the great word of the century, Unity. It will seek to welcome low and high, poor and rich, unbeliever and believer. One who enters its doors flaunting the latest achievements of dressmaker or milliner in such a way as to widen the chasm between her and the family of the honest and earnest poor is guilty of impiety for she flaunts the sanctity of this church.

In Jones' ideal church, moreover, there would be "no rented pews, no ownership of private boxes, where the pride of caste may enter the last hopes of democracy." It would welcome colored folk as well as white, Jews and those of all other denominations and religions "on the basis of a common Humanity, a common Moral Law, Conscience and Duty." Its building would not be "a Gothic sham" but "a secular hall, a workshop, an oratory of the Soul, all in one, where its members may meet for the studying of God's laws, for spiritual culture, for mutual aid and comfort, to do better the work of the world – and for worship."

What would be the theological position of this Ideal Church?

This church will be founded on Reverence. One of its cornerstones will be the besetting presence of that Infinite Sanctity that it cannot escape. Given the freest thought, the widest outlook and the most wholesome desire to help one's kind but wanting that sensitiveness to things divine, the soul is still deficient in character … The time is coming when the church will have but one message to promulgate, namely: "Go, love the Lord thy God with all thy heart, with all thy strength and with all thy mind and thy neighbor as thyself." These Ethical Verities are as eternal as Deity.

If his hearers were moved to say, "I am eager to join such a church – but where is it to be found?" Jones replied by summoning them to work with him to create such a church "in this moment of time, on this spot of ground!"

They accepted the invitation! They started a Sunday school immediately. On December 8, the "Church of All Souls, Unitarian," was organized, with Alexander Thompson as first president. A Unity Club followed in January. Hall rent and other expenses were met by a pledge system in connection with an every-member canvass. On Jones' insistence, the pastor's salary was not a fixed sum but the residue of the income after all other expenses had been paid. The motto of the church was that of

Unity: "Freedom, Fellowship and Character in Religion" and its Bond of Union read:

> We join ourselves together in the interests of Morality and Religion, as interpreted by the growing thought and purest lives of Humanity, hoping thereby to bear one another's burdens and to promote Truth, Love and Righteousness in the world.

By 1885 the Vincennes Avenue hall was bursting at the seams; by 1887 a church building at the corner of Oakwood Boulevard and Langley Avenue was dedicated. In conformity with Jones' ideals, it had no "Gothic pretentiousness [to] frighten away the mechanic and the seamstress; [Gothic] was very costly yet it was useless on week days; it promoted the sense of individual insignificance that served authoritarianism and medieval superstition while its colored windows suggested otherworldliness." Hence the new home of All Souls was flooded with sunlight. Its first floor contained an auditorium, Sunday-school classrooms, parlors, a kitchen, an office, and pastor's study. On the second floor was the parsonage. The *Chicago Tribune* reported that "the architecture had suggestions of a Gothic Cathedral [!] and of a Turkish mosque, according to the point on which you stood to take it in." Never mind! – what vitality throbbed in "The Ideal Church"! Hundreds in the Sunday school, large confirmation classes and services, Unity Club sessions with hundreds of students, a Lens Club, boys' and women's gymnasium classes, a free kindergarten, the Choral Club – and a free public reading room, the special interest of Jones' staunch colleague in church and Conference, Daniel L. Shorey, who had played truant from the Church of the Messiah on fashionable Michigan Avenue, with its *porte-cochère* for parishioners in barouches, and its Easter parade. By 1888 the growth of the All Souls congregation obliged the trustees to enlarge the auditorium to take in the whole first floor; to move the club and classrooms upstairs; and, to Jones' deep regret, to buy a parsonage for the minister to whom, in 1890, the trustees *insisted* on paying a salary of at least $3,000 a year!

Yet for all the meagerness and uncertainty of his salary, Jones had saved enough to buy land upon the Wisconsin River, the country of his boyhood and of his kinfolk. There he had organized a Unitarian church during his summer vacations (at Helena) and had established the Tower Hill community summer school for All Souls members and readers of *Unity* throughout the Conference, where high thinking and plain living, good health and great literature were available at most moderate prices!

[Conclusion]

In 1884 Jones rendered his last report as Secretary of the Conference. The Report called attention to the fact that in 1875, when he began work, there were 43 active societies and 42 ministers in the Conference, with a burden of debt over $100,000. In 1884 there were 87 active societies with 64 ministers, some of whom served two churches; their combined debts amounted to less than $8,000. In 1875 there was but one state conference; in 1884 there were seven state conferences, with seven full- or part-time missionaries. The Sunday School Society started in 1873 was now distributing weekly uniform lessons and thirty or so other publications. The Conference headquarters in Chicago required a staff of four adults and an errand boy; it was thronged daily with volunteers working on tract distribution or the Post Office Mission correspondence, the publication of Unity or the business of scores of Unity Clubs in the West. To bring all this enthusiasm and expansion into being, Jones had traveled at least 122,370 miles, had preached almost 1,500 missionary sermons. Yet for all nine years of his secretaryship, Jones had been a full-time minister (at Janesville) or a part-time minister (at All Souls), and for six of the nine years editor of *Unity*!

The regret of the Conference over his resignation was expressed in a resolution offered by his successor, Rev. J. T. Sunderland:

> This body desires to express to Mr. Jones and put on permanent record its profound appreciation of the zeal, self-sacrifice, devotion and large prophetic vision with which he has planned and labored during these years; and the deep and enduring debt of gratitude which this Conference and Unitarianism in the West owe and ever must owe to him for his long, invaluable service. Further the Conference desires to recognize with heartiness and gratitude its obligations to the unofficial services of Mrs. Jones …

But a better idea of what a visit of Secretary Jones could mean to a little group of liberals in a raw young city on the great

Western plains, beaten down by bank and crop failures, or to a lonely, poorly paid minister in a reactionary environment, is given us by Jones' colleague and comrade, W. C. Gannett:

> One voice, whose bell shall ring away all fear;
> One hand, in which we grasp incarnate cheer;
> One steadfast smile, rayed out from eyes alight,
> To make men say "He's come – now all is right!"

CHAPTER ELEVEN

The Western Issue:
Is Unitarianism Only Christian Theism?

CONSIDERING THE FACT that Rev. Jabez T. Sunderland, a graduate of the Baptist Theological Seminary of the (old) University of Chicago, stood close to Pilot Jones at the helm of the Western Conference from the year 1876 (when Sunderland took over the Fourth Unitarian Church in Chicago from Rev. C. W. Wendte), one would suppose that a resolution from his hand in 1884 praising Jones' "large, prophetic vision" and "long invaluable service" would have both factual knowledge and candid sincerity behind it. From the very start of *Unity* in 1878, Sunderland had been an editorial contributor and must often have read Jones' convictions and aims in the pages of the periodical. From 1878 when Sunderland left Chicago to be minister of the Unitarian church in Ann Arbor, Michigan, as well as the A.U.A.'s missionary in that state, he had worked in close collaboration and apparent harmony with Jones, save for a mild protest against the inadequacy of "Freedom, Fellowship and Character in Religion" as a formal statement of Conference objectives when the incorporation of the Conference was proposed in 1882. Jones and Gannett indeed had wanted to add "the advancement of the cause of intelligence, freedom, reverence, fellowship, character and helpfulness"; but this clause, as well as "the promotion of rational religion" were rejected by a motion of conservative Brooke Herford of Chicago. Sunderland later pointed out in *Unity* that "Freedom and Fellowship" was the motto of the Free Religious Association and that, even in the fine ethical clause which had been rejected, there was lacking something precious that Unitarianism meant to him: "an historic connection with a great past – with what is highest, sweetest, most vital in Christianity." Sunderland confessed his liking for a formula coined by Rev. C. G. Ames:

In the love of truth and in the spirit of Jesus Christ we join for the worship of God and the service of man.

To be sure, Mrs. Sunderland, who, like her husband, had come from a Baptist background, had taken offense at certain radical remarks made at a meeting of the Michigan conference by Rev. Rowland Connor, a missionary salaried by the A.U.A. whom Secretary Jones had attracted from New England to East Saginaw. Connor was a member of the F.R.A. – like Gannett – and a brilliant speaker and writer. Sunderland, however, seems to have kept aloof from his wife's feud with Connor, although in an article published in *The Christian Register* in 1883 on "True and False Liberalism" he had obliquely disparaged Connor's fitness for the Unitarian ministry. Apart from such minor incidents and expressions, therefore, there was nothing to indicate that Sunderland did not feel essentially in agreement with the man whose work he was taking over, and whose "large prophetic vision" and "long, invaluable service" he stressed in the resolution.

But there were other and very good reasons, too, why Jones must have glanced at Sunderland rather quizzically from under his bushy eyebrows when the unctuous resolution was read and passed. Jones was well aware that the old conservative disapproval of the congenital independence and radicalism of the Western Conference was ominously resurgent and that it had, as in the past, Western sympathizers and allies. Samuel K. Lothrop's protégé, Rev. Grindall Reynolds, had succeeded Rev. R. R. Shippen as General Secretary of the A.U.A. Jones and Shippen had worked in mutual understanding and respect. But Reynolds, who was also minister of the church in Concord, depended increasingly on the aid and counsel of the "dark, silent figure," Rev. George W. Fox, permanent Assistant Secretary of the Association, and the conservatives' willing agent in the Year Book episode of 1874-75. Moreover, Henry P. Kidder and his close friend, A. A. Low of Brooklyn – whose insistence on Christian supranaturalism in the first meeting of the National Conference in 1865 had resulted in the formation of the F.R.A. – were President and Vice-President of the A.U.A. In close relations with Secretary Reynolds was W. G. Eliot of St. Louis, who had tried to commit the Western Conference to a supranaturalist Christian position in 1853-54, in contravention of Parkerism. Though Eliot was now chancellor of Washington University, his young colleague, Rev. John Snyder, was definitely a conservative. The same was true of Rev. Brooke Herford, minister of the Church of the Messiah in Chicago, and his leading laymen, C. S. C. Mixer and M. B. Hull – though another "pillar," D. L. Shorey, was showing more and more sympathy with Jones' literary interests and social work at All Souls. In Unity Church, Chicago, which Robert Collyer had left in 1879, the defection of his youthful, handsome, eloquent successor, Rev. George C. Miln (1881-82), to Ingersollism had accentuated the conservatism of the church, with the result that the two following ministers – Rev. George Batchelor (1882-85), Rev. T. G. Milstedt (1885-89) – were called by the congregation more for their sound conservatism than for their conspicuous ability. As a result the church waned into mediocrity and insignificance within two decades.

A hint that this conservatism was being organized as a militant force against "the *Unity* men" came with an address given by Rev. A. P. Putnam, Low's own minister in Brooklyn, before the British and Foreign Unitarian Association in London, in June, 1883, on "The Aspects and Opportunities of Unitarianism in America." Dr. Putnam, who had never attended a Western Conference meeting and knew little about the West in general, lamented that Unitarianism in America had "lost the scepter we ought to hold." Its growth "has ceased to be an object of fear" to orthodoxy as it was in the days of Channing. Many of its birthright sons and daughters were turning to other denominations because American Unitarianism

… has become a medley of doubts and denials, petty criticisms and secular teachings, … never ceases to make war on the miraculous elements in the New Testament … finds fault with Christ Himself or silently leaves Him out of account … especially in its Sunday School literature … neglects the sacraments of Baptism and the Lord's Supper … sinks the Bible to the level of books of other religions.

Old and honored periodicals are dying or have died – *The Christian Examiner, The Liberal Christian, Old and New* – largely because they printed the contributions of unbelievers. "Antioch College, into which the Unitarians have poured untold wealth, has passed under the control of radical managers and instructors and alas! where is it now? ... some Unitarian preachers in the West surpass all others in declaring that God and immortality are but fictions of the mind."

The remedy Putnam offered was – "Go back to Channing!"

If the Unitarian Church of America is to have any great and glorious future, it must cease from its mere criticisms and dead negations, its everlasting platitudes against forms and creeds, its insufferable cant and conceit, its senseless screams for liberty – of which, God knows, we have already had enough! We must retrace our steps and rejoin the Great Church of God with its many banners and Christ the Captain of its salvation.

Although this attack was not directed solely at Western Unitarianism, Jones took up the gauntlet in *Unity* and twitted Putnam as being "blue" and "sick" and making a custom of carrying an "indigo bag" with him on his European travels. W. G. Eliot, however, in a letter to the *Register*, heartily endorsed Putnam's attack: "The church which shakes itself free from Jesus Christ is destined to an early decay and death ... it becomes a lyceum and its religious uses fade away. I have seen the experiment made scores of times."

That the London Unitarian periodical *The Christian Life* should have gone to the expense of mailing its report of this address to every Unitarian minister *in the United States* would seem to afford evidence that powerful interests had inspired Putnam's attack. The method is reminiscent of that used by Rev. C. H. Brigham, the former Western Agent of the A.U.A. and A.U.A. missionary minister in Ann Arbor. One recalls that Rev. A. D. Mayo began the attack on Western Unitarian trends toward Parkerism at the Conference of 1870 in Cleveland with an address on "The Vocation of Western Unitarianism," in which he attributed the failure (as he saw it) of Unitarianism to fulfill its early promise to its departure from the ideas and idioms of Liberal Christianity as Channing conceived it. Brigham followed with a pessimistic report on Western missionary progress. The Conference, as a result, was so divided and demoralized that it almost expired and was only salvaged by the indomitable spirit of Forbush, Hosmer, Wendte, and Jones. Was the pattern to be repeated in 1883?

Jasper Douthit in Shelbyville, likewise an A.U.A. missionary, rejoiced openly in the Putnam "jeremiad." His organ, *Our Best Words*, had been frankly critical of Jones and *Unity* for avoiding doctrinal tenets and theological terms in defining the basis of fellowship and work in the articles of newly formed state conferences and in the covenants of churches. Scarcely an issue of his paper appeared without a comment of this nature, such as a wish "that *Unity* were more useful by being more fervently Christian … The way to build Unitarian churches is to go to work like honest Christians and build them where they are really needed and not anywhere or everywhere that an enthusiastic Spiritualist or a roaring atheist may run out to greet you the first time you preach in a new place." *Unity's* statement in 1882 that the word "Unitarian is broader than the word Christian for it existed before Jesus was born" evoked from Douthit the complaint that "it is hardly fair for *Unity* to be the organ of a Conference of Christian churches while it maintains such a non-Christian attitude." As another brick to throw at *Unity*, Douthit used a sermon by W. G. Eliot in St. Louis, in May, 1883, on "The Coming Church: Will It Be Christian or Not?" in which, after extolling "Jesus Christ as the Messiah of God and the Christian religion as superior to all other religions and systems of morality the world has ever seen," Eliot passed judgment on the Ethical Culture Society in process of formation in his city: "When I have reached the ideal of manhood which the greatest of all prophets has given us, it will be time enough to seek a system of ethical culture more advanced." Douthit supplemented this dictum by admitting that "of course there are good and honest persons who say they do not believe in a God" but "they have inherited their good traits from their Christian parents."

The Christian Life's mailing to all Unitarian ministers in the United States gave Douthit a precedent for doing the same thing with an "extra" of *Our Best Words* of April, 1884. A dramatic letter to Secretary Reynolds explained that Douthit "had become so sick and tired of this sort of business that I cannot in good faith keep silent about it any longer." An equally dramatic letter to Jones reminded him that in June, 1880, Douthit had sent him his resignation from the Western Conference on the ground that

... I do not regard the non-Christian position of the Conference as calculated to enlarge the fellowship ... tens of thousands of needy souls must starve to death for all the good that the Western Unitarian Conference is likely to afford them ... Unitarianism signifies to me Christian liberty, Christian unity, Christian charity and Christian discipleship and character. The Christian fellowship is the largest and most inclusive of all.

To Douthit's agitated soul, the "Issue in the West" presented itself in a series of *ultimata*:

(1) Does Unitarianism mean the Christian religion in its simplicity and purity or does it mean something else?

(2) Are we Unitarians an organized body of Christian believers with the Holy Son of God as our Captain or are we only a nebulous, tenuous mass of humanity, believing anything and everything in general and nothing in particular?

(3) Are Unitarians unequivocally and aggressively Christian in character or are we merely a heterogeneous multitude clamoring for Freedom, Fellowship and Character in Religion with a complacent indifference as to whether the divine religion of Jesus is voted up or down?

In his determination to pledge the Conference – from which he had ostensibly resigned in 1880 – to "outspoken allegiance to the Lord Jesus Christ as sent of God to be our Teacher, Guide and Savior and [as alone] worth living, suffering and dying for," Douthit obviously conceived of the *Unity* men in much the same light as he did the saloon keepers of Shelbyville; and of himself as leading a torchlight parade to the new hymn "Onward, Christian Soldiers" in a campaign in which Christ (i.e. Christian Unitarianism) should be "voted up" and the Devil (Free Religion) should be "voted down" – and *out*, of Shelbyville, i.e. the Western Conference!

"Substantially," wrote W. G. Eliot to Douthit, "I agree with you. The Western Conference is a hindrance and not an aid to our denominational and not less to our spiritual growth."

Jones' editorial reply in *Unity* of May 16, 1884, was both playful and forgiving. As to the shame of belonging simply to "a nebulous, tenuous, mass of humanity," Jones averred that though the adjectives were a bit confusing, nevertheless he liked the idea – for he liked humanity! With regard to the doctrinal issue:

Douthit's religion is larger than his theology. If of our work he can say "my soul abhors it," in his work we can heartily say our souls delight. He may deny the Western Unitarian Conference; I am sure the Western Conference will still delight in him. He may turn us out of his church but he cannot keep himself out of ours. If Freedom, Fellowship and Character are marginal things to him, they are central to us; consequently we must count him in though his "freedom in Christ" counts us out.

Was it possible that Jones' vision of the message and function of Unitarianism, in the West at least, was larger than Douthit's because he had both eyes open and could better understand the significance for the religion of the future of all the crosscurrents of critical, skeptical – and reactionary – thought that were swirling around in "the nebulous, tenuous mass of humanity" in the second half of the nineteenth century? A brief conspectus of the maelstrom may help us at this juncture.

Critics of Doctrinal Christianity, 1870-1900

Never in their history had the Christian church and Christian doctrine been so acutely and even savagely challenged – for never before in any age or country had freedom of thought and expression been so protected by law and public opinion. Metaphorically speaking, palaces, capitals, and even temples were besieged and entered, as in the days of the barbarian invasion. Tennyson had averred in "In Memoriam" (1850) that, since his long conflict with despair after Hallam's death had led him to peace,

> There lives more faith in honest doubt,
> Believe me, than in half the creeds.

But this spelled only a half truth to many honest doubters who could no longer accept any creed of Biblical or Christian faith since geological and biological evolution had invalidated Genesis, and the Higher Criticism had dissected the monolithic Pentateuch and Isaiah into "literary sources," then trimmed their ancient majesty by several centuries. Not only had Deuteronomy lost its halo but the Gospel of John, the most "high church" of the four, had been de-classified as being mostly tendentious fiction and philosophical theology. New Testament scholarship had established the non-apostolicity and relative lateness of the so-called "Apostles' Creed," as well as the priority of the simple

Jewish-Christian "suffering Servant" conception of the Messiah over Pauline soteriology. Not only Jesus' apotheosis, therefore, but even the relevancy for the average mundane person of Jesus' apocalyptic, ascetic, demonological teachings was disputed.

The process of making "honest doubters" was aided by the verdict of physics, chemistry, and biology, establishing the unity of all life and cosmic law through the demonstration of the principle of the conservation of energy; but its massive, impartial operations seemed to many not to be congruous with anthropomorphic conceptions of a fatherly Deity, a benevolent Providence, and the special favor of a felicitous immortality. Nor did the materialism of W. K. Clifford and John Tyndall, with their theories that psychology was properly a branch of physiology, and that both sciences should be studied as phases of sociology, help to persuade honest doubters of the truth of the Christian tenet of the pre-natal and post-mortem existence of the "soul."

Meanwhile the church historians had been disclosing the transformation – or perversion – of early apostolic beliefs by the ideas and idioms of the Stoic and Neo-Platonic philosophies; the historians of European rationalism and morals were emphasizing the almost unvarying opposition of orthodox, ecclesiastical Christianity to the progress of science, social reforms, and political democracy, not only in the Dark and Middle Ages but also in the days of William Lloyd Garrison, Bishop Wilberforce, Pius IX, and [General Georges] Boulanger. "Truth forever on the scaffold, wrong forever on the throne," was an axiom trenchantly reiterated by Ingersoll in the United States, [Charles] Bradlaugh in England, and in more esoteric circles by that brilliant constellation of philosophic liberals in the later Victorian decades – [W. E. H.] Lecky, [Henry Thomas] Buckle, [J. A.] Froude, J. S. Mill, [John] Ruskin, [John] Morley, Walter Pater, Leslie Stephen, Frederic Harrison – none of whom could discern any "God within the shadow, keeping watch above his own."

Nor were the great English poets and novelists who filled the meridian years of Victoria the Good with a rich treasure of Humanist literature a source of support for orthodox Christianity. "In Memoriam" was so elusively Broad Church that the Unitarians hailed it as their own. Matthew Arnold was nominally an Anglican, actually a neo-Stoic. Browning was an ethical pan-psychist, very like Emerson; A. H. Clough, FitzGerald, James Thomson, and Swinburne were all agnostic, though Swinburne and Thomson verged on outright atheism. In the gallery of novelists, Dickens' Christianity consisted chiefly of a veneration of the humanitarian Christ; Thackeray, Disraeli, and Bulwer-Lytton provided no special religious inspiration; George Eliot's noble message was that of an ethical Humanism.

Beautiful quotations might be, and indeed were, made copiously from all these writers in advocacy of the ethical ideals and duties, the moral solemnity, and potential sublimity of human life – even of reverent recognition of an indwelling yet supernal Truth, Beauty, Goodness, and Love, a "Power not ourselves that makes for Righteousness" – but little could be quoted from them on behalf of the major Christian dogmas and the ecclesiastical cultus. The same fact held, of course, for the principal American poets, Bryant, Emerson, Longfellow, Lowell, Holmes, Whittier: they were religious in the deepest sense, but not conventionally so. The C-major key of all their religious utterances was the ethical life, the duty of honorable, tolerant, compassionate conduct and character, harmonious with the spirit and example of Christ, the laws of Nature, the infinite Wisdom and Goodness of God. Always with them, however, the true Christian is "not he who repeateth the Name, but he that doeth the Will." The bold and brave thinkers who knew Whitman heard no church bells in his chants, but they could not miss his natural piety and admiration for the integrated, self-reliant, frank, brotherly individual, man or woman, in whom American democracy came to spiritual flower and fruit.

Jones, the practical man, knew all these writers very well and quoted them as never a Unitarian minister quoted poetry before! Browning was his favorite poet, Emerson was Gannett's, but they were one in their appreciation of Emerson's essays and lectures. For Emerson had from the beginning opened his mind to the truth of evolution, seeing clearly that "striving to be man, the worm mounts through all the spires of form." Quite as early in his career, Emerson embraced another "privilege of the immeasurable mind" – the study and appreciation of non-Christian scriptures of the world. For the Transcendental intuitionism required, like the rationalism and moralism of the old Deists, proofs of the presence of Oversoul beliefs and of the ethical ideas in representative human minds of all ages and lands. Natural Religion's work in the eighteenth century in the discovery and translation of the scriptures of the East was carried on with increasing enthusiasm and productivity in the nineteenth century, culminating in the fifty-one volumes of Max Müller's edition of the *Sacred Books of the East* (from 1875 on). Taken with [E. B.] Tylor's anthropological *Researches [into the Early History of Mankind and the Development of Civilization]* (1865) and *Primitive Culture* (1871), what astonishing analogies were disclosed between the myths, theologies, rites, sectarian rivalries, codes of morality of the Oriental faiths and those of Judaism and Christianity! Yet at the heart of each and all these faiths was the insistence of the Founders on the individual's fidelity to the cardinal ethical verities of truthfulness, the golden mean, the Golden Rule, forgiveness, and boundless compassion.

How was it possible for those who had made themselves conversant with the new knowledge and wide horizons of science, Biblical scholarship, and comparative religion to keep their religious convictions inside the covers of the Bible, the walls of Christian churches, the *Ideenwelt* of Christian creeds and piety? Since cosmic and organic unity of energy, law, and evolutionary process was the new insight, was it not logical that the names "Jewish," "Christian," "Moslem" and the like should have connoted division and sectarian rivalry to those who founded the Free Religious Association in 1867 in protest against the constriction of Unitarian faith and fellowship by the Christian language of Article IX of the National Conference? Observing also the evolutionary obsolescence of any and all the speculative, metaphysical features of religion in history, as well as their all-too-frequent employment as sheep's clothing for wolfish deeds, was it not logical for honest doubters to fall back on what they deemed the abiding ethical core of all religious scriptures as the true basis of faith, fellowship, and aspiration? Of course, if the crucial religious experience of the F.R.A. leaders had been typical Christian emotional-moral conversion, the theological matrix of such an experience would have remained for them sacrosanct, and of exclusive validity, as illustrated by Douthit and his fervent allegiance to the "Captain of his salvation," Jesus Christ. But Jones, Gannett, Blake, Hosmer, Learned, and most of the other *Unity* men had never had such a conversion experience; the provenance of their religious convictions was a gradual intellectual illumination and enlargement, with no fixation in any salvationist Person or theology.

The same may be said of Emerson, the first member and the unofficial patriarch of the F.R.A. – their "great representative of the Absolute in pure thought." Abbot, the dominant philosopher and publicist of the F.R.A., had proclaimed it

… the new Gospel of religion and science, the Gospel of faith in man carried to its extremest consequences – the Gospel of repose in the Infinite Love that works through Universal Law – a Gospel of the enthusiasm of humanity, of the Christianity of Christ's principles, Truth, Righteousness and Love, not of his person.

This was the gravamen, be it noted, of Emerson's Divinity School Address, as well as his essays on "Worship," "The Preacher," "The Sovereignty of Ethics." But the F.R.A. had turned out to be *so* philosophic, *so* individualistic, *so* impractical that it had dwindled by 1882 into virtual impotence and its organ, *The Index*, had to be given up in 1886; meanwhile Abbot's National Liberal League had flickered out in futile debates and negations. In spite of the pleas of Felix Adler, its president from 1879 to 1882, and of the Unitarian Ethical leader, Rev. Anna Garlin Spencer, the "enthusiasm for humanity" of its origin was precluded by hair-splitting individualism of the W. G. Sumner type from participating in most of the humanitarian reforms of the period – Negro education, the temperance movement, labor's fight for justice, international peace.

From such sterility the young doctor of philosophy, Felix Adler, of rabbinical lineage and Kantian scholarship, tried to save the F.R.A. He envisaged a fusion of the social challenge of Amos and Micah and the "scientific" morality of [Herbert] Spencer's theories with Emerson's vision of "a new church founded on moral science." In 1876 he had founded the Society for Ethical Culture in New York City not only for the fostering of personal righteousness but for social and educational reforms. Adler was professedly agnostic with regard to Deity and personal immortality. The Ethical Culture meetings were devoid of the conventional features of worship and prayer, though birth and parental responsibility, vocation and marriage, retirement and death, were ceremonially observed and solemnized, the rationale of such dedications being that "morality becomes religion when it becomes devotion to the eternal Order of the universe, whereby human life achieves meaning, is directed toward moral perfection and in spite of sorrows and afflictions is bound to culminate in a sublime denouement." For the next two decades the extension of the Ethical Culture movement was impressive. Not only did the New York Society flourish and start schools and settlement houses, but similar societies were established in other cities. The founder of that in Philadelphia (1885), S. Burns Weston, had been a graduate of Antioch College and as student in the Harvard Divinity School had brought his study lamp to the School's chapel lectern when Emerson gave his address on "The Preacher" in 1879. W. L. Sheldon, a convert of Weston, founded an Ethical Society in St. Louis in 1886. W. M. Salter, likewise a graduate of the Harvard School, founded the Chicago Ethical Society in 1883. In the constitution of the American Ethical Union of these and other groups, their faith and purposes were clearly stated: "the assertion of the supreme importance of the ethical factor in all relations of life, apart from any theological or metaphysical considerations." The latter were neither debated nor denied in the lectures and classes of the Ethical Culture societies, but simply omitted. The members were not pledged to eschew individual speculative interests, but Adler was careful to see that leadership candidates were not theologically minded.

How congenial the honest doubters and conscientious skeptic found the Ethical Culture fellowship is surely obvious. The affinity it had with the Unitarian radicalism of the West is equally clear. How irritating its very existence and progress were to conservative Unitarians such as Douthit, who doggedly and blindly believed that without Christian piety a high morality and charity were impossible – or impermanent – may be imagined!

Probably never before had such forthright disavowals of traditional Christian doctrines as have been described enjoyed free expression and wide publicity. In two decades agnosticism, Ingersollism, materialistic Free Thought, the Free Religious Association, the Ethical Culture movement had gained such a degree of popular attention and prestige that the conservatives became seriously alarmed. Moreover, economic "anarchy" – for such seemed to be the railroad strikes, the Haymarket riot, Socialist and Single-Tax theories – and the cultural "anarchy" of "realistic" fiction, Whitman's poetry, the French Impressionists, and Woman's Suffrage "bloomers" appeared to be confederates of religious "anarchy" in a dangerous conspiracy against Christ's church and good morals. Orthodoxy met these "anarchist" trends with an authoritarian reaction. Strict doctrinal conformity was required of ministers and members; liberalism was denounced as the source of all evils; heresy trials were resumed. As convenient symbols of such reaction, the names of Pius IX, Boulanger, Bishop Wilberforce, and Charles Spurgeon in England, DeWitt Talmadge, Joseph Cook, and D. L. Moody in this country, may serve us. Official expulsions or voluntary withdrawals from orthodox pulpits became frequent, particularly in the Presbyterian denomination, which forced Professor Charles Briggs out of the New York presbytery and Professor David Swing from that in Chicago. The Congregationalists dismissed Professor Egbert Smith from the Andover Theological Seminary. Voluntary withdrawals included Rev. M. J. Savage, S. M. Crothers, and Reed Stewart (who were gladly welcomed to the Unitarian ministry); and Mangasin Mangasarian and H. W. Thomas who, like Swing, established independent congregations in Chicago. Harvard University, in spite of the wishes of its new Unitarian president, Charles W. Eliot, refused an appointment to a chair in history for John Fiske simply because the latter had too brilliantly given a course of lectures on [Auguste] Comte's Positivism – in which he personally did not believe!

For the victims of these reactionary trends as well as for the unchurched honest doubters of all doctrines who were yet sincere seekers after truth and the good life, Jones wanted Western Unitarianism to offer fellowship – the fellowship of intellectual freedom, fellowship in co-operative character-building, upright and consecrated, which he deemed the central purpose and proof of genuine religion in all ages and lands. Douthit's attack on Jones' dream and work was the Unitarian phase of the conservative reaction occurring in the orthodox denominations.

Sunderland's Crusade Against "Truth, Righteousness and Love"

With the Conference's resolution of thanks in his pocket, but not forgetful of the attacks on his "prophetic vision" and "invaluable work" by Putnam and Douthit, close friends of Sunderland, Jones left the secretaryship and turned to editing *Unity* and making plans for a church building for the rapidly growing All Souls. Sunderland got a substitute for his Ann Arbor pulpit (Rev. J. T. Bixby) and entered upon the schedule of local-church, state-conference, and Boston visitations expected of him. Douthit, who openly rejoiced that the Conference at last had a secretary "with Christian principles," only regretted that Sunderland, in his speech of acceptance, had not made "one loyal or loving reference to Jesus Christ." Douthit rededicated *Our Best Words* to the "Unitarianism that means spiritual unity, freedom, fellowship and character under the *Leadership of Jesus.*" The mere thought of anyone refusing such leadership made Douthit pugnacious: "If this declaration must cause a division, then in God's name and for conscience' sake, let it come!" It was coming, indeed!

Sunderland was in constant touch with Douthit by contributions to *Our Best Words*, by letters and visits to Shelbyville. That they discussed tactics "if a battle is to be fought" – in Sunderland's phrase – is certain. They assured each other that for years past Jones, Gannett, Hosmer, Blake, Learned, and others, including the objectionable Connor in Michigan, had been scheming to transform the Western Conference into a branch of the moribund F.R.A. by exerting a surreptitious spell over the state conferences and the churches to persuade them to rewrite their constitutions, leaving out all theological terms. Jones, like "Satan among the friends of Job," had then persuaded ministers who were members of the F.R.A. to take the pulpits of Western churches and forthwith to dispense with traditional "worship" features – prayers, litanies, hymns, Bible readings – and to lecture, not preach, in denial of personal immortality and a personal God. Since Sunderland, who was somewhat clerical and reserved in manner, was not receiving the welcome and response on his travels among the Western churches that had been accorded to big, hearty "Jenk Jones" – "the suspender Secretary," as some Bostonians called him – he was quite ready to agree with Douthit's suspicions. He had, indeed, known several cases in which birthright Unitarians from the East had joined Western Unitarian churches but had found them little better than conventicles of lower-middle-class radicals, with nothing of the reverence or refinement of the old Colonial shrines in the East, and with nothing but moral lessons in the Sunday schools. No wonder the rate of growth of Unitarianism in the West – though this was even more true of the East – was far below the population growth!

Douthit attended the Conference sessions at St. Louis in 1885 – though he had supposedly "resigned" from the Conference in 1880. Venerable W. G. Eliot, also, was there – for the first time since 1857! Sunderland's report began with a "bright side": he had traveled 21,000 miles, the churches generally were out of debt.

Then, the "dark side": Unitarianism is not gaining as it should because too many of the churches are "utterly heterogeneous. They have been organized on so broad a basis that they include believers and non-believers," and the latter vote themselves into top positions. The children in the Sunday schools get nothing but ethics. "*All* churches stand for ethics!" We should have at least as much theology as is entailed in Jesus' teaching of love to God and love to Man. Some such platform or banner – *not* a creed – is needed to give our work definiteness and direction. Moreover, the office of Western Conference Secretary and Western Agent of the A.U.A. should be united in one man.

The report gave no specific instances; all its generalizations were unsupported by facts. It was a deliberate aspersion upon the societies for whose organization Jones was chiefly responsible – upon the fitness and good faith of their non-Christian radicals, both ministers and members. Ominously, too, the report threatened that "if things went on as they had been going for the past few years the time would come when it would be necessary to divide into two parties, the Ethical Culture one to go by themselves, those who believe in Christianity by themselves" – the Bellows and Eliot threat of schism!

To Sunderland's statement that it would be his policy, if reelected, to accept and recommend to churches only liberal

Christian ministers, James Vila Blake of Chicago's Third Church, who refused to be called a Christian "because the name generally means more than Mr. Sunderland defines it to mean," took serious exception:

"Would you regard me as a suitable man to be received into the Unitarian ministry?"

"Yes," answered Sunderland, "if you asked to be. I have a right to call you a Christian, have I not?"

"But," continued Blake, "would you regard Marcus Aurelius as a Christian?"

Sunderland answered, "Yes."

Blake pressed the point: "Would you help him, a persecutor of the Christians, to a position in a Unitarian pulpit?"

"Yes, if he taught the same now as he did then."

Largely on the strength of this equivocal and inconsistent concession, which would logically include Jones and all the "Ethical Basis" men as well as the agnostic, ethical idealists – even Connor and W. M. Salter – in the roster of Unitarian Christians, Sunderland was elected Secretary for another year, though Jones had opposed his nomination on the ground that his report showed "disbelief in the fundamental principles of Unitarianism" and Gannett protested that Sunderland "was of a reactionary character" and did not represent the bold, progressive spirit of Western Unitarianism.

That Sunderland intended to use his second year of opportunity as militantly as possible was immediately made clear by his reply to an Episcopalian divine of St. Louis who devoted a sermon to gloating over the pessimism in Sunderland's report. The latter informed him:

… the work of our radicalizing leaders has been done so silently that our churches and ministers in general have scarcely been aware of it. In my Report the attention of the denomination was called to it for the first time. Many were startled to find the true condition of things … you may be sure that a reaction will not be slow to set in.

Such an astounding *mélange* of insinuation, egoism, and fiction – had not Sunderland been in the Conference since 1876, and had not Putnam and Douthit been issuing jeremiads since 1880? – quite naturally moved the *Unity* board to ask for Sunderland's resignation as an editorial contributor. No sooner had he given it than he began to lay plans, in concert with Rev. Brooke Herford, the English-born minister of Chicago's Church of the Messiah, for the foundation of a conservative periodical to offset *Unity's* influence in the Conference; *Our Best Words* was too countrified, too blunt – and too Christian! Mrs. Sunderland tried to help the cause by writing a letter to Douthit's paper accusing Rowland Connor, the successful minister since 1885 of the East Saginaw Unitarian Church, of having once been a member of the F.R.A.; of not believing in "love to God," probably because he did not believe in a personal God one could love and worship; of neglecting "religion" in his sermons, "every one of which for three months was on a scientific or literary theme"; of omitting public prayer ("he meditates aloud"); of rejecting personal immortality ("I am told it is no unusual occurrence for his regular hearers to go to an orthodox minister for funeral services for their dead"). Connor protested to Sunderland, who responded not only that he agreed with his wife but that:

> Nobody in the West will be so glad as I if you [give] assurance that you really believe in a God who knows and cares for us as his children; in prayer and immortality. Without such beliefs as foundation for your work I do not believe that your work can be one that ought to be called Unitarian … of course, you can do an F.R.A. or even an Ethical work and I should bid you or any one else Godspeed. I shall very sincerely rejoice in any assurance you may offer that your position and work are those of Christian Theism.

Connor naturally took this as a threat of excommunication. He appealed to the denomination in an "Open Letter to All Unitarian Ministers," in which he did not mince words:

> To me, Mr. Sunderland's opinions have always seemed superficial and narrow … but I never thought of bidding him a Godspeed outside! I fully respected his right to his own opinions. Who gave Mr. Sunderland a right to define Unitarianism? That he fancies from some source the right has been bestowed upon him is apparent in everything he writes or does. Nevertheless I claim an equal right to represent Unitarianism – a right which I proudly share with hundreds of others. I infer from Mr. Sunderland's letter that I might be tolerated if I could arrange to change the expression of my opinions to conform to his verbal moulds. I decline to be tolerated … nor do I think I am called upon to resign my ministry if my preaching is not acceptable to Mr. Sunderland. His policy has the same fatal quality that has fostered intellectual

hypocrisy and moral cowardice in all ages. I know of orthodox churches in which scarcely a single prominent member believes in the written creed or dogmas to which he listens every Sunday. Mr. Sunderland has always been the one discordant element of our State Conference. Again and again he has tried to alter the simple and sufficient constitution of our Conference and replace it with a theological platform of his own construction. His creed crotchet has become his master!

Connor's defiance received wide approval – save from W. G. Eliot, who had led the protest in 1874-75 against the Year Book's exclusion of W. J. Potter! The difference in the cases consisted in the fact that the A.U.A. was aiding the East Saginaw church, whereas that of Potter in New Bedford was independent and affluent. Douthit again uttered the threat of schism, "if any agnostic or atheistic ministers were allowed to remain in our pulpits or if any Unitarian money is paid to a church that refuses to record its belief in God the Father and Jesus Christ as the religious Leader of the race." Should the erstwhile Illinois Fraternity of Liberal Christian Churches – which had exchanged the words "Liberal Christian" for "Unitarian and Other Independent Churches" at its autumn meeting in Geneva (1885) – ask for A.U.A. assistance, "it would be a farce and an outrage"!

Sunderland's strenuous efforts for an anti-*Unity* periodical were consummated in January, 1886, by the appearance of *The Unitarian*, a monthly. Sunderland and Herford were its editors. *The Unitarian* was designed to be "a magazine that shall hold to our old freedom from dogmatic creeds and yet stand clearly for belief in God and worship and the spirit of Christ."

Rumors that Sunderland and Conference President Joseph Shippen were planning a *coup d'état* at the Western Conference meeting to be held in Cincinnati reached Samuel J. Barrows, editor of *The Christian Register*, in February. He decided to throw his influence against methods that seemed to him to be precisely what the Unitarians of 1825 had resisted when used by the Calvinists against them. He noted that the A.U.A. board was quietly following Sunderland's policy and allotting aid only to those churches and missionaries in the West which were avowedly Christian Theist. From the first week in April to the middle of May, the *Register* published not only vigorous editorials to this effect but quoted the covenants of the Western churches to show that most of them contained no theological stipulations for membership whatsoever! It called attention to the fact that of 355 societies listed in the Year Book of the A.U.A., only 127 bore the Unitarian name and only 16 called themselves "Christian." Barrows, who really believed that intellectual (i.e., theological) differences were the source of all the trouble, devised a definition of Unitarianism for comprehending and uniting Christian Theists, Ethical Basis advocates, and Free Religionists:

> Unitarianism is that free and progressive development of historic Christianity which aspires to be synonymous with universal ethics and universal religion.

This was a masterly formula – perhaps the best definition of itself the Unitarian movement has as yet produced – but it had no more effect on the *odium theologicum* in the West than the First Inaugural Address of Lincoln had had on the Southern Confederacy. Barrows then tried copious quotations from the writings of Rev. E. S. Gannett, Channing's colleague and first Secretary of the A.U.A. Gannett, though opposed to Theodore Parker's theology, had objected to his expulsion from the Boston Association of Ministers by the conservatives. How pertinent to the issue were such words as:

> One of the first principles on which we have united, in opposition to the sects about us, is the denial of the right of any denomination to censure its members for mere opinion ... We will let no association of Christians, no company of fellow men, however sincere and honest, come within the walls of any of our congregations and say what shall be believed and what shall be done there. It is very doubtful if any article of theological belief, however intimate its relations may be with piety and virtue, can be made by us the common ground and occasion of effort. Our difference from the sects about us is whether faith or character is the one thing needful. We maintain that it is character which alone can make saints or sinners and therefore it is character which Christianity regards as supremely important.

Had not the first Executive Committee of the A.U.A. stated in 1825 that "we value our doctrines only so far as ... they tend to improve the moral, religious and intellectual character of mankind ... the great end of this Association is the promotion of pure morals and practical piety"? Why else had "Liberty, Holiness and Love" been adopted as the motto of the Association and the *Register*? – as "Freedom, Fellowship and Character in Religion" was that of the Western Conference and *Unity*. Douthit replied to Barrows that, of course, the founders of the Association – whose *first* intention and phrase had been "the promotion of pure and undefiled *religion*" – must have meant "*Christian* Liberty, *Christian* Holiness, *Christian* Love, *Christian* Character." When Douthit was asked the difference between the Christian and non-Christian forms of these virtues, he asserted that *Christian* virtue was meek, humble, and consciously imperfect, while non-Christian virtue was usually smug and complacent.

Conference board meetings must have been rather strained in the spring of 1886. John Snyder of St. Louis, who deprecated Douthit's extreme language, thought he had secured Sunderland's consent to a theological armistice. Let both sides rest content with the Article of 1883 describing the object of the Conference to be "the transaction of business pertaining to the general interests of the societies connected with the Conference." But about a week before the Cincinnati meeting, thousands of copies of a pamphlet entitled *The Issue in the West,* written by Sunderland, were mailed to ministers and prominent members of Unitarian churches and were distributed to delegates as they arrived at the meeting place.

In the pamphlet Sunderland repeated his accusation that a united, purposive, determined group of men – "men we all honor and love" – want to remove Unitarianism off its historic base to Free or Ethical Religion. "Those of us who believe Unitarianism to be Christianity, who believe that to remove it off its Theistic base is to seal its fate as a religious movement would be sinning if we remain silent longer." The issue is not the importance of ethics, or the choice between radicalism and conservatism, dogma, or no dogma, creed or no creed, freedom of fellowship or limitation of fellowship, except in the question of the pulpit. "Shall our pastorates be open to known disbelievers in Christian Theism?" The idea of a Unitarian church which counts nothing essential but ethics and free thought, hence being reduced to virtual Free Religion, is a very recent growth:

I would have the denomination protect itself against it, not by persecutions or heresy trials but by insisting always and everywhere that [the Conference] has always been and still is broadly Christian; that we stand for, at least and everywhere, God and worship, the great immortal hope, the ideal of divine humanity that shines in Christ Jesus – what the A.U.A. stands for. I believe in this in the name of truth, progress, evolution. "Freedom, Fellowship and Character in Religion" is a mistaking of revolution for evolution. All true progress leads to the God idea. The non-Christian attitude puts our movement out of line with the great Christian army, the great band of Christian worshippers and workers, our Universalist brethren, the Broad churchmen of the Episcopal Church, the New Theology men in the Congregationalist body, such Christian independents as Professor Swing and Dr. Thomas. By hauling down our Theistic and Christian flags and running up in their place the Ethical flag only, I am convinced we should seal the fate of Unitarianism in the West.

Sunderland declared that the new watchword was keeping out or driving out multitudes of liberal Christians who had been in the denomination longest and given most of money or labor for its support. As for organizing churches on the Ethical Basis – opening pulpits and membership to all on the sole condition

… that they be men and women of reputable moral character – as well undertake to organize the west wind! Every businessman knows that! Men will labor and give money for definite religious ideas, definite religious institutions, definite discipleship of some great religious Leader [but] to expect men with clear business heads permanently to take interest in such a kind of religion, to give much money or make much sacrifice to support it would seem an absurdity – here is reason run mad!

For such insanity, such revolutionary efforts, the *Unity* brethren were responsible. The simple, primary doctrines of Christian Theism were not "mere opinions" but primary; ethics was secondary.

Moreover, "the result must inevitably be to cut off a large part of missionary revenues." Hence, "there is peace in one direction and only one – and that is what the A.U.A. stands for."

Fervid, eloquent, exigent the pamphlet was, and so plausible and dramatic in its predictions of doom that the delegates might well have gone Sunderland's way. But they did not. Perhaps they reflected that his denunciations of the "revolution" and the "new order" sounded remarkably similar to those directed against Parker in the eighteen-forties, and against Channing in the eighteen-twenties by the conservatives of *those* days. Or they may have reasoned that nothing could be more revolutionary for Unitarianism than a surrender to the old Calvinist consociation method of enforcing a continuing theological Inquisition upon ministers – the very thing that Professor Swing, among, others, had departed from! Would not such a measure result in the exodus from the free churches of the Conference of as many devoted and generous men and women as might come in? Yet why suppose an inrush of conservatives when some of the known Christian Theist churches of the Conference – Keokuk, Milwaukee, Shelbyville, Meadville – were far from conspicuous for popularity and prosperity? Some of the delegates, moreover, may have given heed to the strictures of Henry George, Edward Bellamy, and Washington Gladden, who made no secret of the venial partiality of "big business" for authoritarian, conventional, and supranaturalist Christianity. Could such delegates have been much impressed by Sunderland's appeal to the higher wisdom of businessmen? Were the businessmen of the A.U.A. planning to cut off "a large part of our missionary revenues" if the Conference did not conform?

Whatever the tenor of the delegates' cogitations, the result proved that Sunderland was right on one point, at least: he could not organize the west wind! Gannett led the attack on the pamphlet in valiant fashion:

Is Western Unitarianism ready to give up its Christian character? No! Is it ready to exclude from its full fellowship those who do not take the names of Christian or Theist? No!

A similar answer was given by the delegates to a resolution offered by Rev. Oscar Clute:

The primary object of this Conference is to diffuse the knowledge and promote the interests of pure Christianity

and to a resolution offered by Sunderland:

That while rejecting all creeds and creed limitations the Western Unitarian Conference hereby expresses its purpose as a body to be the promotion of a religion of love to God and love to man.

Then Gannett introduced three resolutions, two of which concerned the appointment of a committee to draw up in simple words "the things most commonly believed among us." These two resolutions were defeated as conceding too much. But the first resolution was passed:

That the Western Unitarian Conference conditions its fellowship on no dogmatic tests but welcomes all who wish to join it to help establish Truth, Righteousness and Love in the world.

Since four sessions of the Conference had been devoted to the issue, faces had grown tired and tense in the hot and stifling church. At the close, Gannett offered a tender prayer for forbearance and brotherhood in the spirit of Jesus despite differences of theological opinion. Sunderland exclaimed to Douthit *sotto voce*: "Oh, that we could only say that to the world!" Douthit – who ostensibly had resigned from the Conference in 1880 – thought of something better to say. "The Conference is now on an atheistical platform," he editorialized in *Our Best Words*:

Our F.R.A. and Ethical friends have taken an action that completes a division in our ranks – as radical a difference as that between Abraham Lincoln and Jefferson Davis. Truth, Righteousness and Love is a humbug basis! Is it not time to organize a Western Unitarian Association to cooperate with the A.U.A.?

The decision of the Conference agitated not only the Unitarian body but the religious press of the country. Barrows of the *Register* outraged the conservatives by avowing that

… the Conference has stood very firmly for the grand principles of Unitarian fellowship. It would not be easy to find three words which contain more of God and Christianity than Truth, Righteousness and Love. [Sunderland's pamphlet] dealt with hypothetical issues. The Western Conference has good reasons for existence and does a useful work.

Barrows clinched his statement by referring the conservatives to *The Thought of God*, a book of poems by Hosmer and Gannett that had just been published. It was radiant with reverence for the Father Spirit and the Man of Nazareth. As for A.U.A. scruples over the phrase "pure Christianity" – had not its board just voted $5,000 to the African Methodist Church? And when Jesus told Pilate that he came "to bear witness to the *truth*"; when he assured John that "it behooveth us to fulfill all *righteousness*"; and when he enjoined his disciples, "By this

shall men know you are my followers – that you *love* one another"
– did Jesus then "stand on a non-Christian basis"?

Douthit's dream and the plans of Sunderland and other conservatives matured in the formation of the Western Unitarian
Association in Chicago on June 21, 1886. Sunderland and
President Joseph Shippen, who had resigned their Conference
offices, became members of the board of the new Association,
whose purpose was "a more definite cooperation with the
A.U.A. in its Western work to diffuse the knowledge and promote the interests of pure Christianity." An eminent lawyer
of Kansas City, George W. McCrary, was elected president.
Other directors were Professor H. H. Barber of the Meadville
School, Douthit, Snyder of St. Louis, M. B. Hull of Chicago,
Janson of Minneapolis. The Association had its own office – in
the Montauk Building on Monroe Street in Chicago. But the
position of General Secretary was left open. Did Sunderland
hope that the Eastern Association would continue him as its
Western Agent and he would then arrange to fill both positions,
as well as to edit *The Unitarian?*

But when the news of this overt secession reached the
A.U.A. board, divided counsels prevailed. Assistant Secretary
Fox and the wealthy donors he represented were quietly jubil-
ant that there was now an organization of sensible Unitarians
in the West with whom they could collaborate. They were glad
to know that *Our Best Words* and *The Unitarian* were urging the
Western churches to divert their contributions to the A.U.A.
and thus starve the Western Conference into submission. When
it was reduced to dependency on the A.U.A. (like the state
conferences) and had to desist from its church extension work,
this work could be wholly centralized in Boston on a truly
religious basis and rich donors would resume their support
of it. The Unitarian patriarchs, Clarke and F. H. Hedge of
Harvard, declared that progress *beyond* Christianity was only
backward and downward; all true religious progress was *within*
Christianity. Clarke preached that, in religion as in other fields,
we, should respect and follow the authority of an expert – and
in religion, Jesus was the acknowledged expert. Hedge was sure
that a city without churches and the worship of God would soon
slip into moral anarchy. Douthit told his readers that just such

a city did exist. It was "Liberal, Missouri," which had been founded by freethinkers, had no churches, and was a sink of iniquity – profanity, drunkenness, illiteracy, vice, and crime flourished there. But the citizens of Liberal persuaded the sheriff of their county to send Douthit a notarized statement to the effect that Liberal was a model town in every respect, particularly in the absence of saloons! Jones pointed out in *Unity* that Abou ben Adhem would have to go with the Ethical Basis folk – the new Christian Association would not have him!

Never was there such a preposterous schism. For, instead of being loud, vulgar, half-educated, shiftless freethinkers, the *Unity* men were mostly Harvard graduates, with very impressive New England pedigrees. All of them were beloved, honored, and efficient in their own churches. Moreover, their personal beliefs were unmistakably Theistic (in the Emersonian sense) and Christian (according to Parker). Their churches were vital and thriving, on the very Ethical Basis so confidently disparaged as the blight and bane of Unitarian growth.

The irony and the tragedy of the schism were deeply felt by most of the board of the A.U.A. Sunderland attended its July meeting and was granted $250 "for services rendered" and a vote of thanks "for the energy, faithfulness and interest with which he has performed his duties as Western Agent." But his appointment was not renewed. That left the Western Association without a General Secretary, and Sunderland moved back to his church in Ann Arbor, taking *The Unitarian's* editorial desk with him.

During the next year (1886-87), pulpits, periodicals, and letters were electric with the controversy. Rev. J. W. Chadwick in Brooklyn, Rev. S. R. Calthrop in Syracuse, Rev. Newton Mann in Rochester, Rev. C. F. Dole and Rev. W. J. Potter in Massachusetts ranged themselves with the Western Conference and found subscribers to the Guarantee Fund raised by Gannett to replace the withheld conservative contributions and provide a salary for Rev. J. R. Effinger, who had been elected to Sunderland's former position. The Meadville School faculty took the lead in organizing and conducting the Lakewood School of the New Theology on Lake Chautauqua for the purpose of indoctrinating young Unitarian ministers with apologetical arguments for Christian Theism. Aging Dr. Clarke gave them a sermon on "The Broad Church" into which he distilled the second volume of his great work on the world's *Ten Great Religions* (1871). He claimed that Christianity could legitimately be interpreted as including the best in Socrates, Plato, Buddha, Confucius, Garibaldi, and Abraham Lincoln – yet the only category in which all these religious leaders could consistently be subsumed was the ethical, not the doctrinal! To Clarke, however, "an Ethical Society seems to resemble a train of cars with no locomotive to make it go!"

Even Barrows of the *Register* deserted the Conference cause for a short time in 1887. He aligned himself with Rev. M. J. Savage, formerly of Chicago, then in Boston, to persuade the Western board to transfer all missionary work to the A.U.A.

> The Western Conference was needed once and has done a noble work but we need to centralize our forces. The A.U.A. has ceased to be a "Boston notion" and has become truly American. It is now ... the voice and hand of our churches. We urge the Western Unitarian Conference at its next meeting to take into consideration the expediency of committing to the A.U.A. its general missionary work ... This is not a proposal of death but of matrimony ...

To press the suit, so to speak, the A.U.A. board sent a committee, headed by Secretary Reynolds, to meet with the Western Conference board in Chicago (April, 1887). Alternative plans were laid before them. Would the Western Conference agree to administer its missionary work and funds on the basis of pure Christianity, making sure in each case that the churches it helped were or became Christian Theist in constitution and character? *Or* – would the Western Conference transfer all missionary work to the A.U.A.? The Western board answered both alternatives negatively, on the ground that to accept and fulfill the first would violate the sacred principle of congregational autonomy, while to accept the second would contravene the constitution of the Conference as amended in 1870. The fact that such a dictatorial policy had been broached by the A.U.A. officials swung the *Register* back to support of the Western Conference position: "If the Board of Directors of the A.U.A. should declare that they would not grant money to any society that would not formally subscribe to 'pure Christianity' in its constitution, they would be guilty of a gross perversion of their responsibilities!"

Douthit, however, was so incensed at the stubbornness of the Conference board that he got out another "Extra" (May, 1887) and with a bundle of copies under his arm started for the Conference meeting in the new building of All Souls Church in Chicago. Sunderland likewise attended and brought a large package of copies of an Address from the Western Unitarian Association to the Conference.

[Things Commonly Believed Among Us]

A third document brought to the Conference was, however, of greater moment than any other. Gannett had drawn up in the face of some criticism a Statement of "Things commonly believed among us" which, over the protests of the Christian Theists, was adopted by a vote of 59 to 13, on the understanding that it did not bind "a single member by declarations concerning fellowship or doctrine, the Statement being always open to re-statement and to be regarded only as the thought of the majority."

Gannett's Statement remains the most comprehensively and nobly conceived, the most justly and persuasively argued, the most ethically inspired and the most beautifully expressed document of its kind in all Unitarian history. Only a full reading of its simple, moving, luminous sequence of almost liturgical paragraphs can do it justice. Every passage is significant, and they are given here to show the magnanimity and breadth of the Statement:

> The Western Conference has neither the wish nor the right to bind a single member by declarations concerning fellowship or doctrine. Yet it thinks some practical good may be done by setting forth in simple words the things most commonly believed among us, – the Statement being always open to re-statement and to be regarded only as the thought of the majority.
>
> All names that divide "religion" are to us of little consequence compared with religion itself. Whoever loves Truth and lives the Good is, in a broad sense, of our religious fellowship; whoever loves the one or lives the other better than ourselves is our teacher, whatever church or age he may belong to.
>
> The general faith is hinted well in words which several of our churches have adopted for their covenant: "In the freedom of the Truth and in the spirit of Jesus Christ, we unite for the worship of God and the service of man." It is hinted in such words as these: "Unitarianism is a religion of love to God and love to man." Because we have no "creed" which we

impose as a condition of fellowship, specific statements of belief abound among us, always somewhat differing, always largely agreeing. One such we offer here:

"We believe that to love the Good and live the Good is the supreme thing in religion;

"We hold reason and conscience to be final authorities in matters of religious belief;

"We honor the Bible and all inspiring scripture, old and new;

"We revere Jesus, and all holy souls that have taught men truth and right-eousness and love, as prophets of religion.

"We believe in the growing nobility of Man;

"We trust the unfolding Universe as beautiful, beneficent, unchanging Order; to know this order is truth; to obey it is right and liberty and stronger life;

"We believe that good and evil invariably carry their own recompense, no good thing being failure and no evil thing success; that heaven and hell are states of being; that no evil can befall the good man in either life or death; that all things work together for the victory of Good.

"We believe that *we* ought to join hands and work to *make* the good things better and the worst good, counting nothing good for self that is not good for all;

"We believe that this self-forgetting, loyal life awakes in man the sense of union here and now with things eternal – the sense of deathlessness; and this sense is to us an earnest of the life to come.

"We worship One-in-All – that life whence suns and stars derive their orbits and the soul of man its Ought, – that Light which lighteth every man that cometh into the world, giving us power to become the sons of God, – that Love with which our souls commune."

Everything excellent in Unitarian history and belief – the free mind, mental integrity, hospitality to the advancing knowledge of science and all culture, ethical ideals, humanitarian service, tolerance and pure mysticism – are noted in the Statement. Commencing with a lucid historical retrospect, it ascends with persuasive logic to a climax, in rhythmic strophes, of moral truths and duties and a doxology of universal hope and aspiration. It includes in sympathetic fellowship the Theist and Christian, the Ethical Humanist, the Universalist, and the non-Christian faiths to which Free Religion reached out fraternally. With such an affirmation, adopted by so large a majority of delegates, how could there be any issue in the West?

But Sunderland and Douthit did not see it that way. *The Unitarian* delayed printing the Statement and seldom referred to it in later years. It was faulty in not being a positive commitment of the Conference to what Sunderland deemed "pure Christianity."

Douthit told the readers of *Our Best Words* that "the dog remains the same kind of dog; they have simply tied a statement on the end of its tail."

The *Register*, on the contrary, was enthusiastic:

> To the demand that the Conference should inscribe its beliefs on its banner – a demand that is the more inexplicable because the A.U.A. has never made any definite statement – the Conference has done so in a grand and noble way. "Things commonly believed among us" is a glorious presentation of Unitarian beliefs which command the allegiance and the love of the human heart and mind.

John White Chadwick took the Statement over to London to read to the British and Foreign Unitarian Association, to which he gave a glowing account of Western Unitarianism and effectually counteracted Putnam's dirge of 1883. But the Statement did not heal the schism, for the latter was not primarily theological in nature. How it grew worse before it was finally transcended in 1894 is now to be told.

CHAPTER TWELVE

Progress through Storm

WHILE THE TRENCH MORTARS of "pure Christianity" from the redoubts in Shelbyville, Ann Arbor, Meadville, and Boston are bombarding the citadel of "Truth, Righteousness and Love" in Chicago, let us turn to the life and work of the Western churches as reflected in their literary, educational, and humanitarian activities.

[Literature]

Considering the torrent of publications that flowed from the liberal presses of the Colegrove Book Concern and the C. H. Kerr Publishing Company in Chicago, as well as the George H. Ellis and James H. West publishing companies in Boston, it seems probable that there was never a period in Unitarian history of greater literary production in respect not only to quantity but to quality as well. In the first category there were books of sermons, poems, and liturgics, as well as tracts – the Unity Short Tract and Unity Mission Tract series, Sunday school texts and study guides, Unity Club program and study outlines. In the second category there are originality, variety, erudition, and literary excellence. Every church had its literature table, its loan library, and its weekday Post Office Mission and Cheerful Letter groups; the last work owed its origin to the determination of elderly, poor, lonely, and invalid Sallie Ellis of Cincinnati, whose will to serve the liberal cause by letter-writing and tract distribution transcended her afflictions – even the incurable disease that ended her earthly life. Since the editors of the periodicals – *Unity, Our Best Words, The Unitarian* – took pains to give cordially appreciative reviews to the productions of their theological opponents, the purchase and use of all this theological literature were virtually assured even though most of it was the work of the *Unity* men and women. Save for a *Unitarian or Free Christian Catechism* prepared by Douthit (1888) and a book of transitional sermons preached by Rev. Minot J. Savage in his first Unitarian pastorate, *Christianity, the Science of Manhood* (1873), as well as some short homiletical presentations by Rev. Joseph H. Crooker – *Jesus Brought Back* (1889), *Different New Testament Views of Jesus* (1891), *The New Bible and Its New Uses* (1893) – the Christian Basis seems to have inspired almost nothing in quantity and nothing at all in quality to compare with the productions of the embattled Ethical Basis proponents. To be sure, in Boston, James Freeman Clarke, who had declared that "some kind of creed is inevitable – some articles affirming the supranatural character of Christianity and the superhuman nature of Jesus, to exclude radicals and to unite those who are sound on these points," entered the struggle in his beloved Western field with two apologetical weapons: *A Manual of Unitarian Belief* (1884) and in 1886 *Vexed Questions in Theology*, the first chapter of which contained the "Five Points of Unitarianism": the Fatherhood of God, the Brotherhood of Man, the Leadership of Jesus, Salvation by Character, the Progress of Mankind onward and upward forever. How significant it was that Clarke, the devoted friend of Emerson – who, in the great Divinity School Address of 1838 had averred that "the sentiment of virtue is the essence of religion, at once divine and deifying" – did not sympathize with the Ethical Basis Emersonians of the Western Conference but justified Channing's lament of 1840: "Unitarianism now has a new orthodoxy"!

But the books by the Ethical Basis leaders were written not so much to defend their position as to propagate their progressive, optimistic, democratic "new religion" – as Sunderland called it, with the hauteur toward heresy that he possibly had derived from his former Baptist orthodoxy. A "new religion" it certainly was, if thought transfusions from Spencer, Darwin, [Charles] Lyell, [T. H.] Huxley, Tylor, Max Müller, and the New Testament critics ([F. C.] Baur, [Karl von] Hase, [Ernest] Renan) could make it so. Yet it was much more than Free Religion of the Francis E. Abbot type; for the *Unity* men were emphatically and enthusiastically churchmen – men of mystical and emotional disposition, ministers of implicit and pronounced pastoral and social devotion, rather than detached, iconoclastic philosophers. All of them – most notably Jones, Gannett, Blake, Hosmer, Simmons, Mann, Learned, Judy – and of the women ministers, Miss Safford, Miss Gordon, Miss Hultin, were beloved by their congregations, honored by long pastorates, successful in building up churches. In their writings they essayed the task of co-ordinating religious feeling with the insights of the new knowledge – primarily evolution, secondly social psychology, Biblical criticism, comparative religion. For such a task they were especially fitted by virtue of their Transcendental convictions: the Divine immanence, the absolute intuitions of truth and goodness, the universality and continuity of Revelation, the divine power and impulse of creative good in every human being. Union with the One-in-All through a reverent appreciation of Cosmic Grandeur, Law, and Beauty; through a grateful recognition of the ultimate beneficence of Cosmic Law and its impersonal Providence; through a hearty, hopeful co-operation with the Divine Plan in making "the good things better and the worst good" in personal growth and in the social order – such was the "new religion" of the adherents of the Ethical Basis. It was a rational faith, yet intensely rapturous and lyrical; science and philosophy were fused in it with genuine religious fervor, as Hosmer's great hymn so well illustrates:

> O prophet souls of all the years
> Bend o'er us from above;
> Your far-off vision, toils and tears
> Now to fulfillment move!
>
> From tropic clime and zones of frost
> They come, of every name,–
> This, this our day of Pentecost,
> The Spirit's tongue of flame.
>
> One Life together we confess,
> One all-indwelling Word,
> One holy Call to righteousness
> Within the silence heard;
>
> One Law that guides the shining spheres
> As one through space they roll,
> And speaks in flaming characters
> On Sinais of the soul;
>
> One Love, unfathomed, measureless,
> An ever-flowing sea,
> That holds within its vast embrace
> Time and eternity.

With the morale of such faith the Western Unitarians advanced, at the first alarm, upon the alleged dragon of evolution who was expected to ravish and devour religion – and evolution was converted into an ally and friend of true religion! Almost three decades before Henry Ward Beecher "accepted" evolution (1883) and four decades in advance of Lyman Abbott's *Theology of an Evolutionist* (1897), Newton M. Mann and Moncure D. Conway in Cincinnati had begun the campaign against the alleged dragon – predicting, indeed, the devastating impact of evolution on orthodox mythologies and doctrines, but arguing that though Christian theology might be shaken, true religion, primarily Jesus' spiritual and ethical teachings, had nothing to fear. Throughout the eighteen-sixties, Unitarian pulpits and periodicals were tribunes of such reassuring pronouncements; but the conservatives either disregarded such heterodox literature, or, like the modern historians of American theology, read the books and articles, yet kept silence about them.

Many were the articles and discussions on evolution at the Radical Club meeting at the Sargent home in Boston after 1865, in *The Radical* and in *The Index* after 1867. Jones' piece at the Meadville School Commencement in 1870 dealt with the same theme, which was introduced into the program of the Western Conference in 1869 by Rev. H. H. Powers with a paper on "Evolution and Immortality," followed in 1875 by one on "Evolution and Religion" by Rev. T. B. Forbush – so excellent that it was printed in full in *The Chicago Times* the next day. The sermons in *The Religion of Evolution* (1876) by Rev. M. J. Savage present science as a beneficent ally of man, and its disclosures a proper concern of religion:

Science has heightened infinitely the objects of religion, giving us a grander God, a nobler humanity, a more magnificent universe as the theatre for social action. Science has [hitherto] destroyed the doctrine of astrology, of demoniacal possession, of witchcraft; and now, the fatalistic doctrine of an irretrievable fall into evil of Man's nature in the Garden of Eden. Evil is nothing more than human maladjustment to laws which, when known and kept, are the mighty helpers of humanity. Faith, Duty, Love, worship, prayer, God are demonstrable realities, changing and yet unchanged through the aeons.

How evolution aided a reasonable understanding and evaluation of the Bible was indicated by Newton M. Mann in his

Rational View of the Bible (1879), which was later developed in Sunday school studies for the *Unity* course and appeared, expanded and enriched, in *The Evolution of a Great Literature* (1904).

Perhaps no better indication of how the "new religion" synthesized the momentous disclosures of modern science with the religious sentiments into a natural religion of cosmic horizons and harmonies may be chosen than *The Unending Genesis* (1882) by Rev. Henry M. Simmons of Minneapolis. Was ever such a plenitude of scientific knowledge blended so lucidly and eloquently with reverence and moral truth and duty? And in a more concise literary form, in Gannett's hymn poems, "He hides within the lily" and "Bring, O morn, thy music"; and in J. V. Blake's "O Eternal Life, whose power gathers ages to a span." Samuel Johnson's "Life of ages, richly poured" and J. W. Chadwick's "Thou, whose spirit dwells in all" voiced with equal elevation the evolution faith. Though these last two authors were Easterners, they were *Unity* men in spirit.

Did this synthesis of science with reverence, this stress on moral values and quests as a sufficient fellowship bond for churches, really spell atheism – as Douthit insinuated? Did its motto of "Freedom, Fellowship and Character in Religion" and its aim of "Truth, Righteousness and Love" connote a disregard of God, immortality, and worship – as Sunderland claimed? To illustrate how these values were retained and enriched in the "new religion," the *Unity* men published several sermonic and poetic symposia of noble thought and literary artistry. Such was *Show Us the Father* (1888), a sheaf of six sermons by M. J. Savage, S. R. Calthrop, J. W. Chadwick, H. M. Simmons, W. C. Gannett, J. L. Jones – and each sermon memorable. Another symposium was *The Faith That Makes Faithful* (1886), to which Jones and Gannett contributed sermons of such practical spiritual uplift, (for example, "Blessed Be Drudgery" by Gannett, "Faithfulness" by Jones) that by 1899 over 27,000 copies had been sold. Jones' talks on *Practical Piety* (1887) were almost as popular. To Eastern Unitarians, who believed that Gannett and Hosmer must be unbelievers, if not worse, Editor Barrows of the *Register* recommended their joint collection of original religious poems, *The Thought of God* (first published in 1885), a treasure of beautiful hymns and of tender, whimsical occasional poems. Many of these hymns, as well as others by Chadwick, Whittier, Samuel Longfellow, Blake, Samuel Johnson, and other liberal Theists, were incorporated in *Unity Hymns and Chorals* (1880). Following its 259 hymns were choral chants and doxologies.

In the 1911 edition of the book [*Unity Hymns and Chorals: A book for heart, home, church*] – which in its original form had been used extensively in the Western churches for 30 years – Gannett disclosed the rationale of hymn selection:

> Our hymns reflect the religious feelings of moral longing and conse-cration, of dependence on the One-in-all, of happy thankfulness, of free communing between man and man in brotherhood. There is more than the usual proportion of herald songs – songs of the good-to-be. More, also, than is common of hymns touched with the wonder and beauty of nature. Songs suffused with the thought and feeling, without the name, of God will be used increasingly as hymns, we think. The imagery of Christian hymns has been largely borrowed from a drama of salvation now passing out of credence; its place will be taken by imagery drawn from Nature and life.

In this [revised and enlarged] edition, Gannett included liturgical materials which had been developed in the Western Unitarian churches over three decades and braided them into fourteen regular and festival services, with choral responses. There was also a body of prayers of equally high spiritual and poetic merit. A novel feature consisted of the hymn words from *Unity Tract #28* ("Love to God and Love to Man"), which had been set to the popular hymn tunes of Moody and Sankey's *Gospel Hymns*, such as "In the sweet by and by," "He leadeth me," "What a Friend we have in Jesus," "I love to tell the story," and others. Hosmer's "Forward through the ages" adopted the tune but avoided the monarchist and militaristic idioms of "Onward, Christian soldiers." With Blake's *Unity Festivals* (1878) for congregation and Sunday school, and Hosmer's Sunday school hymnal *The Way of Life*, and *Unity Hymns*, the Western Theistic churches were provided with an opulence of noble liturgical material that conformed to the best criteria of the art, yet were non-traditional in thought and language.

A unique characteristic was the inclusion of several hymns whose theme was the appreciation of truth in non-Christian religions – such as Samuel Longfellow's "Light of ages and of nations" and Gannett's "It sounds along the ages." Nor was the vision of the Church Universal omitted. Samuel Johnson's "City of God, how broad and fair," Longfellow's "One Holy Church of God appears through every age and race" and Felix Adler's "Hail the glorious, golden City" were paeans of the church of Humanity to be.

The "Ethical Basis" was primarily a conviction, not a notion. Its defenders, though intellectuals par excellence, were spiritual democrats in the sense that they knew and respected, inside and outside of religious institutions, many thoughtful men and women of high character who were infidels and agnostics. Such folk they wanted to include in Unitarian fellowship without necessity of any compromise of mental and verbal honesty. Jones' feelings on this point are well illustrated in the sermon chapters of *Jess: Bits of Wayside Gospel* (1899) and *A Search for an Infidel* (1901). Never did he miss an opportunity to invite his close friend, the Ethical Culture lecturer William Salter, as well as the great liberal rabbis of Chicago – Hirsch, Rosenthal, and Stolz – to speak at special occasions at All Souls Church and Western Conference programs. When the emancipated Presbyterian, David Swing, sought to organize a Liberal Ministers Association in Chicago, Jones and Blake stood aloof since Salter and the rabbis were not invited. Temperamentally, however, Blake was not a natural democrat like Jones, but a litterateur of neo-Stoic beliefs, mellow culture, and remarkable literary versatility, whose auctorial output resembles that of George William Curtis, the Unitarian editor for many years of *Harper's Weekly*. He published almost thirty books, whose titles range from *Manual Training in Education* (1886) through *Essays* (1887), *St. Solifer* (1891), *Poems* (1887), *Songs* (1902), to *Lady Bertha's Honey Broth*, a poetic drama (1911) and *Sonnets from Marcus Aurelius* (1920). Like his essays, Blake's sermons, as sampled in *A Grateful Spirit* (1889), *Happiness from Thoughts* (1891), *Natural Religion* (1892) were masterpieces of broad, philosophic reflection, mature culture, and yet of homely, practical wisdom – an esoteric blend, indeed!

Blake, like Jones, was a social radical in fidelity to the long Channing-Parker tradition in American Unitarianism, which antedated by decades the Social Gospel of Washington Gladden and Walter Rauschenbusch, the Christian Socialism of W. D. P. Bliss and of George D. Herron. Perhaps the provenance of this attitude of Jones, in addition to his farm and war experiences, was in the lectures on social and economic problems that President Livermore of the Meadville School had given in his courses on ethics in the late eighteen-sixties.

For another student, Rev. George W. Cooke, this instruction had opened vistas of the collectivist principle in economics, politics, and religion. During his pastorates in Michigan and Indianapolis, Cooke wrote much on this subject for *Unity*, *The Chautauquan*, and other periodicals. His destiny, however, was to lie in the field of literary history and criticism, the first step being his highly acclaimed *Ralph Waldo Emerson: His Life, Writings and Philosophy* (1881). Though he soon after left Indianapolis for New England, he returned to Cleveland in 1902 to edit the Rowfant Club's edition of *The Dial*, and to write for it his comprehensive *Historical and Biographical Introduction* (1902).

Cooke's mature thought found expression in *The Social Evolution of Religion* – an interest he shared with Rev. Joseph H. Crooker, whose *Problems of American Society* (1889), social studies dealing with scientific charity, the root of the temperance problem, moral and religious instruction in the public schools, predicted his later amplification of such themes, while a minister in Topeka, Kansas, in *Religious Freedom in American Education* (1903) and *Shall I Drink?* (1914). Another author of acknowledged merit in the field of social problems was Rev. Nicholas P. Gilman of Antioch College, later of the Meadville School, who applied himself to considering alternatives to Socialism such as *Profit Sharing* (1889). His book on *Socialism and the American Spirit* (1893), a shrewd analysis of the incompatibility of the two factors, was widely read.

In the educational field, Western Unitarianism continued its long tradition of intellectual activity and influence. Though the Chicago Literary Club (1874) was and is undenominational, Robert Collyer was its first president and a large number of its early members were Unitarians. One of them, Daniel Lewis Shorey, president of the Western Conference during twenty critical years, took the lead in founding the Chicago Public Library and in getting a state law passed permitting municipalities to levy taxes for the support of public libraries. Indeed, in most of the communities in the West where a Unitarian church was located, the free lending library and reading room, privately supported in the early years, owed its existence and development – often, before Carnegie's day, even its housing – to Unitarian initiative and aid. The Unity Club programs fostered the study of great authors and promoted community commemoration services for Emerson, Browning, George Eliot, and other great lights of literature.

Curiously enough, however, Unitarian ministers – save Blake – seldom adventured any literary form but the sermon and the hymn poem. Robert Collyer, indeed, developed a charming lecture style, half fiction, half fact, and wrought the touching story of John Oliver Reed's conversion by Jasper Douthit into *A Story of the Prairies*, which circulated by thousands in this country and England. Moral earnestness supplied the motive of the three novels of Rev. Celia Parker Woolley, who, after a short pastorate in Geneva, Illinois, settled in Chicago, where she became a notable figure in educational reform, Women's Rights, and interracial equality. As president of the Chicago Women's Club (1888-90) she led in the founding of the Glenwood School of Industrial Training for delinquent boys. Three novels of serious purpose and of literary merit diminished only by their obvious didacticism came from her pen in this period: *Love and Theology* (1887) (republished as *Rachel Armstrong*); *A Girl Graduate* (1889); *Roger Hunt* (1893).

Humanitarian Work

Mrs. Woolley's novels, however, found but limited acceptance. The contrary was the case with those of Helen Hunt Jackson, a Colorado Unitarian of New England birth. Many and excellent were the verses, short stories, and novels – especially *Mercy Philbrick's Choice* (1876) – she wrote in the days of friendship with Emily Dickinson and Thomas Wentworth Higginson; but the mistreatment of the Indians in the Far West and in California brought out her deeper powers. *A Century of Dishonor* (1881) (a formidable arsenal of facts, scathingly presented, of our country's injustice and inhumanity toward the Indians) having failed of the effect she sought, *Ramona* (1884) followed – a tale of the mission Indians of California. It stirred public indignation to demand reforms to eliminate the poverty and illiteracy of the natives. One result of her crusade was the establishment in 1887 by Eastern and Western Unitarians of the Montana Industrial School on the reservation of the Crow Indians, with Rev. and Mrs. Henry F. Bond in charge. Rev. Samuel A. Eliot, then the Unitarian minister in Denver, continued the interest he developed in this reform in a long term of service as a Federal Commissioner on Indian Affairs.

Another of Eliot's services to Denver was his successful labor for the organization of the Associated Charities, the first offshoot in the Far West of a movement started in Boston in 1866 by Dr. Samuel G. Howe, F. B. Sanborn, John A. Andrew, G. W. Curtis, and [Samuel Eliot, a cousin] of the Denver pastor. Its aims were to reform the prevailing hit-and-miss methods of poor relief by centralizing and co-ordinating as many relief agencies as possible, in the hope of discouraging pauperism by preventing duplication of relief; and of restoring self-dependence through adequate, scientific methods of rehabilitation. Through the influence of this new American Social Science Association and its *Journal*, the National Conference of Charities (and Correction), the National Prison Association, and the national drive for local Associated Charities or Charity Organization Societies came into being. The first of the local bodies was organized by Rev. Charles G. Ames in Germantown, Pennsylvania, in 1874. Buffalo Unitarians were foremost in the same cause in their city in 1877; Philadelphia and Cincinnati followed suit in 1878 and 1879. Brooklyn, New York, achieved a Bureau of Charities in 1879 through the initiative of Alfred T. White, a member of the First Unitarian Church, whose noble record of wise beneficence caused him to be acclaimed in later years as "the great heart and master mind of Brooklyn's better self." Coming westward, the reform was introduced in Cleveland, Detroit, Milwaukee, St. Paul, Minneapolis, Omaha, and Denver, largely by the enterprise of the Unitarian ministers in those communities.

Similar pioneer work was done in the field of the humane treatment of animals by the organization of state and local branches of the American Humane Society, which owed its inception to Henry Bergh, a member of All Souls Church (H. W. Bellows) in New York City, who organized the first Society for the Prevention of Cruelty to Animals in 1866. Of the American Humane Society, the national organization of such efforts, Rev. G. E. Gordon of the church in Milwaukee was president for some years, and similar leadership on the state and community level was furnished by other Western Unitarians. Gordon was likewise active in promoting the American Association of the Red Cross, of which the Universalist Clara Barton was founder and first president, with Gordon as a member of its first board of directors.

The promotion of civil-service reform was another phase of Unitarian pioneering in the West, as well as in the East, in the two decades of effort which elapsed between the first proposal laid before a hostile Congress in 1863 by Charles Sumner and the passage of the Pendleton Act in 1882. The persistent advocacy of the reform by George William Curtis, political editor of *Harper's Weekly* from 1863, moved President Grant to appoint him chairman of the first Commission on Civil Service Reform. Assisted by Dorman B. Eaton of All Souls Church in New York City, where the experiment of competitive examinations for appointment and promotion was first tried, Curtis pushed the reform by his editorials and lectures throughout the country until at last a reluctant Congress – shocked by the assassination of President Garfield at the hands of a disappointed office seeker – passed the Pendleton Bill. To ensure its honest enforcement and further extension, the National Civil Service Reform League was organized in 1881; Curtis was made president for life. During three decades virtually every Unitarian pulpit, forum, Unity Club program, in the West agitated for the reform; innumerable sermons were preached, tracts distributed, articles written.

Another concern of denominational preoccupation was the total-abstinence and local-option movement against alcoholism that focused in the Unitarian Temperance Society (1886), of which the Westerners Jones, Crooker, H. H. Barber, C. G. Ames, and W. C. Gannett were early directors, and whose programs had a place in the annual Conference sessions for many years. Needless to say, even greater attention was paid to the Women's Rights movement, of which the Women's Western Unitarian Conference (1877) was practically a bi-lateral Chicago headquarters, working in close agreement with most of the Ladies Aid groups in the local churches and providing the latter with plenary resources of lectures and literature. One pities any Western Unitarian minister who – after his installation – opposed the movement!

The women ministers of the Iowa Association were, of course, prominent in the work and took the greatest satisfaction in the success which attended the efforts of one of their number, Rev. Caroline Bartlett at Kalamazoo, Michigan (1889-99). Inspired by the "institutional church" pattern of All Souls in Chicago, Miss Bartlett – later Mrs. Crane – persuaded Silas Hubbard, who had been a member of the church for over thirty years, to give what he estimated he had saved during that time by abstinence from liquor and tobacco for the erection of a commodious "People's Church" (1894) with a seven-day-a-week program of activities. These included a free kindergarten – another pioneer venture of the liberal churches in the West, as in the East – manual training, domestic science, gymnasium, music classes, a Frederick Douglass Club for Negro women, and an attractive Unity Club schedule offering not only the usual study classes in evolution, current literature, and comparative religions but also a "lend-a-hand" program of philanthropic work according to the scheme devised by Rev. Edward E. Hale of Boston and adopted by many of the Western Unitarian churches. The free reading room of the People's Church, whose innovations and efficient operation received national attention, developed, through the generosity of members of the church, into a well-housed public library.

All Souls Church in Chicago had been interracial from the beginning. The same was true of the Chicago Athenaeum, an institution founded in 1871 as "The Christian Union" for young people in an effort to alleviate post-Fire conditions of a social and educational nature. Through the generosity of William H. Baldwin and other Boston Unitarians, and under the direction of W. C. Wendte, the Union developed into the Chicago Athenaeum, a kind of downtown "Workingmen's College," providing a broad curriculum, chiefly in evening classes, of high-school subjects, with collateral lecture courses on contemporary literature, current affairs, and ethical problems, given by scholars from Northwestern University or local ministers. Rev. T. B.

Forbush followed Wendte in the superintendency (1876-80) and was succeeded by Rev. E. I. Galvin (1880-94). Byron P. Moulton of the First Unitarian Church served as president of the Athenaeum for many years, and then gave place to Judge Henry Booth of the Ethical Society. Over its nearly forty years of work, the Athenaeum numbered its students by tens of thousands and filled an admitted need in the city – since, unlike the Y.M.C.A., it was non-sectarian, interracial, and admitted women as well as men to classes and the faculty. Changing conditions and budgetary problems led finally to the merger of the Athenaeum with a Loop business college after 1910.

Another pioneer philanthropy of the decades under review was the Eli Bates Settlement House and Industrial School, on Chicago's north side. Like the North Star Dispensary, it had been started by the Liberal Christian League of Unity Church as a broad-gauge continuation of Robert Collyer's early Ministry to the Poor. Bates' generous legacy to the work consummated his loyal support of it during his life. After almost sixty years of service to the Italian immigrants and other new Americans employed in the factories and warehouses along the north branch of the Chicago River, it surrendered to the encroachment of industry, the hostile attitude of the great Roman Catholic parishes of the vicinity, and the declining support from Unity Church members. Eventually its work was taken over by the Chicago Boys Club Association; the original endowment is now held jointly by the trustees of the Unity Church and the Northern Trust Company.

For the Negroes settling perforce in the decayed districts on the south side of Chicago, Mrs. Celia Parker Woolley and her husband founded in 1904 the interracial Frederick Douglass Center at 3032 South Wabash Avenue. Her purpose was "to promote a just and amicable relation between white and colored people; to remove the disabilities which the latter suffer in their civil, cultural and economic life; to establish a center of friendly helpfulness and influence and for mutual cooperation in the ends of right living and a higher citizenship." Along these lines Mrs. Woolley worked for almost fifteen years, winning the gratitude and affection of thousands of Negroes whose burdens she helped to bear. After her death in 1918 the work was taken over by the Chicago Urban League and has been carried on in the spirit of the words of Booker T. Washington inscribed over the Center's fireplace: "I am determined that no man shall drag me down by making me hate him."

The World Parliament of Religions

The ideal of human unity on the higher levels of ethical and spiritual aspiration and endeavor that we have seen embodied in the various reforms and institutions reviewed above found its religious counterpart and climax in the World Parliament of Religions held in conjunction with the World's Columbian Exposition of 1893 in Chicago. The magnitude of the conception, of its execution, and of its success made it the crowning event of the great Exposition. By general agreement with the top officials of the Exposition, the Parliament was carried out on a strictly non-sectarian basis. To avoid any possible boycott of the Parliament and its ancillary Congresses, Rev. John Henry Barrows of the First Presbyterian Church, Chicago, was made chairman of the general committee and Jenkin Lloyd Jones its secretary – although to Jones' kindling enthusiasm the idea owed its realization, and to his executive ability was due the efficient performance of most of its administrative duties. He was fully aware that such a Parliament of Religions had been predicted by W. J. Potter, secretary of the Free Religious Association, in 1872:

> Some of us here may live to see the day when there shall be a world's convention ... of representatives of all the great religions of the globe, coming together in, a spirit of mutual respect, confidence and amity ... not to make a common creed ... but emancipated from all bondage to creed and sect, to join hands in a common effort to help mankind to higher truth and nobler living. It may be that the work of this Association will culminate in such a world's convention.

The idea of a Parliament of all world religions instead of merely a Congress of the Christian denominations in this country seems to have originated in a conference between Jones and Rev. David Utter of the First Unitarian Church in Chicago. They agreed that an exposition of the world's material progress should be elevated by a presentation of the spiritual beliefs of the world's religions. Utter left Chicago for Salt Lake City in

1891, and the negotiations for the project fell upon Jones' shoulders. With admirable finesse and self-effacement, he secured the co-operation of eminent liberal denominational leaders of Chicago and the country, as well as the approval of the high officials of the Exposition. By 1892 Jones was deeply involved in the vast and complex work of organizing the Parliament and the subsidiary Congresses. Invitations were sent through the State Department to all the nations and religious bodies of the world, asking for assurances of support and for the appointment of official delegates, who should assemble "to deepen the spirit of brotherhood among the religious men of diverse faiths; to indicate the impregnable foundations of Theism and the reasons for man's faith in immortality; to strengthen the forces adverse to materialism."

Favorable replies were received from virtually all those approached save the Sultan of Turkey, the Archbishop of Canterbury, and the General Assembly of the Presbyterian Church in the United States. But many of the Episcopal bishops in this country disregarded the English Primate and, like the leading liberal Presbyterians, participated in the Parliament; while the Roman Catholic bishops both approved and attended the Parliament. The register of noted prelates, scholars, rabbis, and ministers who came from all parts of the world covers six pages in the two massive volumes of the proceedings of *The World's Parliament of Religions* edited by J. H. Barrows (1893), beside which we have a thousand-page volume, *The World's Congress of Religions*, edited by J. W. Hanson (1894).

The opening session was brilliant in the extreme. A processional of over three hundred of the most eminent religious leaders in the multi-colored vestments of their offices entered the great Hall of Columbus in the Art Institute on Michigan Boulevard, whose seating capacity of four thousand was increasingly inadequate to accommodate the crowds attending the sessions from September 11 to the 29th. Cardinal Gibbons of Baltimore led in the reading of the Universal Prayer that opened the first session; Rabbi Emil G. Hirsch of Chicago led in the recitation of the Lord's Prayer that closed the last session. The most significant utterances, especially those of the representative of the Brahmo Somaj of India, Protap Chunder Mozoomdar, and of the disciple of

Ramakrishna, Swami Vivekananda, which made a deep impression, are included in the very satisfactory literary souvenir of the Parliament, *A Chorus of Faith* (1893), compiled by Jones and containing 167 extracts from notable speeches. Between the topical chapters are appropriate poems which appeared in the official program of the Parliament, some used as hymns by the audiences. Their authors were Gannett, Hosmer, Samuel Longfellow, Leigh Hunt, David A. Wasson, Emerson. He also included the hymns already cited in this chapter on the theme of universal religion by Gannett, Hosmer, Samuel Longfellow, Samuel Johnson, and others, which were sung by the vast audiences at the sessions.

To Jones, the Parliament demonstrated clearly the three underlying Unities of Religion: Brotherhood, Character, Reverence. As for the last: "The day set apart for the discussion of the Divine Nature was the least fruitful – a rather dry day. The Parliament was most triumphant when it took God for granted." It was hard, to be sure, for certain Christian leaders to refrain from revivalist attempts to convert the heathen when they had such an opportunity. But in only two instances did Christian superciliousness and imperiousness break out! Although the carefully planned Unitarian Congress (an unofficial session of the National Conference) was a dismal failure, since most of the speakers failed to appear, and the Unitarian laity were mostly to be found in the Parliament sessions, the denomination was otherwise well represented. In the Liberal Arts Palace in Jackson Park (now the Museum of Science and Industry), the Unitarians had a small Greek temple to house busts and publications. The Tower Hill Sunday School Institute held lectures and classes in the *Unity* building on Sixty-third Street near the Fair's main entrance. The headquarters of the Western Conference at 175 Dearborn Street, which had been newly decorated through the combined efforts of "pure Christian" and "Ethical Basis" Unitarians of Chicago, were thronged by visitors the summer long.

At the closing session of the Parliament, "busy, ubiquitous Secretary Jones, happier than he had ever been before" – to use the words of W. W. Fenn in his report to the *Register* – was given an ovation, to which he replied simply: "I am sufficiently happy in the knowledge that I have been enabled to be to a certain extent the feet of this great triumph." Fenn interpreted the triumph thus:

Every Unitarian has a right to be proud of the fact that this Parliament of Religions was possible because Channing and Emerson have lived. These have been their coronation days.

The Supplementary Resolution of 1892

Beyond doubt the Issue was the subject of much discussion among Unitarians from all parts of the country who met in these centers to rest their weary feet after days and miles of sightseeing in the White City. At the Conference headquarters they might have picked up copies of the statement of "Things commonly believed among us" of 1887, which now bore the Supplementary Resolution of 1892:

Resolved: that the Western Unitarian Conference hereby declares it to be its general aim and purpose to promulgate a religion in harmony with the foregoing Preamble and Statement.

Since the latter was not only a synopsis of the tenets of early Unitarianism and of congregational polity but also an exhibit of specimen Christian Theist, Universal Theist, and Ethical Basis church covenants, all of this material prefaced by a declaration that none was authoritative – a vote to "promulgate" it only added to the irony of the situation! Why was it passed?

To explain this, a review of developments between 1887 and 1892 will be helpful.

In the fall of 1887, the A.U.A. decided to consult no longer with the directors of the Western Conference as to financial aid to missions and churches in the Central West but to deal directly with the state conferences – although their delegates, too, had voted for "Truth, Righteousness and Love" in 1886! Rev. George Batchelor was appointed Western Agent, but on the pretense of "neutrality" he did not use the address of the Western Unitarian Association in Chicago. For two years he traveled about in the West, visiting conservative churches chiefly and pushing the "neutrality" policy so far that he never visited the Conference headquarters and refused its invitation to preach at the annual meeting of 1888. Having failed to disintegrate the Ethical Basis *bloc*, which went about its work frugally but sturdily with Shorey as President and Effinger as Secretary, Batchelor resigned in 1889. The A.U.A., in a fresh attempt to divide the *Unity* men, nominated Hosmer for its board in 1890. But Hosmer, at the May Meeting of 1890, firmly declined to desert his comrades and reproached the A.U.A. for its policy of snubbing and sabotage, which was the more flagrant because Batchelor had preached in orthodox churches, though he would not come near the Western Conference pulpit! During the heated debate it was divulged that the Ethical Basis group were regarded as "cantankerous recalcitrants" because they would not yield to the Association's demand that they consent to at least *use* Christian Theist phraseology, so that the A.U.A. directors (as Secretary Reynolds dramatically pleaded) might not incur jail sentences on the charge of aiding churches on the "Truth, Righteousness and Love" basis with funds which were given for the promotion of "pure Christianity"!

The Association then adopted the policy of out-flanking and isolating the Conference. Rev. T. B. Forbush, who, like Sunderland and most of the conservatives, could not admit the validity of any position beyond Parkerism, and who had long held, with M. J. Savage, that the Conference should surrender its missionary work to the A.U.A., was appointed Western Superintendent. He arranged for a Western Missionary Mass Meeting in Chicago (October, 1890), to which the officials of the Western Conference were given a kind of left-handed invitation which they declined to accept, on the ground that the Conference itself was *the* Western missionary body and none other was needed. The chief accomplishment of Forbush was the formation, in 1890, of the Rocky Mountain Conference of nine churches. He had the co-operation of Rev. S. A. Eliot of Denver who, like Professor F. H. Hedge, was "intellectually radical but ecclesiastically conservative."

Since most of these churches, like Sunderland's and Douthit's, were subsidized by the A.U.A., Gannett claimed that "from first to last the real strength of the A.U.A. has been in the East, not the West ... The A.U.A. has been their main dependence. Its antecedents and its temperament compel it to withhold sympathy from a forward movement until the public opinion of Unitarianism in Massachusetts declares for it." Gannett, perceiving clearly that financial strength was a factor in the struggle, summoned the Conference to complete its endowment fund of $50,000, "to make a vigorous independent center in the West, turn the great valley of the Mississippi into a home mission field, help to nationalize Unitarianism by de-Bostonizing it – though not forgetting the honor and gratitude due the old homestead."

Through 1891 the situation was deadlocked. Forbush established an A.U.A. office in Chicago, but its lack of activity contrasted dismally with the busy, cheerful rooms of the Conference in the Loop. The attitude of Eastern Unitarians was changing, however. Chadwick, whose non-doctrinal Second Church in Brooklyn had always generally supported the position and the treasury of the Western Conference, visited its sessions in 1890 and wrote the *Register*:

If at any time Boston runs out of "pure Christianity" or Christian Unitarianism it has only to send to the Western Unitarian Conference for a supply. I have never attended a meeting where there was a more lively sense of the dignity and glory of Unitarianism; a more awed sense of Infinite and Eternal things; a more hopeful outlook on the other side of death; a more simply natural and human reverence for Jesus of Nazareth. The difference is the smallest that ever kept men apart who belong together.

With the coming of Rev. W. W. Fenn to Chicago's First Church and his co-operation with Rev. S. M. Crothers of St. Paul, the ice jam began to break up. At the session of the Conference in 1892, they moved and seconded the Supplementary Resolution, which had been prepared by Sunderland with Forbush's approval and which they now appeared in person to urge on the Conference. Sunderland conceded that "it is time the separation should cease." He added that he desired only that the Conference should declare that it was going to *work* for the things it believed in.

The paradox of this demand of Sunderland – who had begun and who had fostered the "separation" over five years – would have wrecked all hope of reconciliation had not Fenn and Crothers hastened to assure the Conference that the Supplementary Resolution did not exclude giving aid to churches and ministers that did not accept the Statement of 1887. Then lawyer

Shorey assured the Ethical Basis adherents that the Resolution did not mean anything legally since it would not be part of the constitution of the Conference. It was nothing more than an olive branch, with Sunderland as the dove proffering it! Blake, Jones, Gannett, and others liked the olive-branch idea but had some doubts about the dove's designs. But the Supplementary Resolution was finally passed – though with less than a two-thirds' majority.

Douthit deemed the action a victory for the Ethical Basis! Gannett regarded the latter as now a "Dimmed Ideal." He regretted "this miserable and ignoble theory of a *working* basis as distinct from a *talking* basis; now we are told that the 'haze' in the Resolution is its peace value! [But] thank God, for six years the Conference has braved the misrepresentation and indifference and loneliness that Eastern Unitarians have accorded it."

The Reconciliation at Saratoga, 1894

Besides giving the Association the excuse it desired for aiding Ethical Basis churches in the West without risking a jail sentence – real or imaginary – for its directors, the Supplementary Resolution seemed to have accomplished little else. The A.U.A., in spite of the necessity for drawing on its General Fund as the business depression of the nineties progressed, continued Forbush in office; instead of accepting the suggestion of the Conference that he make his headquarters with them, he kept his own office in Chicago. Conference Secretary Effinger was not restored to a place on the (Ministerial) Fellowship Committee of the National Conference, which passed on the qualifications of candidates for Western pulpits.

But the Parliament of Religions in 1893 – where it was made obvious that world unity in religion could rest only on a universal Ethical Theism unconstricted by sectarian loyalties to this or that prophet, saint or sage – gave Eastern Unitarians a new conception of the potential inclusiveness of their denominational name, as well as an insight into the vision and hope of the Ethical Basis brethren in the West. Moreover, the "theological scare," as Jones called it, of the eighteen-eighties had largely subsided; for Ingersollism, secularism, Ethical Culture, as well as evolution, Biblical criticism, and the study of ethnic religions, had now become accepted or at least respectable. What was quite as important, the revolutionary aspects of anarchism, Socialism, and the labor movement had settled down into a steady, orderly opposition to the *status quo*. With all these "dangerous" radicalisms the Ethical Basis party had been vaguely though unjustly associated. Since the "New Theology" of the liberal orthodox churches had domesticated evolution – with the aid of [Asa] Gray, Fiske, [Henry] Drummond, [Benjamin] Kidd, Lyman Abbott – its advocacy could no longer be regarded as an assault on any Bostonian's family tree. The Free Religious Association was languishing, and its philosopher, Francis E. Abbot, had openly attacked the Ethical Basis.

In 1891 a Committee on Revision of the Preamble and Constitution of the National Conference had been appointed, with Savage as its chairman, Professor C. C. Everett, C. G. Ames (Clarke's successor in the Church of the Disciples), J. W. Chadwick, E. E. Hale, W. B. Weeden, and other moderates as members. In the spring of 1894 the committee published in the *Register* a preliminary draft of its work, only to have it condemned by Rector H. N. Brown of King's Chapel, J. T. Sunderland, Douthit, and others because it dropped the Christian name and all Theistic phrases – a "cowardly thing" to do, wrote Sunderland, bound to be "widely misunderstood."

Another draft was prepared, and when it was submitted to the morning business session of the National Conference in Saratoga, October, 1894, an immediate vote was called for. Gannett, Hosmer, and Chadwick pleaded for time to consider it. The temper of the Conference may be judged by the fact that 278 acquiesced, though 117 opposed delay. So anxious were Savage and his committee to meet the views of the Western delegates that a further revision of the Preamble was made during the noon recess. By Chadwick's counsel the second half of the present Preamble dealing with congregational and individual freedom was placed in juxtaposition with the statement that "these churches accept the religion of Jesus, holding, in accordance with his teaching, that practical religion is summed up in love to God and love to man." For the benefit of those who might object to this as caging Unitarianism within Christianity, Rev. C. G. Ames explained to the Conference: "We are members of the church of Jesus Christ as we are members of the Republic of George Washington." Ames paid tribute to the "wisdom, tact, good nature and persistence of one layman" – George H. Ellis, publisher of the *Register*, by whom "many men of many minds had been brought within reach of each other and so have attained the impossible."

There was a breathless moment when the chairman, after a volume of "Ayes" for the new Preamble, called for the "Nays." Not one was heard, possibly because Jones was in Chicago! What he later called "a unanimity of concession" the other Ethical Basis men deemed keeping the unity of the Spirit in the bond of peace. No wonder the assembly sang the Doxology with streaming eyes; for after fifty years of tension and division, the lesson of unity had been learned by the Unitarians: no quarrels over minor theological differences!

The wording of the new Preamble, as finally ratified, was as follows:

> The Conference of Unitarian and other Christian Churches was formed in the year 1865 for the purpose of strengthening the churches and societies which should unite in it for more and better work for the kingdom of God.
>
> These churches accept the religion of Jesus, holding, in accordance with his teaching, that practical religion is summed up in love to God and love to man.
>
> The Conference recognizes the fact that its constituency is Congregational in tradition and polity. Therefore it declares that nothing in this constitution is to be construed as an authoritative test; and we cordially invite to our working fellowship any who, while differing from us in belief, are in general sympathy with our spirit and our practical aims.

In the high tide of good will, Mrs. [Mary Thorne Lewis] Gannett, D. L. Shorey, and Hosmer were elected to the board of the National Conference, Miss Safford and W. W. Fenn to the (Ministerial) Fellowship Committee. A Missionary Council was soon devised, consisting of a delegate from each of the nine state conferences, the Secretary of the Western Conference, and the Secretary of the A.U.A. Its office was in the Conference headquarters in Chicago. Forbush resigned as Western Superintendent, but Rev. A. W. Gould, a close friend of Jones, remained as Conference Secretary – although Douthit's distrust of their good faith burst forth in another "Extra" of *Our Best Words*. Douthit, however, now had to fight the battle of the angels alone; Sunderland had resigned the editorship of *The Unitarian* in December, 1895, claiming that "the recent action of the denomination at Saratoga, placing it unequivocally on the Christian basis," justified his release. Shortly after, he was given a leave of absence from his church in Ann Arbor and was sent to India as the ambassador of the A.U.A. to the Brahmo Somaj Theistic Society, with whose president, Mozoomdar, he had become acquainted during the Parliament of Religions.

Jones never accepted Saratoga. He remained true to the Ethical Basis, with what results we shall see in our next chapter.

PART IV

THE FRUITS OF HARMONY (1894-1952)

CHAPTER THIRTEEN

Integration and Expansion

CLIO, SAID A FRENCH SAGE, would be undone were it not for hostility. But there had been very little personal and partisan hostility in the theological battles of the Western Issue, and what there was had been factitious and imported. Heightened seriousness and resolution, however, generated an evangelical energy that resulted, during the captainties of Jones (1878-84) and of Grindall Reynolds (1881-94) in an increased tempo of church founding as well as of literary propaganda – a tempo stimulated by the lush economic prosperity of the eighteen-eighties, but retarded and in some respects halted by the depression of the nineties.

[New Beginnings in Pittsburgh, Indianapolis, and Elsewhere]

Until 1904 the new churches in the Meadville area were members of the Western Conference. That at Dunkirk had been organized in 1880. Rev. James G. Townsend, who passed from Methodism to Unitarianism while a preacher in Buffalo, founded the First Unitarian Church of Jamestown, New York, in 1885. Particularly gratifying was his success in strongly Presbyterian Pittsburgh, where three former Unitarian movements had failed (1820, 1849, 1860). The fourth venture commenced with a newspaper notice inserted by Townsend which drew together a dozen or more liberals, who began public meetings in private homes and a third-floor hall – the time-honored pioneer method! Four of the incorporators of the First Unitarian Church (May 8, 1890) had been connected with previous efforts: A. F. Marthens, Mr. and Mrs. R. M. McCargo, and Miss Martha Glass. Soon Mrs. R. H. Lee, a granddaughter of John Campbell, the pioneer of the eighteen-twenties, came in. The unique wording of the church's charter to the effect that it "is formed for the worship of Almighty God according to the *faith, doctrine, discipline* and *usages* of the Unitarian Church" doubtless betrays

Townsend's Methodist background; but it so pleased the as yet unjailed directors of the A.U.A. that the church received generous aid from 1890 to 1897. This made possible the replacement of Townsend, whose health had failed, by Rev. Charles E. St. John. His hard work and inspiring words got a neat wooden church built in 1893 and a Citizens' League organized; the League both initiated and designed the filtering plant for a pure water supply, which ended the city's perennial scourge of typhoid-fever epidemics. During the long, devoted, and efficient ministry of Rev. L. Walter Mason, "Father of the City Playgrounds" (1910-29), the church steadily gained strength and also a new building (1904), funds for which had been secured largely through the minister's astute negotiations in selling the former site to the Roman Catholic archbishop for $60,000! To Mason's initiative were largely due not only the city's Associated Charities and Juvenile Court Association, but the Northside Unitarian Church (1906), planned for community center work in an industrial area. Mason's legacy of efficient church organization, genial fellowship, humanitarian vision, and service has been cherished and augmented by his successors, Rev. Frank E. Smith (1929-43) and Rev. Irving R. Murray.

Indianapolis, like Pittsburgh, had been recommended by the A.U.A. prospectors – M. G. Thomas in 1829, F. W. Holland in 1849 – as having strategic promise; and an attempt had been made in 1869 to start a Unitarian movement there by three lawyers (J. D. Holland, George Perrin, Judge David McDonald) and by Miss Mary E. Nicholson, principal of the normal school. They organized the First Unitarian Church, rented the Academy of Music, and engaged Rev. Henry Blanchard, who succeeded in attracting large congregations and buying the former Universalist church. But the depression of the eighteen-seventies halted the work in 1877. Then Secretary Jones came, revived the movement as "Unity Church," and secured Rev. George W. Cooke for its ministry (1878-80). Cooke's abilities and interests, however, were philosophic and literary rather than administrative and pastoral. Strenuously through he preached and lectured on such subjects as [Auguste] Comte, Spinoza, [Gottholt] Lessing, Spencer,

Darwin, Emerson; and though Unity Church had no creed, "believes more in works than doctrines … is independent and free … does earnestly believe in morality, character, manhood, love to all men," the grain was, obviously, "tossed too high in the cribs for the critters" in Indianapolis! Cooke resigned and the church was closed. For the next fifteen years the Unitarian contingent rallied to a young radical minister, Oscar McCulloch, who had made the Plymouth Congregational Church into a non-denominational "Church of the Open Door." After his tragic death, the chairman, Horace McKay, appealed to Boston and Chicago for aid; and from the Western Conference came its then secretary, Rev. Fred V. Hawley, to appraise the situation. Meetings held in the Jewish temple had such good response that Rev. E. E. Newbert was sent from Boston for organizational work, facilitated immeasurably by McKay's personal purchase of a vacant Presbyterian church building to be held for the Unitarians. This gesture of faith was decisive. On May 9, 1903, bearing huge branches of dogwood, the little band of Unitarians found the Jewish temple filled for the installation of Newbert, with Hawley preaching the sermon. By June, 1904, All Souls Unitarian Church permanently occupied the building that McKay's foresight and generosity had procured for it on the site where its larger successor now stands.

Then history began ominously to repeat itself, for Newbert resigned in two years and went back to New England! But Secretary Hawley averted the omen by recommending Rev. Frank S. C. Wicks, a graduate of Meadville School. In the autumn he began a ministry of thirty-three years, during which the congregation not only grew in numbers and resources but also advanced to a high position of civic prominence and responsibility. It has been active in the founding of the Playground Association, the Children's Aid Association, the Family Welfare Society, and the Public Health Nursing Association. Wicks has been board member and president of the Riley Hospital for Children, the Art Institute, the Coleman Home for Unmarried Mothers, the Literary and Contemporary Clubs. Under the leadership of Rev. E. Burdette Backus (1938) the church's character as "a religious center with a civic circumference" has been enhanced through its vital concern with the defense of civil rights, non-sectarianism in tax-supported public education, and a just and humane status in community and church for the Negro.

A similar record of early disappointment and later success is held by the First Unitarian Church of Youngstown, Ohio, 1904, preceded in 1892 by the Unitarian Society of Youngstown; the Unitarian Society of Fort Wayne, Indiana, 1939, preceded by the First Unitarian Society, 1875; the First Unitarian Church of Dayton, Ohio, 1910, preceded by the Unitarian Congregational Society, 1846; the First Unitarian Church of Columbus, Ohio, preceded by a movement of the same name in 1869. The economic and cultural population growth of these railroad centers is largely responsible for a better showing in recent years. But the factor of improvement in missionary methods should not be overlooked nor should the more typically Midwestern character of the new societies, which are not composed so largely of New England expatriates as was the case in former decades.

[The Scandinavian Unitarian Missions]

Similar success in regaining the lost ground has not as yet been attained with the Scandinavian Unitarian missions which, beginning with the work of the Norwegian, Kristofer Janson, continued through the eighteen-eighties, the nineties, and the early nineteen hundreds. Of Janson's mission churches, those at Underwood, Minnesota (Free Christian Church, 1890), and Hanska, Minnesota (Nora Free Christian Church, 1882) have continued in existence, chiefly through the efforts of Rev. Amandus H. Norman. But the Swedish Unitarian churches in Denver (1892), Minneapolis (1890), Chicago (1904), Springvale, Minnesota (1909), to which August Dellquist, Axel Lundberg, August Dellgren, O. E. Helsing, and David Holmgren ministered, have not survived.

The Finnish Mission has met with better fortune. Though the work in Red Lodge, Montana (1913), and Iddington, Minnesota (1924), has been suspended, that of the Free Christian Church of Virginia, Minnesota (1911), continues by dint of the diligent, consecrated leadership of Rev. Risto Lappala and his wife, Rev. Milma S. Lappala Erkkila, whose joint ministry in the Finnish language extended from 1910 to 1941. By 1913 an attractive church had been built and a parsonage purchased. When Risto Lappala died in 1923, Mrs. Lappala, who had started the Alongo

Unitarian Church in Angora, Minnesota (1916), carried the responsibility for both churches until 1941. Services in English had been started in Virginia by the Unitarian minister in Duluth, Rev. Robert E. Romig, and under Rev. Kenneth J. Smith of Duluth the precedent has become an effective dual ministry.

[Developments in Chicago]

Howsoever discouraging to the Western Secretaries of the two decades between 1890 and 1910 – J. R. Effinger, F. L. Hosmer, A. W. Gould, F. C. Southworth, F. V. Hawley, W. M. Backus, E. C. Smith – the ebbing tide of the Scandinavian Mission must have been, to say nothing of the demise of many embryonic churches in Michigan, Indiana, Illinois, Iowa, and Kansas, slain by the business depression of the nineties, the progress of Unitarianism in Chicago must have renewed their optimism. Since 1888, when the Federation of Liberal Religious Societies was organized, Jones' inclusive spirit had rejoiced in publishing a weekly register of their names, locations, and leaders in *Unity*. By 1896 the list had grown to twenty. Among the number were the three liberal Jewish temples, with their eminent rabbis, Hirsch, Stolz, and Felsenthal; the Ethical Society, whose leader was Mangasin Mangasarian, a convert from Presbyterianism; the People's Church meeting in McVickers Theatre, the congregation of H. W. Thomas; four Universalist churches, the largest of which was that on Stewart Avenue in Englewood led by Rufus A. White; and seven Unitarian churches – the Church of the Messiah, or First; Unity, or Second; the Third, on the west side; All Souls, replacing the old Fourth; an Independent Liberal Church in Lake View, a suburb on the north side; the churches in Hinsdale and Evanston.

Two major developments in the period under review merit special description: (a) the growth of All Souls Church to the point where a new and larger edifice was needed and eventually provided; (b) the removal of the First Unitarian Society from the ornate and majestic Church of the Messiah on Michigan Avenue at Twenty-third Street to a new chapel and parish house on East Fifty-seventh Street between University Avenue and Woodlawn Avenue.

Jenkin Lloyd Jones had felt that while the Supplementary Resolution of 1892 went a step toward doctrinalism, the Saratoga

Preamble of 1894 definitely constricted the meaning of "Unitarian" by a theological phraseology to which his close friend W. M. Salter and the three rabbis just mentioned could not give assent. Jones hitched the wagon of his allegiance only to "the Free Church of the Spirit, based on the eternal demands of the Ethical Law alone ... whose purposes, aspirations and helpfulness reach out not only from Unitarians to Christians but from Christians to Jew and Pagan." To such amplitude of sympathy a Unitarianism committed to the religion of Jesus could not attain, for "this religion of Jesus is an ambiguous term. Unitarians are disposed to interpret it not by what is unique in it but by the elements it has in common with other religions. [Yet] Christianity triumphed and made its estate first by a messianic, then by a mediatorial element that most Unitarians discard."

Hence, though Jones held All Souls Church loyally in the Western Conference, his enthusiasm shifted from the National Conference to a new body inspired by the World Parliament of Religions. The American Congress of Liberal Religious Societies – which H. W. Thomas, 28 rabbis, 70 Unitarian ministers, 12 Universalist ministers and 4 Ethical leaders had convened by manifesto – held its first meeting in Sinai Temple, Chicago, May 22, 1894, for the purpose of uniting "in a larger fellowship and cooperation those of us who are in sympathy with the movement toward undogmatic religion." It was hoped that the Congress would "foster and encourage the organization of non-sectarian churches and kindred societies on the basis of absolute freedom ... by developing the Church of Humanity, democratic in organization, progressive in thought, cherishing the spiritual traditions and experiences of the past but keeping itself open to all new light."

Thomas was elected president, Jones secretary of the Congress, which All Souls Church immediately joined and supported liberally. A corollary of the new affiliation was the voluntary repayment to the A.U.A. and other Unitarian donors of the $4,000 they had given All Souls in 1886-87 toward its building. Another, though temporary, result of the Congress affiliation was the conversion of *Unity* into *The New Unity*, a connection that lasted only three years (1895-98). A. M. Judy's periodical *Old and New*, published at Davenport, Iowa, became the official Western

Conference organ. *The New Unity*, promised Jones, "would be disloyal to no Unitarian interests save those that are identified with sectarianism and a dogmatic position." Although the Congress had little or no success in starting churches, temples, or any sort of liberal group, the *Christian Register* dubbed it "American Denomination No. 148" – the more unnecessary "because the A.U.A. is so broad and catholic that nothing could be broader." How the A.U.A., with its commitments to "pure Christianity" and "the religion of Jesus" could spend its funds for liberal Jewish congregations or Ethical Societies was an enigma to Jones. Since, however, the pogroms in Russia were intensifying Jewish isolationism to such a point that even the liberal Jews drew together in the Central Conference of American Rabbis (1889), and since Felix Adler's jealousy of rival leaderships discouraged Ethical participation in the Congress, the latter eventually shared the fate of the Free Religious Association and that of the National Federation of Religious Liberals organized by C. W. Wendte in 1908 – the fate of prophetic but premature truth.

The star of All Souls Church, however, continued to rise. Its Sunday congregations had passed five hundred, its educational and philanthropic activities were equally well attended and supported. In memory of Dr. Helen Heath, who had virtually sacrificed her life in work during the hard winter of 1893-94 for the foreign-born of the warehouse and stockyard district on Chicago's south side, a settlement house was opened at 831 West Thirty-third Place, with a program of classes in domestic science, physical hygiene, music, and civics – as well as an interracial social club and a pioneer parent-teacher group. To continue to serve the polyglot neighborhood, the work was organized independently of All Souls Church in 1904 by Mrs. Marion H. Perkins and Mrs. Bronson Peck. Fellowship House has continued Helen Heath's memory in sacrificial service to tens of thousands of under-privileged fellow humans in the miserably crowded and cheerless section east of Halsted Street.

Jones' dream of a new and larger home for All Souls envisaged a great community-center building at the heart of which should be the interracial, non-sectarian church, with a fitting sanctuary and auditorium for lectures and concerts as well as worship and sermons. Almost ten years of planning and fund-raising culminated on Easter Sunday, 1905, in the occupancy of the massive building named Abraham Lincoln Centre, directly across the street from the original home of the congregation at South Langley Avenue and Oakwood Boulevard. The six stories and basement contained, from top to bottom, gymnasium, domestic-science classrooms, residents' apartments – including a "parsonage" and a guest room – Emerson and Browning study and lecture halls, large and small dining rooms, a picture gallery, a music room, a minister's study, offices, a public reading room, editorial offices for *Unity*, manual-training shops, game rooms, a dark room for the Camera Club. In all, the Centre was the most complete institutional church in the Midwest. By giving the property and its endowment fund separate incorporation from All Souls Church, Jones and his colleagues designed to make the Centre an independent institution of secular, ethical religion; and such has been its character since its opening.

Jones' Editorship of Unity

From 1905 to his death in 1918, Jones dwelt, preached, lectured, and edited *Unity* in the Centre as in a citadel of unrimmed Freedom, Truth, and Humanity. Through the forty years of his editorship of *Unity* (1878-1918) no periodical in the United States had such a long, consistent record of championship of wronged and exploited human beings – the Chicago anarchists, the victims of distillers and saloon-keepers, the Zulus and Boers, the Chinese enslaved by the British opium interests, the solider victims of "embalmed beef" and other forms of war graft, the Philippine patriots under [Emilio] Aguinaldo, the oppressed peoples of India, the Jews slaughtered by Czar and Sultan, the American Indians, steel workers and packinghouse workers, Socialist and pacifist speakers and ministers silenced by reactionary forces. Nor had any periodical in this country advocated so many reforms that have eventually been accepted and legalized: the Froebel method [of preschool education]; education in sex hygiene; industrial training in the schools; credit unions and the Co-operative movement; profit-sharing and employees' welfare plans; Federal laws against lynching; Federal, state, and municipal control of public utilities; organized charity; juvenile courts; Civil Service; women's educational, economic, and electoral rights and equality; the Hague

Peace Congresses and the World Court – to name but a few of the most hotly contested issues. Not an illiberal, inhumane, sycophantic, or prudentially compromising editorial or article is to be found in *Unity's* pages in all those forty years.

Two episodes in *Unity's* history deserve special attention. In 1904, on one of his "March escapes," Jones made a pilgrimage to Hodgenville, Kentucky, where Lincoln had been born. He found the site of the log cabin marked by a stake in the midst of a muddy field – the cabin itself had been taken to New York for exhibition in a Broadway museum. The spring nearby was a wallow for hogs; the farm was for sale by the sheriff. Jones expressed his sorrowful indignation over such neglect of a spot where Nancy Hanks gave her son the fundamental lessons in character and literacy. Jones' son, Richard, then a tyro on the staff of *Collier's Weekly*, brought the article in *Unity* ("A Neglected Shrine," March 4, 1904) to the attention of his chief. The latter started a campaign in the pages of *Collier's Weekly* to raise a national fund to buy the farm, bring back the old cabin, and dedicate both as a National Memorial. All this was duly accomplished; and on November 16, 1916, a stately granite temple enclosing the cabin, together with the now park-like farm – paid for chiefly by the pennies of American school children! – was accepted for the nation by President Wilson. In February, 1917, *Unity* organized a pilgrimage by special train from Chicago to the "restored shrine," whose interior walls were inscribed with Lincoln's tribute to his mother. At the memorial service (February 12) Hosmer's hymn was sung:

> The prairies to the mountains call,
> The mountains to the sea;
> From shore to shore a nation keeps
> Her martyr's memory.
>
> Land of our loyal love and hope,
> O Land he died to save,
> Bow down, renew today thy vows
> Beside his sacred grave.

The second episode in *Unity's* history under Jones' editorship is related to his resolute opposition to war. The conclusion reached by the young Wisconsin artilleryman in 1865 – "it was such a wrong way of doing the right thing" – remained his deep conviction until death. So insistent was he that opposition to war was thoroughly patriotic and manly that the theme was omnipresent in sermons, editorials, lectures, prayers. One of the last, which he gave at a Union Thanksgiving Service in 1906, inspired Rev. William Pierson Merrill, a Presbyterian neighbor, to write his famous patriotic hymn "Not alone for mighty empire." In 1898 Jones, like most of his brethren in the West, had denounced and resisted the Hearst-Hanna aggression against Spain and her colonial possessions which, he thought, like the Negro slaves in the South, would better have been purchased at any price than fought over. On the same principle and for the same reasons he resisted propaganda for preparedness in 1914 which, he was convinced, was certain to involve our country in war. As early as 1879 he had written: "Where are the newspapers that will anticipate the ghastliness of the battlefields, the gruesomeness of the hospitals? Let artist, orator, teacher, lawyer and above all, ministers of religion speak out!" Innumerable are the editorials in *Unity* from then on, deploring the Spanish-American, the Boer, the Russo-Japanese wars.

After the outbreak of the First World War his vehemence increased: "The hypocrisy of the Christianity that invokes the blessing of the Prince of Peace on the devilish instrumentalities of destruction! Innocent men are killing and being killed and no righteous cause is being promoted thereby!" When Henry Ford's invitation came to him to join the Peace Ship Expedition (December, 1915) to the warring countries of Europe, Jones accepted "not because we believe that it will have much influence on the war-maddened countries but because the Cause is so ill spoken of; because what we believe to be sincere principles ... are made the butt of flippant newspaper ridicule. We are glad to enroll ourselves among the unarmed army who seek truth, justice and right."

Returning to this country Jones declared: "I am glad I went ... I have no apologies to offer ... I have been at the storm center of sarcasm and ridicule and feel better for it!" To President Wilson he addressed many editorial letters pleading against provocatory words – "the five hundred American lives more or less cannot be brought back by offering tens of thousands more of innocent lives on the Moloch altar of war." To members of Congress: "I am opposing war as the survival of the beast that is ever followed by a trail of woe, degradation, demoralization." *Unity* saluted ministers whose opposition to war and the anti-German hysteria brought dismissal from their pulpits. Among the Unitarians there were Frank C. Doan, Alson H. Robinson, C. R. Joy, George R. Gebauer, H. W. Pinkham, Arthur B. Heeb. When the A.U.A. board of directors voted on April 9, 1918, "that any Society which employs a minister who is not a willing, earnest and outspoken supporter of the United States in the vigorous and resolute prosecution of the war cannot be considered eligible for aid from the Association," Jones recalled previous instances in which the Association had sought to use financial power to coerce conscience and violate congregational autonomy. He predicted, however, that sooner or later this latest ruling would be reversed – as indeed it was in 1936 by the Pinkham resolution, which regretted the action of the 1918 board "as contrary to the fundamental Unitarian principle of freedom of thought and conscience" and pledged "that never in the future shall the economic power of the organization be used to influence the opinion or conduct of any minister or society." In 1916 Jones published *Love for the Battle-torn Peoples* in a valiant attempt to stem the flames of prejudice and hatred fanned by propagandists. "Why Love Germany?" was included among chapters interpreting the history, the culture, the people of the great European countries in a friendly and appreciative spirit. "The way to world peace lies through the hearts and minds of the *people*."

All this sounded subversive to Washington authorities, and the Post Office Department suspended the mailing privilege of *Unity* from the issue of July 4, 1918, to that of August 29, 1918. But Jones would not withdraw a word he had written or promise to suppress his pacifist views for the future. The extra correspondence and excitement aggravated heart trouble from which he had been suffering. Finally the Post Office relented – the war was almost over, anyway – and released the August 29 edition, a copy of which reached Jones at Tower Hill on the morning of September 10. He read it through carefully, pointed out the inevitable typographical error, chuckled a bit over his victory, fell into a deep slumber, and died in his sleep. For his epitaph in the old Welsh Burying Ground at Tower Hill, he had selected Lincoln's words: "He sought to pull up a thistle and plant a flower wherever a flower would grow."

Though Rev. John Haynes Holmes – who had been editorial contributor to *Unity* since 1910 and between whom and Jones there had existed a profound unanimity – assumed the editorship of *Unity* with Francis Neilson as associate, he declined a call to the ministry of All Souls Church. Rev. J. M. Evans became its minister until 1922. He was succeeded by Rev. Fred Merrifield, who persuaded the dwindling congregation to contribute its membership and capital to aid in the formation of the Jackson Park Community Church at Blackstone Avenue and East Sixty-Sixth Place. In spite of a large building investment by the A.U.A. and an encouraging start, the new society could not weather the depression of 1929 and went out of existence in 1932 – another proof of the desirability for a great leader to select a congenial, competent, and consecrated associate before his powers wane, if the institution he has created is to survive. Abraham Lincoln Centre was saved from the fate of All Souls Church by the election of Rev. Curtis W. Reese, Western Conference Secretary, as its dean in 1930.

The Hull Memorial Chapel and the University of Chicago

Chicago's Church of the Messiah, whose flamboyant, neo-Gothic structure had towered above the corner of South Michigan Avenue and East Twenty-third Street since 1873, would have shared the decline of Unity Church on the north side – whose congregation had to sell Collyer's famous sanctuary to the Knights Templar in 1904 – had not the First Church's minister, Rev. W. W. Fenn (1891-1901), been a practical and determined visionary. This characteristic he shared with the chairman of his board, Daniel L. Shorey, who was also a member of the first board of trustees of the new University of Chicago. Like the Universalist, Charles L. Hutchinson, donor of the Hutchinson Commons, Shorey, the Unitarian, was a sympathetic and tireless collaborator with the good Baptist, President Harper. He was instrumental in securing for the University from the first Marshall Field the segment of the present campus lying along the Midway. As chairman of the buildings and grounds committee for seven years, he rendered such generous and efficient service that when he died in 1899 Harper resorted to superlatives in acknowledging its value:

> He exhibited a devotion to [the University's] interests which may not be described in words. In consequence of his long and varied experience in the practice of law he was able to give clear and valuable advice upon the many technical problems which frequently arose. How carefully he followed the workmen in the erection of every building now standing on the University grounds; how diligently and successfully he planned and executed the work of filling and planning trees and shrubbery and the general laying-out of the grounds. But his contribution was, if possible, still greater in the heartiness with which he co-operated with every effort to realize the highest educational ideals in the work of organizing the University. His large experience with University men and his great faith in the University's ideas and ideals enabled him to render service of an invaluable character in the birth period of the University. Mr. Shorey's influence in the early history of the University can never be effaced; his memory among those who associated with him in this important work can never be forgotten.

This interest in the new institution in Hyde Park, where Shorey lived, was of course a cardinal factor in the project to which he had drawn Fenn's attention: the establishment of a chapel-of-ease of the Church of the Messiah in close proximity to the new University. A third aspect of his dream was the conviction that the Meadville Theological School should be moved to Chicago – a conviction and a hope that originated as far back as 1870. In that year, Artemus Carter, President of the Conference, with the aid of his minister, Robert Collyer, raised a fund from Chicago Unitarians of $50,000 to underwrite the relocation of Meadville in Chicago in proximity to the old University. To secure Western Conference endorsement of the plan, Carter prepared a masterly analysis of "The Want of Ministers in the West and How to Supply It," in which he criticized the rural situation of the Meadville School:

> The students should have opportunity all along in their course to practice the art of preaching and of the pastor's life. As well let a man sleep a week and work two as keep the student hived three years in his dormitory and recitation room and then send him among people as a pastor and preacher. A great and populous city is the only place for his proper training.

Bellows of New York vigorously supported Carter's project, but the family pride and possessiveness of the Huidekopers, in which their kinsman J. F. Clarke concurred, blocked the movement. Another opportunity to move the School to a large city was offered in 1882 by Jeptha H. Wade, a Unitarian of Cleveland, Ohio. He proposed to give the school at least $150,000 and several acres of land opposite Adelbert College on Euclid Avenue – the site now occupied by Symphony Hall – if, in addition to training ministers, the School would establish a chair in psychical research, a subject in which he was deeply interested. Barrows of the *Register*, Jones of *Unity* urged the acceptance of Wade's offer. Jones characterized the School as "staid, solid and conservative ... the course of study, even the textbooks, is the same as we had seventeen years ago." Such backwardness he attributed to the paternalism of the conservative Huidekoper family's control of the board of trustees – a control that again asserted itself in the rejection of Wade's proposal.

All this background of his persistent hope Shorey told Fenn, and the latter threw himself loyally into its fulfillment. Commencing with a meeting at the home of Rev. J. R. Effinger in Hyde Park in 1894, Fenn held afternoon services in Masonic Hall on East Fifty-seventh Street near Harper Avenue. The expenses of these services were met by the church treasurer, Morton B. Hull, but he and his wife died in 1895. At the sixtieth anniversary of the church in 1896, Chairman Shorey earnestly pressed the Hyde Park extension work and paid a glowing tribute to the interest of Mr. and Mrs. Hull in it. A few days later, their son, Morton Denison Hull, and his sister Eudora offered to build a memorial chapel and parish house in memory of their parents on a lot purchased for the purpose on Fifty-seventh Street and South Woodlawn Avenue. Hull Chapel was dedicated in 1897 and was immediately successful in terms of large congregations, many coming from the University, and of a progressive religious-education program. To superintend the latter, Fenn had the assistance of a young Harvard graduate, Charles E. Park, whose ministerial training Fenn was guiding in connection with the University's Divinity School faculty. In 1899 Park received his diploma and accepted a call to the Unitarian church in Geneva, where he was ordained in 1899. This left Fenn with the care of the mother Church of the Messiah on Michigan Avenue, where he preached Sunday mornings and evenings, giving the afternoons to Hull Chapel work. All this, beside weekly lectures at both posts, did not prevent his serving on the boards of the Conference and of the A.U.A., lecturing at Meadville School, and having a considerable part in the Conference reconciliations of 1892 and 1894. In 1901 he resigned to accept Harvard's call to the Bussey chair of theology.

The Removal of the Meadville School to Chicago

But the task of fulfilling Shorey's and his dream for the removal of the Meadville School to Chicago he had committed to the new chairman of the church board, Morton D. Hull, and to his Harvard classmate, Rev. Franklin C. Southworth, then Secretary of the Western Conference. On the resignation of George L. Cary from the presidency of the School in 1902, Southworth was elected to the office. His service of twenty-seven years (1902-29) was the most vigorous and progressive in the School's history. It was also, as we shall see, the most dramatic. For, after a faithful attempt to attract college graduates to its student body and teachers of admitted excellence to its faculty, while the School was located in Meadville the struggle was seen to be a losing one and a sharp legal battle ensued in the Supreme Court of Pennsylvania. Let us follow the salient stages of this development to the final decision.

Jones had not been wholly just in assaying the School in 1882 as "staid, solid and conservative." The last it undoubtedly was; but the Christian Theism of gracious, venerable President Livermore was warmly humane and, within limits, intellectually hospitable. In comparison with contemporary seminaries, even the more liberal, the School was a pioneer in several respects. We have already noted the admission of women in 1868 and Livermore's inclusion of the tenets of non-Christian religions in his earliest lectures. Only Paris and Geneva antedated the School in establishing a chair of ethnic religions (1879), and it was one of the organizers of the American Lectures on the History of Religions, through which the most eminent scholars of Europe and America in this subject came in successive years to the School for a week of brilliant lectures. From the time that Parker pressed the application of Jesus' teachings to social conditions in the 1840's and 1850's, various phases – Abolition, the temperance movement, the humane treatment of criminals and the insane, the condition of the local prisons, the relief of poverty and unemployment – received constant and careful attention in conferences and lectures, long before Bliss, Gladden, Herron, and Rauschenbusch introduced these subjects into the more conservative seminaries. In 1881 regular lectures on "charities and corrective methods" were begun by Edward Everett Hale, and the interest shown by the students resulted in the endowment of the Adin Ballou Lectures in Christian Sociology (1892) and the Caleb Brewster Hackley chair of sociology (1895), the first occupant of which was Rev. Nicholas Paine Gilman, editor of *The New World*.

In the field of Biblical study "probably no theological faculty in the world enjoyed such untrammeled freedom." In Old Testament, Professors G. R. Freeman (1890-98), Henry Preserved Smith (1907-13) – an eminent Presbyterian scholar dismissed by Lane Seminary – Theophile J. Meek (1918-22) made their students acquainted with the latest researches and most radical theories. In New Testament, Professor Cary (1862-1905), with ripe scholarship – as his *The Synoptic Gospels* (1900) attests – kept the students abreast of the rapid progress of criticism and documentary discoveries; while Professors Francis A. Christie (1893-1924) and Clayton R. Bowen (1905-34) presented the views of [Guillaume] Baldensperger, [Bernhard] Weiss, [Adolf von] Harnack, [Wilhelm] Bousset, [Alfred] Loisy, [Albert] Schweitzer, which disturbed traditional positions after 1888. In the psychology and philosophy of religion, Professors Livermore, James T. Bixby (1879-83), Thomas H. Hill (1881-91), Henry H. Barber (1884-1904), Frank C. Doan (1904-13) had presented the thought of [Sir William] Hamilton, Spencer, [John Stuart] Mill, Huxley, Fiske, [Ernst] Haeckel, [Edward] Caird, T. H. Green, [James] Martineau, [Hermann] Lotze, [Gustav] Fechner, [Henri] Bergson, [William] James, [Wilhelm] Wundt to the minds of the students, whose freedom of speculation and discussion was probably unequaled in any seminary in the land.

Although President Southworth was a man of scholarly attainments in theology and literature, he came to his duties fresh from the Western secretaryships and had acquired very practical ideas on the kind of training a modern liberal minister needed, not only in the conventional theological disciplines, but in general literary culture, religious education, and preaching. An energetic campaign of recruitment was launched; scholarly effort was stimulated by the Robert H. Billings endowment for prizes and the Harriet Otis Crufts Fellowship for study abroad (1895). Increased instruction in preaching was augmented by professional training in voice and expressional techniques. A course in religious education not only for the men students but to prepare young women for that work was introduced, and a summer institute largely devoted to work with the youth of the church was held from 1908 to 1912. Social problems and institutions were thoroughly handled by Professor Gilman, under whose guidance the senior class spent three weeks in one of the great cities, visiting and studying typical social agencies and activities. These curriculum provisions for the students' training were supplemented by the cultural offerings in music and drama available at nearby Allegheny College and the interesting procession of denominational officials, visiting alumni, and scholarly lecturers who occupied the guest suite in Divinity Hall and ate with the students in the stately refectory in Hunnewell Hall or played tennis on its adjacent courts or handball in its gymnasium. Moreover, the location of the faculty homes on or near the campus, with their unlimited hospitality, gave added opportunity for close and cordial relations between students and teachers. It would seem that the utmost had been done to attract college graduates to the School and the ministry. Yet few came!

Another attempt to move the School to Chicago was made in 1911, in the confidence that with Morton D. Hull and Dean Fenn on the board the resistance of the local trustees would be overcome – a futile hope! Again President Southworth accepted the reverse and faithfully applied himself to strengthening the faculty. Rev. Robert J. Hutcheon of Toronto, Canada, was appointed to the chair of psychology and philosophy of religion, from which Professor Doan had resigned. Rev. Anna Garlin Spencer, Unitarian minister, Ethical leader, and a sociologist of national reputation, became professor of social ethics (1913-18), the chair vacated by the death of Professor Gilman in 1912. To advertise the School's broad and progressive spirit, two faculty symposia were published: *Religion and Life* (1909) and *Theological Study Today* (1921). To illustrate the high and liberal scholarship standards of the faculty, Professor Bowen published his able critical study of *The Resurrection in the New Testament* (1911), while Professor Francis A. Christie's articles on Arminianism in New England and Catholic social action in Europe and this country attracted wide attention. In 1914, on the initiative of Professor Anna Garlin Spencer, the experiment was tried of transporting the collegiate student body to Chicago for the summer term of the University Divinity School. The broadened outlook and intellectual stimulus thus afforded resulted in the Chicago summer term being made a permanent feature of the School curriculum, requiring the purchase (1921) of a large residence near the campus (now Meadville House) for dormitory, social, and office purposes – the camel's nose in the tent!

The results of this experiment were so favorable, and the proportion of alumni trustees on the board was so large, that the time seemed propitious for the introduction of a resolution favoring the removal of the School and authorizing a canvass of the comparative advantages of Ann Arbor, Michigan; Cleveland, Ohio; and Ithaca, New York, as well as Chicago. This decision was the signal for a sharp legal battle in the Supreme Court of Pennsylvania, which resulted in a decision – as predicted long before by Shorey – that the trustees, as directors of a corporation, had the right to determine where its work (that is, the fulfillment of the purposes of its endowments) could best be performed, provided the legal residence of the corporation remained in Pennsylvania subject to the oversight of its Supreme Court. With the fear of the forfeiture of any endowments thus allayed, the board proceeded in February, 1926, to order the removal of the School to Chicago, a choice indicated by the predilections of President Southworth, Secretary Reese, and others of the trustees – who were also influenced by the offers of generous financial assistance from Morton D. Hull. Arrangements rapidly proceeded to put the resolution into effect; a lot and two more large residences in Chicago were purchased; the School's property in Meadville was sold, and the School left its beautiful campus hilltop, hallowed by over seven decades of precious personal and spiritual memories, to open the following September in its new home at the Unitarian "four corners" of Woodlawn Avenue and East Fifty-seventh Street, Chicago.

The new location had many advantages, one of which was the opportunity of developing a system of graded field work for the students in the liberal churches and the settlement houses of Chicago. A hearty welcome was extended the School by the Divinity School faculty, whose Dean was then Shailer Mathews. The pressing need of an academic building necessitated a financial campaign, which was conducted by President Southworth's successor, Rev. Sydney B. Snow (1929-44), and brought the School almost $400,000 from Unitarians throughout the country. Southworth, Hull, and Fenn, to whose invincible faith and indefatigable efforts the removal was chiefly due, had the pleasure of taking part in the dedication of the new Academic Building in February, 1932. Coincident with its erection, an exceptionally imposing new church and parish house in Early English Gothic had been given the First Unitarian Society by Morton D. Hull, the Memorial Chapel of 1897 being preserved and allotted to the use of the Meadville School for daily Vespers.

Art and Religion in the New Church

The stately architecture of the new sanctuary provided Rev. Von Ogden Vogt, who succeeded Rev. W. Hanson Pulsford (1901-23), with a worthy setting the enriched and modernized liturgical worship he had advocated in *Art and Religion* (1921). For many years its author, who began his career in the Congregational ministry, had deplored the aesthetic poverty of American Protestant churches of the Puritan lineage, in respect to both their architecture and their forms of worship. Deeply sensitive to the beautiful in art and to the ceremonial aspects of religion, Vogt had made a thorough study of the psychology and historic rites of religion, as well as of its architecture and symbolism. This study bore fruit in the conviction that "Chicago needs a great church of liberal thought ... It is the poorest churched big city in the world ... No other big city has so few impressive church buildings." Such a "civic cathedral" as he envisaged should have "no creed except to seek and serve truth, goodness and beauty." It should house, at different hours on Sunday, all forms of worship – "ritualistic, improved American [Protestant], popular evangelistic; also civic forum meetings and dramatic, musical, pictorial presentations." On weekdays one would find within its walls religious-education classes, health guilds, cultural study, and pastoral ministrations. The nation's work life – farming, the industries, transportation – and the realms of nature and science should be appropriately symbolized and glorified by murals, statues, mosaics. To preserve the sentiment and sanctity connoted in the contiguity of graveyards with churches in New England and the Old World, this "civic cathedral" should contain a burial crypt for those who might desire to rest forever after death near the spot where they worshipped in life. The building should also contain accommodations for the activities of community and labor organizations, in keeping with the prophetic social message of its pulpit.

Art and Religion (second edition, 1948) – later amplified and illustrated in *Modern Worship* (1927), *Cult and Culture* (1951) – was acclaimed at once as a fresh interpretation and a revitalization of the function of the arts in and for the religious experience, hence a brave stimulus to creativity on the part of both the liturgist and the architect. The latter, Denison B. Hull, muted the traditional Protestant emphasis on preaching by making the altar the chancel focus. Mosaic symbols bordered the marble reredos and appeared in a frieze above the piers of the nave. A columbarium was provided in the crypt. The symmetry of a graceful stone spire, two hundred feet in height, was added to the cluster of Gothic towers that give one of the most liberal and progressive universities in the world the semblance of medieval Oxford. *Ordinaries of Worship*, containing much original and beautiful liturgical material expressive of modern thought and life, was printed; new musical settings for such traditional elements of the liturgy as the introits and versicles were composed by Organist Robert L. Sanders.

Interest in the experiment spread quickly in many Protestant denominations, possibly because it was hoped that more ritual would raise Protestant church attendance to the Catholic churches' plenitude, possibly also because radical prophetic preaching was boring complacent Protestants. Many, of course, recognized the functional truth in Vogt's suggestions, and his book was acclaimed as "the classic expression of the philosophy behind the rebirth of the church arts in America." The author was invited to lecture in several Protestant seminaries and to give a series of Lowell Lectures. In the construction or reconstruction of scores of church buildings he has been a consultant or an arbiter, as "the acknowledged Nestor of the movement for the Church Beautiful." The new momentum of the Unitarian Religious Arts Guild owes much to his inspiration.

To his church, Morton D. Hull left not only a large endowment but a legacy of twenty-seven years of disinterested and distinguished public service, the thorough integrity and high intelligence of which was so generally acknowledged that for several terms of his re-election to Congress as representative of his district the Democratic party opposed no candidate of its own. Through his substantial support of the League of Nations Association, he carried on Judge Shorey's earlier interest in World Peace and the Hague Tribunal. These precedents have been continued in the active participation of the church and its present minister, Rev. Leslie T. Pennington, in the United Nations Association and in local community problems, particularly in the integration of Negroes in the church membership and the community and interracial co-operation in the maintenance of neighborhood standards. Moreover, through the excellence of the religious-education and adolescent-youth programs, under the direction of Dr. Edna Acheson, as well as the free and stimulating discussions of the Channing Club for campus folk, the University constituency has been increasingly responsive to the message of Free Religion.

In both developments just narrated – the removal of the Meadville School to Chicago and the colligation of the vision of Von Ogden Vogt with the far-sighted and generous loyalty of Morton D. Hull – Curtis W. Reese, Secretary of the Western Conference since 1919, had rendered unobtrusive but patently effective service. The further debt of the Conference and the denomination to his religious statesmanship and conciliative spirit, particularly during the ominous tensions of the controversy over religious Humanism, will be disclosed in the next chapter.

CHAPTER FOURTEEN

Western Freedom for Religious Humanism

My concern is for Humanism as a philosophy of life – in sharp contrast with opposing schools of thought – able to challenge the traditional philosophies and ethnic religions, having a program covering all aspects of human well-being, and aiming at the complete possession of the territory of the human spirit.

Curtis W. Reese

THE LOSS OF ENTHUSIASM AND MOMENTUM, to say nothing of physical assets and community influence, that results through tardy, inept organization has been – as our survey has plainly disclosed – a major handicap of Western Unitarianism. It has traditionally been difficult to organize radical religious individualism, but the Western Conference has succeeded in doing so for a longer period and on a larger scale than any other experiment of the sort in either this country or Europe. On the other hand, too much institutionalization of any religious inspiration, particularly that of free religion, risks quenching spontaneity and halting progress either through complacent relaxation or through discreet conformity. For both reasons the pace of Unitarian expansion during the decade before the First World War was slackening ominously. Apart from outposts of the Scandinavian Mission in Montana (Red Lodge, 1913) and Wisconsin (The Danish-Norwegian Free Church of Superior, 1911), only two churches were founded in the West between 1910 and 1920; The First Unitarian Society of Dayton, Ohio (1910), by Secretary E. C. Smith's initiative; and the First Unitarian Church of Canton, Ohio (1916) – but the latter soon expired! To some extent, no doubt, this lethargy was due to the First World War; to a greater extent it can be explained by the Association's policy of centering missionary effort in large cities and university

238

centers. Since most of them already had Unitarian churches, further possibilities seemed limited after the Unitarian Church of Urbana, Illinois, had been founded in 1907 by a faculty group headed by Professors Morgan Brooks and Thomas K. Oliver of the University of Illinois.

At Lincoln, Nebraska, seat of the state university, All Souls Unitarian Church, which had limped along for ten years by the aid of professors' lectures and the neighborly ministrations of Rev. Newton Mann from Omaha, responded admirably to the leadership of Rev. Arthur L. Weatherly (1908-20, 1929-42). With a group of its members, he organized the Initiative and Referendum League, which succeeded in writing its reform into the new state constitution. To their initiative was due also a workingmen's compensation law and the formation of the Nebraska Peace Society, as delegates of which Weatherly and C. A. Sorenson were invited by Henry Ford to join his Peace Ship company in 1915. The city of Lincoln is also under obligations to Weatherly and All Souls Church for spearheading the organization of the Urban League, the Charity and Child Welfare Societies, the Maternal Health Clinic, the Lincoln City Club, the Chamber of Commerce, and the Lincoln General Hospital. Weatherly's pioneering in such forms of social action has been emulated by his successors, Rev. Carl A. Storm (1942-47) and Rev. Philip Schug (1947-52); the latter's work in Lincoln, however, can never surpass in importance the crucial assistance he rendered, while minister in Urbana, Illinois (1943-47), to Mrs. Vashti McCollum in her valiant and successful campaign to secure a decision from the U. S. Supreme Court forbidding religious education in public schools.

Further evidence that the creative impulse of free religion had not atrophied, in spite of the apparent inanition of official missionary zeal, is afforded by the founding of the Peoples Church on Chicago's north side in 1912 by a young man from Michigan, Preston Bradley, who from early youth had wanted to be a preacher and had come to the great city to study the art of public speaking. The Presbytery of Chicago licensed him for the ministry of the Church of Providence but presently reversed its action because of doctrinal irregularities and Bradley's tendency to preach on such secular subjects as "Life Values,"

"Education," "Science" – and to quote Emerson, David Swing, Robert Ingersoll, and other non-Calvinist sages! Followed by the great majority of his congregation, Bradley organized a creed-less church around a Declaration of Principles as liberal as the *"Unity* men" themselves could have composed:

The purpose of the church is to deal with the supreme things in human life as measured by the rational conclusions of science and history. It is essentially religious, not in the traditional but in the scientific and ethical sense of the word. It regards religion as spiritual energy directing itself toward the enrichment of the individual life and the perfection of the social order. This church assumes the right of everyone to think his or her own thoughts and expects the greatest progress to follow from entire intellectual liberty and perfect freedom of judgment. It welcomes to its membership all who wish to cooperate in making a world which shall be enlightened by knowledge, guided by reason and animated by good will.

Services were begun in Arcola Hall on North Clark Street, then moved to larger and larger theaters as attendance increased. Among the early recruits were about thirty former members of the Peoples Church of Rev. Hiram W. Thomas – including Mrs. Thomas herself – which had expired after several ministries, Dr. Frank Crane's among them, and a migration from downtown McVickers Theatre to Woodlawn Masonic Temple on the south side. Former members of Robert Collyer's congregation also rallied to the new movement, whose strength steadily increased until in 1926 the present imposing and spacious church was erected on Lawrence Avenue.

In 1924 Bradley began broadcasting his entire Sunday-morning service, thus adding to the thousands who attended the two services on Sunday a radio congregation of many hundreds of thousands. Not only is this radio ministry the largest in the Midwest in number of hearers, but it is the oldest in the United States.

Preston Bradley has continued and extended the liberal message and influence of Collyer and Thomas not only by the spoken and written word but by civic service as well. Since 1924 he has been a member of the board of trustees of the Chicago Public Library and chairman of its book committee for almost as long. His chairmanship of the faculty committee of the State Normal School board recalls the contributions of Jesse W. Fell; while Unitarian literary traditions are worthily perpetuated in his Wednesday-evening book lectures at the church – the most largely attended events of their kind in the Midwest.

In golden letters on the great proscenium of the Peoples Church are inscribed in the words of Channing:

Live a life of Faith and Hope
Believe in the mighty power of Truth and Love

The inscription denotes not only the dynamic liberalism preached in the pulpit beneath it, but the profound appreciation felt by Dr. Bradley for the Unitarian heritage. As was Collyer, he is warmly welcomed by the Unitarians of Ulster and Britain, as well as by the Dutch, Danish, Norwegian, Czechoslovakian, and Transylvanian members of the International Association of Free Christian and Other Religious Liberals. On the other hand, his broad sympathies and genial spirit make him a welcome guest in many liberal Congregational, Methodist, and even Presbyterian churches in the Midwest.

Up to 1923 the Peoples Church had remained unaffiliated with any denomination. To the out-reaching policies of the new Secretary of the Conference, Curtis W. Reese, were due the acceptance by Preston Bradley of Unitarian ministerial fellowship and the connection of his church with the Conference and the A.U.A. in 1923. Similar action was taken in 1928 by the Peoples Church of Cedar Rapids, Iowa, which had started in 1869 as a Universalist congregation. Its example was followed by the Peoples Liberal Church of Englewood on Chicago's south side, which, under the name of Stewart Avenue Universalist Church, through the forty-four-year ministry of Rev. Rufus A. White, adhered to the Fraternity of Liberal Churches headed by Hiram W. Thomas and Jenkin Lloyd Jones. Unitarian affiliation, therefore, commencing with the Chicago Unitarian Conference (1938) and culminating, during the ministry of Rev. Donald Harrington (1939-44), with the Conference and the A.U.A., came logically and easily for the church. With A.U.A. aid, it then proliferated (1942) in the suburban Beverly Unitarian Fellowship.

Other accessions that attested the comprehensive vision and executive tact of Secretary Reese were that of St. John's Church in Cincinnati (1923), a root of the old Protestantische Bund, whose ministers, Rev. Hugo G. Eisenlohr (1884-1931) and Rev. Julius F. Krolfifer (1931 on), loyally oriented the German-American congregation in its new associations; that of the Westermann Memorial Church of Louisville, Kentucky (1903), which became the Clifton Unitarian Church in 1922 during the ministry of Rev. G. Theodore Hempelmann (1911-28, 1935 on); that of the Church of the Christian Union in Rockford, Illinois, whose ministry Rev. Thomas Kerr, the comrade of the "*Unity* men," had handed on to Rev. Charles P. Connolly (1913-42), under whom the church became Unitarian in 1928; that of the Independent Religious Society of Chicago, which came into the Conference in 1922 during the leadership of the ex-Presbyterian minister, M. M. Mangasarian. Moreover, the feathers ruffled by the Western Issue having been smoothed down, Reese succeeded in doing what Jones had dreamed of – the reception of the leader of the Chicago Ethical Society into Unitarian ministerial fellowship by ordination in 1924.

Reese's transit from the Baptist to the Unitarian fellowship was largely due to the effect of the Higher Criticism of the Bible upon the orthodox teachings of his seminary, the Southern Baptist at Louisville, Kentucky. His record of constructive social action as Unitarian minister in Alton, Illinois (1913-15), on behalf of municipal law enforcement, and in Des Moines, Iowa (1915-19), on behalf of the state's first housing law – for the enforcement of which he became a state commissioner – was prophetic of the energy with which he proceeded, when elected Secretary of the Conference in 1919, to cope with the problems of a stagnant if not declining movement, about a fifth of whose pulpits were vacant. Prophetic also of the widening horizons of the Conference during the successive phases of his connection with it – the Secretary (1919-30), Executive Director (1941-43), President (1938 on) – was the action of the annual meeting at Minneapolis in 1920, simplifying the statement of purpose in its revised constitution:

The object of the Western Unitarian Conference is to foster religion through the organization and support of liberal churches within the limits of the Conference, and to transact business pertaining to the general interest of the societies connected therewith.

Though the battle-scarred standard of 1886, "Truth, Righteousness and Love," was thus relegated to the rotunda beside its predecessor of 1875, "the Kingdom of God," there was no alteration of the free spirit of the Conference:

> Our interpretation of religion has long been beyond Christianity and beyond any historic religion. We cut loose from no history that has contributed to our growth but we seek to make new history that will contribute to the growth of the future. We feel most at home in territory where the winds of the spirit move from many directions.

To just such resolute open-mindedness and equanimity the Conference had been conditioned by the experience of seven decades. Hence, when the low- and high-pressure areas of Theism and Humanism met on its plateau in 1920, there was little acrimony in the encounter and less danger of a break in the ranks – although the issue of Humanism challenged tradition and attracted outside attention to a far greater degree than had the Ethical Basis of 1886.

Religious Humanism

Non-Theistic views had been broached in Unitarian circles for many years before the conservatives brought them into public controversy. Their compost had for the most part been the Pragmatism of William James and of F. S. C. Schiller, although Comte's Positivism and the agnostic, humanitarian liberalism of John Morley, [C. H.] Tyndall, W. K. Clifford were also sources of inspiration. A disciple of James in the chair of the psychology and philosophy of religion at the Meadville School, Professor Frank C. Doan (1904-13), persuaded many of his students who eventually passed into the Unitarian ministry – including J. A. C. F. Auer, later of the Harvard Divinity School faculty and Charles H. Lyttle, later of the faculty of Meadville – of the unreality of the concept of an omnipotent, omniscient Deity, which Doan replaced by the Cosmic Humanism expounded in his *Religion and the Modern Mind* (1909). As early as 1916, Lyttle delivered a lecture at Cooper Institute in New York City on "Humanism, America's Real Religion." Doan's thought, reinforced by Schiller's *Studies in Humanism* and by Professor F. G. Peabody's writings on the social gospel, augmented convictions already maturing in the mind of Rev. Curtis W. Reese, then at Des Moines, Iowa, which he embodied in a sermon tract, "A Democratic View of Religion" (1916), and distributed to delegates of the Western Unitarian Conference meeting in his church – one of whom was Rev. John H. Dietrich of Minneapolis. Dietrich, who had been excommunicated by the Dutch Reformed Classis of Pittsburgh, Pennsylvania, became a Unitarian minister in Spokane, Washington. By the road of ethical Theism, comparative religion, Spencer, Huxley, the publications of the Rationalist Press Association of London, the lectures of Frederic Harrison and Frederick J. Gould on the Religion of Humanity, Dietrich arrived at what he regarded as a new synthesis of the best in all these and other similar points of view: non-Theist, scientific, religious Humanism: "a vision of what life might be upon this planet if all our intelligence were brought to bear upon its improvement" and "a faith that this vision may be realized through the responsibility and effort of men themselves." Called to the ministry of the Unitarian church in Minneapolis in 1916, he unequivocally announced his intention of shifting "the emphasis of thought from the traditional to the scientific, from the theological to the historical, from the supernatural to the natural," in the hope that the Society might better "serve as a kind of dynamo to generate power and enthusiasm to cope with existing evils and to work for the ideal good."

In the case of Dietrich, who resolutely opposed war in 1916, and of other Humanists who, like him, regarded war as the apogee of inhumanity and folly, the general invocation of divine sanction and support for the battling causes and armies by the Theists of the various nations strengthened their Humanist convictions, since traditional Theism so readily served human enmity and destruction. In spite of Dietrich's pacifism and Humanism, increasing congregations soon required the abandonment of the old church building for a large downtown theater.

Though Minneapolis Unitarians accepted Dietrich's radicalism with little opposition, their Eastern brethren were startled

by an address given at the Harvard Summer School of Theology
in July, 1920, by Secretary Reese:

> In the past, the basic content of most religions had been the submission
> of persons to supernatural agencies … There was submission from below
> and control from above. The monarchic view of religion rose to its noblest
> height in the expression "Thy will be done." [But] the realm of the divine
> is now subject to investigation … Liberalism is now building a religion that
> would not be shaken if the old thought of God is outgrown. With this must
> go most of the nomenclature and many of the forms of worship.

Reese ended his remarks with a Humanist aspiration: "To know
oneself as inherently worthful; to find fullest self-expression in the
noblest human service, and consciously to become a co-worker
with cosmic processes which human minds have associated with
their noblest thought of God, is spiritual experience deep and
abiding."

But his critics did not think so! One of them felt that
"Reese came perilously near saying he did not believe in God
[yet] belief in God is the only sure foundation for any religion." To Rev. Augustus P. Reccord of Detroit, Michigan,
Reese's remarks revealed "a condition of spiritual poverty
that is almost disheartening" – and augured no good for the
Layman's League's campaign for three million dollars! True to
form, the Meadville School was so alarmed that it summoned a
Presbyterian theologian from the Union Theological Seminary
to assure the autumn convocation that the new age, far from
being Humanistic, would worship a God who is personal,
austere, majestic, yet responsive to mystical intercourse with
his worshippers.

By a curious coincidence the editor of the *Register*, Rev.
Albert C. Dieffenbach, was as hospitable to the Humanist view
as his predecessor, Rev. Samuel J. Barrows, had been toward
the Ethical Basis thirty years before. In a crisp editorial on "A
Theological Flurry," Dieffenbach rejoiced that "we are cutting
down on the primacy of adoration and increasing the necessity for cooperation … placing less responsibility on God and
more on our own self-dependent minds and wills." Dieffenbach
reminded the Theists that Reese's position was virtually that
of the Unitarian poet William Henry Carruth, whose famous
"Each in his own tongue" they so greatly admired and often

quoted. In another editorial a month later, he took occasion to remark that "the Western Unitarian Conference was never more ably directed than it is today by Mr. Reese."

With such encouragement, Reese felt justified in asking Dietrich to follow Rev. Earl F. Cook's address on "The Outlook for Industry" at the Western Conference session in Chicago, May 16, 1921, with one on "The Outlook for Religion." Unlike the judicial, optative style of Reese, Dietrich spoke boldly, almost peremptorily. In his opinion the religion of the future would be strictly naturalistic, not supernatural – Humanist, not Theist.

Perhaps the political perturbations of the time – the disappointment over the Versailles Treaty, the Senate's desertion of the League of Nations, the successes of atheistic Russian Communism – set folks' nerves on edge. In any case, a heated controversy of denominational and extra-denominational dimensions flared up. Rev. George A. Dodson, professor of philosophy in Washington University, an Absolute Idealist, resented Dietrich's insistence that "Theism must be given up, that the thought of God will have to go and that the future belongs to non-Theistic Humanism." He protested to Secretary Reese that "such addresses ought not to be given under circumstances in which they would naturally be regarded as representative." Was this the A. Mitchell Palmer influence? Reese defended programming Dietrich on the ground that the Conference stood for liberty. To Dodson, whose provenance was Eastern, such a stand for liberty was impermissible in an official "whose business was largely that of securing ministers for churches." These views Dodson took the liberty of expressing in a letter to the *Christian Register* under the caption "Clear Thinking or Death" – the last word meaning, of course, the imminent demise of a Unitarianism that tolerated such radicalism! Dodson claimed that "it now seems clear that we must avow our faith in God even if that faith may remind us of a creed." Alluding to a campaign for missionary funds by the Unitarian Laymen's League "to promote the worship of God and the love and service of mankind in the spirit of Jesus," Dodson wondered "how much money Unitarian laymen will give to promote the view that Jesus was under the spell of a pathetic delusion when he spoke of his communion with God." It may be observed, however, that the laymen excelled the minister in their fidelity to freedom – or in their approval of Humanism – for the campaign was gratifyingly successful!

During the summer of 1921, the *Register* printed many letters *pro* and *con* Dietrich's position from agitated theologians. Rev. Richard W. Boynton, Unitarian minister in Buffalo, New York, and professor of philosophy at the city's university, together with Rev. Robert S. Loring, Unitarian minister at Milwaukee, Wisconsin, agreed in a desire for "a variety of theological belief, even reverent agnosticism," though they themselves found Theism a "better support for programmes of individual and social reform than anything that Pragmatism has to offer." Rev. Walter S. Swisher of Wellesley Hills, Massachusetts, called Dodson's attention to the Humanist implications of *The Finality of the Christian Religion* (1906), by Professor George B. Foster of the University of Chicago's Divinity School.

At the opposite pole of such tolerance stood a recent convert to Unitarianism from Roman Catholicism, Rev. William Laurence Sullivan. Formerly a Preceptor at the College of the Paulist Fathers in Georgetown, Sullivan had received a thorough training in scholastic theology and pulpit eloquence. He had refused to sign the anti-Modernist oath imposed by Pius X upon all Catholic teachers in 1907. Rev. Minot Simons rescued him from poverty and illness in Cleveland, Ohio, and persuaded him to continue his ministerial vocation – for which his sympathetic personality, rich intellectual culture, and impressive pulpit artistry so well fitted him – in the Unitarian body. These gifts advanced him quickly from the ministry of the Unitarian church in Schenectady, New York, to that of All Souls in New York City. Sullivan combined in his preaching the moral theology of James Martineau with the rapt, uplifted, oracular solemnity of John Henry Newman. Like both these great Theists, Sullivan was predominantly concerned with personal righteousness and its transcendental pietism rather than with the militant social meliorism of Reese, Dietrich, and most of the other Humanists. This concern with the individual's inner moral struggles and their traditional Theistic *morale* concepts, as well as Sullivan's exceptional pulpit power and popularity, led the Unitarian Laymen's League – whose post-war financial opulence made possible the establishment of a Midwest office in Chicago (1921) – to appoint Sullivan as their Missionary at Large (1922-24).

Long schooling in the classic orthodox thesis that all heresy is mere conceit and superficiality betrayed Sullivan into rushing to Dodson's support in a *Register* article, "God, No-God, Half-God," replete with sarcastic aspersions on Dietrich's "romantic atheism" and Doan's "evolving God," together with artful colligations of Reese's "religion of democracy" with the equalitarian delusions of "Ivan Ivanovitch." Reese's objective comment that while "Theism is philosophically possible it is not religiously necessary" did not halt Dodson's and Sullivan's plan to submit to the forthcoming National Conference meeting in Detroit an "affirmation of what most Unitarians believe" that would rhyme with the Laymen's League's assurances that "we worship the Living God, our Father and our Friend." Sunderland's old ally, Rev. Joseph H. Crooker, reminded *Register* readers, however, that considering the congregational autonomy of the denomination it would not be feasible to pass anything more than a simple descriptive statement to the effect that "our churches do now as in the past stand for faith in God, for hope of eternal life, for love of Jesus." Then "all ministers who fail at these points will go where they belong." For Rev. W. A. Vrooman this meant a well-deserved extrusion from Unitarian churches: "Unitarians who cease to believe in God in the Theistic sense have no right to propagate a philosophy of agnosticism or atheism under the protection of historic names."

How reminiscent are all these theological denunciations, innuendos, and creedal projects "of old unhappy, far-off things and battles long ago"! Had Unitarians learned nothing and forgotten everything?

The answer to this challenge came, *first*, in the failure of the Dodson-Sullivan creedal plan at the National Conference at Detroit in October, 1921; *second*, in the rapid, forthright, and unchecked growth of Humanism among Unitarians, especially of the Western Conference, from 1921 on; *third*, in the election to the presidency of the American Unitarian Association of Rev. Frederick May Eliot, Unitarian minister in St. Paul, Minnesota, from 1917 to 1937. Though a Theist, he was nevertheless a staunch advocate of the Western Conference principles; intellectual freedom, fellowship in the spirit, the activation of religion in character and service.

The National Conference, Detroit, 1921

While we are waiting for the start of the evening session of the Conference on Wednesday, October 5 – when Rev. Dilworth R. Lupton of Cleveland, Ohio, Dietrich, and Sullivan are to give their versions of "The Faith That Is In Us" – it is interesting to reflect how logical it is that within the Western Conference, of all church organizations in the world, Humanist religion should have first been freely broached and sympathetically considered. Had not the pioneers – Pierpont, Clarke, Hosmer, Eliot – preached the dignity of human intelligence, its right to freedom and growth, the obligation of true Christians to do all in their power to create a more just, brighter social order? Had not the doctrinal elements of Christianity been progressively minimized since 1854? Was not Emerson's summons to self-reliance and non-conformity audible in Humanism? Had not the synthesis of Transcendentalism and Evolution in immanental Theism predisposed to Humanism? Was not the Ethical Basis a propaedeutic of Humanism? When Gannett, in his memorable sermon on "Incarnation," hailed all men as Immanuel Messiahs, born to make the good things better and the worst good, did he not still further open the trail for Humanism's advent? When Jones spoke on "Religion From the Near End" to the Berry Street Conference in 1886, asserting the primacy and centrality of the natural, homely, human values and idioms in genuine religion, and consenting that his own poetic Theism should be deemed preferential, not essential, was he very far from the Humanist position? By their acknowledgement of the wisdom and nobility of Buddha's teachings, did not Conway, Hosmer, Blake, and Jones predispose Western Unitarians favorably toward non-Theistic Humanism?

Dietrich's presentation of the faith in him was made in simple, direct terms:

We, as Unitarians, have faith that the pain and suffering, the poverty and misery, the hatred and strife, the ignorance and squalor … that afflict humanity can be overcome; that a new order can be introduced which shall bring peace, security and happiness to the whole of mankind. [But] this grand faith which must be the strength of humanity, the popular religion has not given us and apparently has no aim of giving us. Its dream of a perfect social order has its accomplishment somewhere else. The kind of world we live in depends not upon some God outside of man but upon man himself, or, as some of us would put it, the God that dwells in humanity. Neither can we believe any longer in some supreme Cosmic Principle that is working inevitably along lines of progress toward a better era regardless of what man does or fails to do. In fact we believe that such a faith is a menace to the world as it teaches men to depend on God for what they should do themselves. Let men hold their idea of God if they will; but we insist that whatever God does, he does *through* men and not *for* men.

The majority of the Conference program committee were for Theism, but they made a fatal mistake in entrusting its case to Sullivan rather than to Dodson. For at a time when the younger Unitarians, at least, were thinking of the exigent social problems of the hour – disarmament, the Hoover Commission's work in feeding European children, America's participation in attacks on the Russian Revolution, Henry Cabot Lodge's sabotage of Wilson's idealism, the current depression – Sullivan, after disparaging the denominational aversion to anything resembling a creed, proceeded to argue academically for a supranatural source for the Moral Law implicit in conscience:

Man is under a law which he has got to obey … a law that prescribes right for souls must come from a source that has the right and authority to command souls, therefore is itself *at least* a Soul. It is the Living God before whom I shall stand, and you; and every lie will be chastised and every deliberate wrong shall receive its meed, as it ought and must!

Without this basic truth, Sullivan insisted, speeches about democracy were more or less amateur and those about social righteousness more or less dilettante! Then, with increasingly fervid rhetoric, he went on to attack Dietrich, in thinly veiled phrases, as a theological upstart and revolutionist.

Some of the delegates were so affected by Sullivan's eloquence that the move to draft him as Missionary at Large began that very night! But the large majority of the audience were not satisfied with his conventional emphasis on personal righteousness and its naïve metaphysics and total neglect of social problems and reforms. Sullivan, though personally tolerant and lovable, seemed to them an embodiment of medieval authoritarianism, which had ever exploited the guilt complex and immemorially represented poverty, ignorance, slavery, and war as God's will and way of punishment for sin and probation for heaven; which had obstructed scientific inquiry, condemned religious freedom and heretics – even as Sullivan had scolded Dietrich.

So adverse, indeed, was the reaction of the delegates that the Dodson-Sullivan resolution committing Unitarianism to Theism was not even presented at the business session the next day.

The Growth and Recognition of Humanism (1921-37)

The President of the American Unitarian Association during the first quarter of the century was Rev. Samuel A. Eliot. Though inclined, by the circumstances of his birth and education, to conservative views, yet while a minister in Denver, Colorado (1889-93), he had held aloof from partisanship during the Western Issue, consistently holding and pleading that congregational autonomy should be respected and trusted. Such doctrinal and administrative policies he continued during the twenty years of his A.U.A. presidency. Hence he placed no obstacles in the way of the growth of Humanism. Subventions were generously granted to any needy church, regardless of its theological climate, provided only that its emphasis and work were spiritual and ethical, its minister earnest and effective. This policy was carried on by his successor, Rev. Louis C. Cornish (1927-37). There were, to be sure, Unitarian churches and Conference programs which were closed to Humanists; Dietrich, for instance, was never invited to give the Anniversary Sermon of the A.U.A. (but neither was Theodore Parker nor Jenkin Lloyd Jones) – though Sullivan was bidden twice! Since Chicago, with Reese at Conference headquarters and [A. E.] Haydon at the University, seemed a hotbed of Humanism, Sullivan opposed the removal of the Meadville School thither. It should be noted that the school gave honorary doctorates in divinity to Reese in 1927 and Dietrich in 1932, a significant victory for freedom, since Jones had been denied all such academic and sermonic honors by his alma mater.

This progress was achieved not only by Secretary Reese's scrupulous fidelity to congregational principles in assisting Western churches to secure ministers theologically harmonious, but by the less iconoclastic and more positive tone of the presentations of Humanism that issued from the press after 1921. This was especially true of M. C. Otto's *Things and Ideals* (1924) and *Natural Laws and Human Hopes* (1926), both of which were written in a gracious, sympathetic style and spirit which may partly account for the early bent of the Unitarian church in Madison, Wisconsin, toward Humanism, since Otto was on the University faculty there. His literary mellowness was followed by the philosophic objectivity of Reese's *Humanism* (1926), which proved to be the reveille for two decades of accelerating activity in publication and organization. Dietrich began his Humanist Pulpit series of sermon tracts in 1927. *The New Humanist*, conducted by a group of Unitarian ministers – Harold Buschman, Edwin H. Wilson, Raymond B. Bragg, former students of Professor Haydon – made its appearance the same year, with the Humanist Press Association (1928) as its financial sponsor. In 1927, also, the Open Court Publishing Company issued *Humanist Sermons*, edited and prefaced by Reese with interestingly diverse contributions by John Haynes Holmes, C. H. Lyttle, E. S. Hodgin, A. W. Slaten, J. H. Dietrich, Earl F. Cook, L. M. Birkhead, E. M. Cosgrove, E. Caldecott, S. S. Robins, F. M. Eliot, J. H. Hart, F. S. C. Wicks, F. C. Doan, A. L. Weatherly, A. E. Haydon. Reese's Preface underscores the general attitude:

> The Humanist is keenly conscious of the present [world] situation. He feels that personal and social values should speed ahead ... He finds no compensation in unfolding cosmic purposes, no cosmic compensation for the dead scattered over a thousand battlefields nor for the living dead in a million homes. The Humanist does not want to wait for the slow processes of nature or nurture. Rather would he speed up nurture itself in the development of the young; and in the development of the elders he would seek psychological new births. Man is capable of achieving things heretofore thought impossible. It but remains for religion to place human responsibility at the heart of its gospel.

As if to give the *Sermons* the support of science, Julian Huxley's *Religion Without Revelation* appeared almost simultaneously.

In 1928-29 the pace of Humanist publication quickened. H. E. Barnes' *The Twilight of Christianity* (1929) sounded above the growling threats of Fascism and Nazism like the opening Fate chords of Beethoven's Fifth Symphony. But R. W. Sellars' *Religion Coming of Age* (1928), A. E. Haydon's lucid and genial *Quest of the Ages* (1929), Walter Lippman's *Preface to Morals* (1929), H. A. Overstreet's *The Enduring Quest* (1929), were all prescient and descriptive of religious Humanism, whose more precise features were presented by Reese in *Humanist Religion* (1931) and by C. F. Potter in *Humanism, A New Religion* (1930). For the first time in its own name, Humanism had been institutionalized by Potter, formerly the minister of the West Side Unitarian Church, in the First Humanist Society of New York (1929).

By this time the Christian theologians had awakened to the desirability of trying to thrust back the "Humanist hurricane" which W. M. Horton, in *Theism and the Modern Mood* (1930), feared "would strike all Christendom before long – the theistic faith [being] under a cloud just now." So Edward Scribner Ames defended the God idea as the socialization and personalization of reality (*Humanism*, 1931). *Humanism: Another Battle Line* (1931) marshaled an imposing squadron of Christian theologians, but their concessions to the Humanist position amounted to a retreat. A similar effect was produced by the excogitations of two gentle liberals, Professor Robert J. Hutcheon (*Humanism in Religion Examined*) and Rev. Minot Simons (*A Modern Theism*). Both defined their Theistic faith as "Humanism plus."

What with Hutcheon, the Meadville School's professor of religious philosophy, and its president, Rev. Sydney B. Snow, both professing "Humanism plus," while Lyttle, in the chair of church history, was teaching the provenance of Humanism from Graeco-Roman ethical philosophy and the Christian Humanism of the Renaissance; with Haydon in the chair of the history of non-Christian religions at the Divinity School of the University of Chicago, and Professor Shirley Jackson Case stressing the Humanist elements in early Christianity – it is easily understandable that so many graduates of these institutions later avowed Humanism. A similar situation was created in the Harvard Divinity School by the presence of Professors Auer and J. S. Bixler on the faculty, although their influence was countered by that of crypto-conservative Dean W. L. Sperry, who criticized the Western Humanists as brash and individualistic.

Dietrich was now requested to provide the Unitarians with a specific definition of Humanism, and his response was issued as an A.U.A. tract in 1934. Dietrich distinguished cultural Humanism, humanitarianism, and "Humanism plus" from religious or scientific Humanism, which he defended from the charge of atheism:

> It simply ignores the existence of God, failing to find any evidence of intelligent purpose in the Universe, which is surely the minimum basis of Theism. Its attitude is one of open-mindedness and inquiry, not of denial. Its whole program is based on the assumption of an indifferent universe ... in which man must carve out his own destiny. [Today] men and women are naturalistic in their everyday affairs; they have the enhancement of human life as their goal. In all their activities, except religion, people rely upon human experience and inquiry for their knowledge ...Only in religion do they pretend to get knowledge from some supernatural source, have the glorification of that source as their goal and depend upon it for guidance and help ... Two ideas are here in conflict: on the one hand, man organizing and directing his own life, on the other, professing to believe that a deity orders it for him.

Dietrich argued that in the resources of modern science, sociology, and psychology "we have in our own hands the direction of human development."

How challenging a call, in terms of personal responsibility not only to serve the present but to conserve the best of the past and to transmit it enriched to the future, his new outlook gave him, Dietrich revealed in his concluding words:

> To feel that I am a contributor to the splendor of that distant goal which I descry is to find myself lifted to the possibilities of purest and bravest life. Man, struggling with an indifferent Universe and Prometheus-like wresting from it his destiny – this gives me light in these hours of darkness when great things are demanded of us and we are called to heroic labors.

Enthusiasm over the victory of the New Deal in the elections of 1932, in contrast with reactionary trends in Europe, was partly responsible for the promulgation of the "Humanist Manifesto" by R. W. Sellars and Rev. Raymond B. Bragg, Reese's successor in the secretaryship of the Western Conference. Its timeliness was underscored by the report of Professor J. H. Leuba of his researches into the religious convictions of college students which he published in *God or Man* (1933). The "Manifesto" was also prompted by the widespread havoc wrought in human faith and hope by the great depression. It sought to replace despondency and doubt of God's loving Providence by confidence in the power of human intelligence and co-operative good will to become its own Providence. Thirteen Unitarian ministers, one Universalist, one Jewish rabbi, eleven university professors, two Ethical leaders, and sundry others, such as Harry Elmer Barnes and Rev. A. C. Dieffenbach of the *Register*, signed the "Manifesto." Since it attracted widespread attention and comment, its major theses deserve summation.

Article I declared that "Religious Humanists regard the Universe as self-existing, not created"; Article V: "the nature of the Universe, as depicted by modern science, makes unacceptable any supernatural or cosmic guarantees of human values"; Article VI: "the time has passed for Theism, Deism, Modernism and the several varieties of 'New Thought'"; Article VII: "the distinction between the secular and the sacred can no longer be maintained"; Article IX: "in place of the old attitudes involved in worship and prayer, the Humanist finds his religious emotions expressed in a heightened sense of personal life and in a cooperative effort to promote social well-being"; Article XI: "Humanism will take the path of social and mental hygiene and discourage sentimental and unreal hopes and wishful thinking"; Article XIII: "religious institutions, their ritualistic forms, ecclesiastical methods and communal activities must be reconstructed as rapidly as possible in order to function effectively in the modern world"; Article XIV: "existing acquisitive and profit-motivated society has shown itself to be inadequate … radical changes in methods, controls and motives must be instituted … a socialized and cooperative economic social order must be established for the goal of a free and universal society in which people voluntarily and intelligently cooperate for the common good … to establish the conditions of a satisfactory life for all, not merely the few."

In practical recognition of their acceptance of these convictions, the Unitarian churches in Los Angeles, California; Kansas City, Missouri; Ann Arbor, Michigan; Madison, Wisconsin; Evanston, Illinois; Salt Lake City, Utah; and the Third Unitarian Church in Chicago followed the Minneapolis church in adopting the Humanist position. In another year All Souls in Indianapolis, Indiana, joined the number. Meanwhile Reese was experimenting with Humanist meetings at Abraham Lincoln Centre in Chicago (1932), and in the city's downtown section Rev. E. Burdette Backus was developing the First Humanist Society (1933). In spite of the fact that Reinhold Niebuhr (*Moral Man and Immoral Society*, 1932) and Fulton J. Sheen (*Religion Without God*, 1928) were exploiting the confusion and cynicism of the nineteen-thirties for the benefit of the Christian guilt complex, to the discouragement of the hope that Jesus' precepts and prophecies of the Kingdom of God on earth could be realized by the endeavors of unregenerate men and by the wisdom of "godless" scientists; in spite also of the disheartening evidence of the vicious propensities in human nature furnished by totalitarian tyranny abroad, more and more Unitarian ministers and congregations were turning to Humanism. The disclosures of depth psychology as to the psychogenic origins (Freud, *The Future of an Illusion*, 1928) of supranaturalist religious ideas were undoubtedly conducive to this trend. In 1936-37 the equality of status of Humanism with Theism in the denomination became a political issue.

The Eliot-Joy Contest for the A.U.A. Presidency (1937)

A recession in denominational morale and expansion led, in 1934, to the appointment of a Commission of Appraisal, of which Rev. Frederick May Eliot of St. Paul, Minnesota, was chairman. Its report, *Unitarians Face A New Age* (1936), contained, in addition to practical administrative recommendations, a chapter on doctrine, in which the points on which "Unitarians agree" were defined in non-theological terms, while in the category of disagreements was "the expediency of using the traditional vocabulary of religion within a fellowship which includes many who have rejected the ideas commonly associated with such words as 'God,' 'prayer,' 'communion,' 'salvation,' 'immortality.'" The report led to the resignation of President Cornish and the nomination of Eliot for the office. A group of Theists challenged many of the practical recommendations of the report and the large concessions, if not priorities, given Humanism, by nominating Rev. Charles R. Joy, a Theist. It was pointed out that Eliot had declared himself a Humanist by contributing to *Humanist Sermons* in 1927 and by passages in a sermon on "The Reality of God" (1930) in which he spoke of the Humanists as "a growing minority [which] includes some of the most clear-headed and conscientious among the younger men and women of today, whose point of view [should be recognized] as being equally valid with that of the acceptance of traditional beliefs."

In accepting the Theists' nomination, Joy did so as a theological partisan: "Dr. Eliot states frankly that 'it is because Humanism can serve human needs far better than any other sort of faith that I hold it myself and preach it from this pulpit, [though] we may rightly use "God" as a symbol of our loftiest aspirations and deepest faith.'" Joy quoted from the 1930 sermon further: "I do not believe in personal immortality; the passionate desire for the survival of an individual life seems to me a relic of the childish days of early humanity." Joy questioned, therefore,

… whether the time has come when the Unitarian fellowship wishes to be represented by a president whose religious views seem to be at variance with those held by a vast majority of our people, approximately nine-tenths of them according to the Commission's own estimate; since, according to the report, leadership is only possible with a group that shares a common faith and a common enthusiasm.

Was the denomination to be torn by another doctrinal conflict? Had Unitarians not learned, after more than a century of experience, that such conflicts were utterly and ironically incompatible with their principle of the free mind and conscience, their subordination of theological speculation to ethical and spiritual bases of faith and fellowship?

It transpired within a month that the overwhelming sentiment of the denomination was against a theological battle. The leaders of both factions met in conference; Joy was persuaded to withdraw his name and Eliot was elected without a contest.

Since the Humanists had been solidly behind Eliot, his election meant that henceforward their views would be respected and recognized in denominational literature, programs, officialdom. The suggestion of the report that a doctrinal consensus should be co-operatively developed was quietly dropped. Substantial evidence of the new dispensation was the collaboration of the Humanist leader, Reese, with Von Ogden Vogt and other latitudinarian Theists in the compilation of *Hymns of the Spirit* (1937), in which a generous quota of Humanist hymns, responsive readings, doxologies, and benedictions was placed side by side with those of the Theistic language and thought. The Beacon Course of religious-education texts was revised in accordance with the philosophy of John Dewey. The reinvigorated Beacon Press proceeded to publish Humanist books, among which should be mentioned the poems of Rev. Kenneth L. Patton of Madison, Wisconsin, *Hello, Man* (1946), and *The Meaning of Humanism* (1945) by Curtis W. Reese – perhaps the most informing and inspiring survey, interpretation, and forecast the movement has thus far produced. Beyond the scope of this history is any further mention of the library of Humanist publications, which now comprises scores of books by non-Unitarian authors not only in the fields of religion and philosophy but in education, the social sciences, and psychiatry.

The Western Conference, where modern religious Humanism was first explicitly formulated and freely accepted, remains the seat of its national organization. The American Humanist Association, which was organized in 1943, has its offices in Yellow Springs, Ohio, in proximity to Antioch College. Its executive director, Rev. Edwin H. Wilson, serves also as editor of its bi-monthly organ, *The Humanist*. Almost half of the ministers of the Western Conference are Humanists, as well as the Leader of the Chicago Ethical Society, A.E. Haydon.

CHAPTER FIFTEEN

The Century's Consummations

To thy fellow countrymen thou shalt preach the gospel of the New World: that here, here in America, is the home of man; that here is the promise of a new and more excellent social state than history has recorded.

Emerson

THE HUMANIST MOVEMENT ACCENTUATED the democratic character of Western Unitarianism. Since the days of the ascendancy of Parkerism and the "grass-roots" independence of Secretary Jones, this democratic character – so noticeably different from the lingering upper-class traditions of Federalist Massachusetts Unitarianism – had been developing apace. While cultural Humanism had its genesis in the aristocratic circles of the Renaissance, religious Humanism had been, perforce, the covert faith of the thinking bourgeois and non-clerical intelligentsia of Europe; whence it passed to the freethinkers, the secularists, the scientists and social philosophers of evolution. With the insistence of Humanism – the "religion of democracy," in Reese's earliest phrasing – upon human competence and duty to improve the human estate, the Western spirit of pioneer self-reliance and frontier adventure was perfectly congenial. These traits, so manifest in Pierpont, Clarke, and Hosmer, Huidekoper, Eliot, and Conant, provide the spiritual logic of the advent of religious Humanism in the Conference they founded.

In institutional matters this democratic strength and self-reliance was demonstrated by the ability of the Western churches to surmount the great depression of 1929 without the losses that had occurred in the depressions of the eighteen-fifties, sixties, seventies, and nineties. Critical moments there were, to be sure, especially for such churches as had just incurred heavy building debts; yet in all but three cases they weathered the storm and have grown steadily stronger ever since. Reese's successors in the office of Secretary – Rev. Raymond B. Bragg (1930-35), Rev. Lon Ray Call (1935-41), Rev. Randall S. Hilton (1943-on) – have been capable executives. In co-operation with the Department of Church Extension of the A.U.A., they have succeeded in getting churches organized in Flint, Michigan (the Congregational-Unitarian Church, 1930); in Fort Wayne, Indiana (the Unitarian Society, 1939); in Grosse Pointe, Michigan (the Unitarian Church, 1939, missionized by Rev. Augustus P. Reccord from Detroit); in Columbus, Ohio (the First Unitarian Church, 1940); in Chicago, Illinois (the Beverly Unitarian Fellowship, 1942); in Indianapolis, Indiana (the North Unitarian Church, 1950); in South Bend, Indiana (the First Unitarian Church of South Bend, 1952). Of particular interest is the Free Religious Fellowship of Chicago, an interracial body organized in 1947 by the efforts of Harry I. Jones, Rev. Kenneth L. Patton from Madison, Wisconsin, and Rev. Lewis McGee – the last becoming its minister. Two of the several students of the Meadville School who became members of this Fellowship have been given ordination to the ministry: Rev. Maryell Cleary and Rev. Hugo P. Leaming. With historic appropriateness its work is carried on at Abraham Lincoln Centre.

Consulting the surveys and predictions made by Thomas in 1829, Briggs in 1837, and Holland in 1849, we find that with the exceptions of Steubenville, Zanesville, Oxford, and Sandusky, in Ohio; Wheeling, West Virginia; St. Charles, Missouri; Janesville, Wisconsin; and a number of small cities and towns in central Illinois, there is now in existence in every community whose liberal promise was stressed by the three surveyors a Unitarian or a Universalist church or a Unitarian Fellowship. There are Fellowship groups in Boulder, Colorado; Jamestown, North Dakota; Minnehaha County, South Dakota; Park Forest, Illinois; Bloomington, Evansville, and West Lafayette, in Indiana; Ames, Burlington, and Cedar Falls, in Iowa; Topeka, Kansas; Lexington and Paducah, in Kentucky; Birmingham and East Lansing, in Michigan; Columbia, Missouri; Bowling Green and Springfield, in Ohio. It is likely that several of these units will follow the example of South Bend, Indiana, and acquire full church status before long.

The idea – and the existence – of such pre-church Fellowships is truly Western, for in scores of remote settlements even before the eighteen-fifties small liberal groups came together and sustained their convictions by reading the sermons of Channing, Walker, [Orville] Dewey, and Gannett; by reading the *Christian Register*; by drinking in the words of itinerant missionaries; by tracts from the Chicago office of the Conference after 1865 and the Post Office Mission committees of the city churches. How sacred the flame on these little, transient altars of spiritual freedom! How precious these opportunities of untrammeled learning and discussion on high intellectual and cultural planes and themes! It is another happy consummation of the century's growth that in 1944 there was brought about the establishment of the Unitarian Church of the Larger Fellowship, whose members are committed to no doctrinal bias, but avow simply "our earnest desire to lead pure, reverent and useful lives [and] seek together the love with quickens fellowship and the truth which makes men free." Nowhere in the nation is there a richer field for the Fellowships than the great states beyond the Mississippi and Missouri rivers.

Another Western experiment in larger fellowship that is coming to consummation on a national scale is the union of the Universalists with the Unitarians. While theological and even social barriers long impeded such a *rapprochement* in the East, the freer and friendlier spirit of Western Unitarianism was sweeping them away as early as the eighteen-fifties. With this more inclusive attitude the affinity between Channing's ecumenical vision and that of the Christian movement had much to do – an affinity urged and embodied by Clarke, Huidekoper, Stebbins, Conant, and others.

In preceding chapters we have frequently noted instances of co-operation and even fusion between Unitarians and Universalists in struggles to start and to maintain liberal churches. It is probable that over a third of the present Unitarian churches in the Conference are in constituency what those at Detroit and Cleveland are in legal title – "Universalist-Unitarian." Seventeen Universalist ministers in the West now hold dual fellowship; seven Unitarians have the same relationship with the Universalists. The Chicago Liberal Ministers Association and the Prairie Group – formed in 1951 for the study and discussion of religious subjects – enjoy cordial inter-denominational fraternity. Universalist church delegates have worked with their Unitarian brethren to create and support the Midwest Council of Religious Liberals (1951). The Michigan Area Unitarian Conference met for several years in conjunction with the Universalist State Convention. Like comity has obtained in the Iowa Unitarian Conference, whose fellowship and work have continued with unabated loyalty during the secretaryship of Rev. Charles E. Snyder of Sioux City and Davenport, with Henry H. Griffiths as treasurer for thirty-eight years.

The Association sponsored from 1924 to 1930 a summer Institute for Religious Education and Youth Fellowship at Humboldt, a continuance of less formal gatherings held there for decades. In 1930 the Youth Fellowship was transferred to McGregor, Iowa, on the upper Mississippi. In 1937 this enterprise coalesced with the Midwest Unitarian-Universalist summer conference at the Turkey Run and Shakamak State Parks, Indiana (1937-38), with renewed emphasis on religious education, under the leadership of Rev. Lon R. Call, then Secretary of the Western Conference, and with the untiring aid of Miss Bertha C. Finger, Registrar of the Institute. A final transfer of the location of the venture to Lake Geneva, Wisconsin, was made in 1939. Call's successor, Secretary Hilton, assisted by Mrs. Esther L. Heinrichs as Registrar, has labored with vision, persistence, and effectiveness to assure the summer assembly of the Western Conference a richer program and increasing attendance as a focus of education, fellowship, and inspiration.

Exclusive of the growing library of Humanist publications, the literary activity of Western Conference Unitarians has continued in good volume and high quality. The historiographer is heartened by the availability of such an autobiography as *Jasper Douthit's Story* (1909), with its moving appreciative preface by Jenkin Lloyd Jones. The wealth of data and appraisal, not only of religious matters but of national history, that W. G. Eliot's journals contain was suggested by his daughter, Charlotte C. Eliot, in her biography, *William Greenleaf Eliot*, published in 1904. Nina Moore Tiffany and Francis Tiffany's *Harm Jan Huidekoper* (1904) and F. M. I. Morehouse's *Life of Jesse W. Fell* (1916) worthily portray these two frontier philanthropists and educators. Fell's political and religious influence on Abraham Lincoln is related with scholarly power in R. D. Richardson's *Abraham Lincoln's Autobiography* (1947), which also contains a facsimile of the priceless document now in the keeping of the Library of Congress by gift of the Fell-Richardson family. Of outstanding value is J. H. Holmes' *Life and Letters of Robert Collyer* (two volumes, 1917), a masterpiece of narration, quotation, and interpretation.

A vivid account of the early days of Humanism in the West is given in Carleton Winston's biography of John H. Dietrich, *This Circle of Earth* (1942), a useful prologue to which is R. B. Bragg's [sermon on] *Henry M. Simmons* (1944); while sidelights on Unitarianism in Minneapolis are furnished by O. W. Firkins' *Memoirs and Letters* (1934).

Biographical in method but theological in content is F. A. Christie's *Makers of the Meadville Theological School* (1927), which sketches the School's intellectual history and contingent publications up to about 1920. Since that year has appeared *Religion and Life* (1921), a summarization of the progress of religious thought for the School's seventy-fifth anniversary. Professor R. J. Hutcheon edited a memorial volume of *Studies in the New Testament* (1936) by his colleague, C. R. Bowen, which bears ample witness to the latter's deep and mellow religious feeling and scholarship. Hutcheon's own convictions are set forth in his *Frankness in Religion* (1929).

Carrying on the traditional Meadville interest in German liberal theology – an interest actualized in the appointment of Carl Greve and Immanuel Benzinger from the Deutsche Evangelische Synod to the faculty (1910-18) – Professor J. L. Adams published in 1945 a study of *Paul Tillich's Philosophy of Culture, Science and Religion* and in 1948 a translation with introduction of Tillich's *The Protestant Era*.

The revelation of the profound religious philosophies of India that came to Rev. J. T. Sunderland at the World Parliament of Religions, and that led in following years to two visits to India, resulted in his *India in Bondage* (1928), a moving expression of his tireless propaganda extending over thirty years to arouse American sympathy for India's struggle for independence. Like concern for India led John Haynes Holmes to an intimate acquaintance with Mahatma Gandhi – for whose autobiographical *Story of My Experiments with Truth* Holmes secured exclusive American publication rights in *Unity* (1926-27). Gandhi's principle of non-violent resistance found another disciple in Rev. Homer A. Jack, whose discriminating book of selections, *The Wit and Wisdom of Gandhi*, came out in 1951.

In contrast with preceding periods, the last quarter of the century under discussion has been less prolific in religious poetry, although in terms of popular appeal its productions rank first. The title poem of *Each in His Own Tongue* (1908) by William H. Carruth, and "God Bless You" in the same volume, appear in many anthologies and are quoted by many speakers. This is true also of Edmund Rowland Sill's "The Fool's Prayer" and "Opportunity" from his *Poetical Works* (1906). Quite different in character is the philosophic poem *And Thus Was Adam* (1943) by Rev. Ralph E. Bailey. At opposite poles of thought and form is *The Visitor* and *Hello, Man* (1947) by Rev. Kenneth L. Patton, and the enlarged and revised edition of *The Thought of God* (1918), Hosmer's and Gannett's symposium of hymn poems that first appeared in 1885. So many of them have been gratefully appropriated by other denominations that the symposium's only American rival in this respect is *Gospel Hymns* by Moody and Sankey! The only Humanist hymn of Western Conference genesis enjoying extra-denominational popularity is "Wonders still the world shall witness," first printed in *Songs and Readings* (1937) by Rev. Jacob Trapp.

The genteel old custom of publishing plump volumes of beautifully written sermons chosen by the minister's congregation as his best efforts seems to be obsolete. The radio and the new psychology dictate brevity and practicality. Such are the merits of Rev. Dilworth Lupton's *Religion Says You Can!* (1938). Rev. Robert L. Sonen, in *A Unitarian States His Case* (1947), made a forceful presentation of liberal principles especially fitted for Fundamentalist minds in the Southwest. A more diversified spectrum of Unitarian theological and social opinion appears in *Together We Advance* (1946), edited by Rev. S. H. Fritchman. "A Time for Liberal Action," the 1947 A.U.A. Anniversary Sermon of Rev. Curtis W. Reese, was in the second of the two volumes of *Voices of Liberalism* (1947-48), which also contained sermons by such Western leaders as E. Burdette Backus, E. T. Buehrer, J. L. Adams, H. A. Jack, R. L. Mondale, A. W. Olsen, and L. T. Pennington.

Radio broadcasting of religious messages has created a new type of literature – the brochure of short, pithy scripts. Those of Rev. Walton E. Cole – *The American Way of Life* (1939), *The Choice Before Us* (1940) – recall the victorious resistance he organized against the demagogic anti-Semitism of the Roman Catholic radio priest, Father Coughlin, in Detroit. The rector of the Little Flower Church was forbidden to broadcast by his archbishop soon after Cole aroused national attention and indignation. A similarly militant summons against orthodox aggression was sounded in the broadcasts gathered into *If Thought Be Free* (1946) and *The Sheep and the Goats* (1948), by Rev. E. Burdette Backus, of All Souls Church of Indianapolis, one of eight Western Unitarian churches carrying on a radio ministry, the others being in Denver, Colorado; Omaha, Nebraska; Sioux City, Iowa; Madison, Wisconsin; Fort Wayne, Indiana; Toledo, Ohio; and the Peoples Church, Chicago. Preston Bradley has multiplied the influence of his sermon broadcasts by his books, *Mastering Fear, Courage for Today, Life and You, Power from Right Thinking, New Wealth for You, My Daily Strength*, and *Meditations*, which have had hundreds of thousands of readers.

After the unusual volume of writing on behalf of evolution during the preceding period, it is not surprising to find that outside the Humanist school few works in the field of the philosophy of religion were produced from 1900 on. J. T. Sunderland's earlier and very popular work on evolution, *The Spark in the Clod* (1902), was reissued as *Evolution and Religion* (1925), while John H. Dietrich's *Fathers of Evolution* (1927) also aided the allies of progress, the Unitarian echelon of which at the celebrated Scopes trial at Dayton, Tennessee, in 1925 was led by Rev. Charles F. Potter. Another reminder of former days and issues was George R. Dodson's *The Sympathy of Religions* (1917), though its tendentious manipulation of facts in favor of Western Theism was not in the spirit of the "*Unity*" men." Yet Dodson's interpretation of *Bergson and the Modern Spirit* (1913) used Gannett's hymn poem, "He hides within the lily" for a coda. Neither Theist nor Humanist, strictly speaking, was Rev. Duren

J. H. Ward, a Unitarian minister of Iowa, later of Denver, Colo-rado. To insure the survival of science, after the cataclysm of civilization predicted in his *A Receivership for Civilization* (1922), Dr. Ward spent his last years in storing an encyclopedic record of modern knowledge in two mausoleums in Denver, to be opened in 2000 A.D.

The modern age has witnessed the adoption by the churches of the custom of weekly bulletins carrying not only local but denominational news. Large resources of endowment or sub-scription income are required to meet the greatly increased cost of publication of periodicals. Consequently the efforts of the Meadville School to provide a medium of theological study and discussion in its *Quarterly Bulletin* (1906-30), its *Journal* (1930-33), were decreasingly successful from the point of view of circulation, although the quality of contributions was high. It co-operated with the Unitarian Ministers Association in the publication of the *Journal of Liberal Religion* (1939-43), under the editorship of J. L. Adams. The *Journal of Liberal Religion* was continued by the Ministers Association with E. T. Buehrer as editor until 1949. The Conference had a similarly discouraging experience with its news organs, *The Western Unitarian Bulletin* (1920-21) and *The Western Unitarian* (1922-28). Without compromising its independence, *Unity* has become the medium of Conference announcements and news.

From 1919 to 1926 this "Journal of the Religion of Demo-cracy" had as its co-editors John Haynes Holmes, Francis Neilson, Mrs. Edith Lloyd Jones, Rabbi Louis I. Mann, and Curtis W. Reese. In 1926 Holmes became editor-in-chief, with a distinguished staff of editorial contributors and foreign corre-spondents – E. D. Morel, Sydney Strong, Romain Rolland, Stefan Zweig, and Rabindranath Tagore among them. The fearless advocacy of justice and humanity in all areas of life, the forthright condemnation of all forms of political and eco-nomic exploitation and oppression, continued to be *Unity's* policy, which was brilliantly executed. Absolute opposition to war, as in Jones' years of editorship, remained its primary principle; but its coverage of other social issues was as wide as the world. The progress of Communism in Russia, the Sacco-Vanzetti tragedy, the menace of Japanese militarism, the ominous restlessness in China, the iniquity of the British opium trade, lynching in the United States, the betrayal of the League of Nations, the unholy munitions business – all were subjects of report and comment, so that *Unity* served as a bi-weekly Judgment Day for social wrongdoers! Contributors of poetry from Zona Gale, Edwin Markham, Robert Haven Schauffler, Angela Morgan, Edith Lovejoy Pierce, Ralph Chaplin, came gratis to its pages, as well as stirring hymn poems on peace and economic justice by its editor. Perhaps the most notable reform sponsored by *Unity* in this period was that for the outlawing of war, originated by Salmon O. Levinson and aided by Senator William O. Borah and President David Starr Jordan of the University of California. Their efforts culminated in the Pact of Paris of 1927, signed by sixty-three nations represented by such leaders as Secretary Frank B. Kellogg, Aristide Briande, and Lord Lothian. Its intent was nullified during the following decade by the bellicose threats and aggressive measures of Fascism, Nazism, and the Japanese imperialists. An interesting by-product, however, of the close association of Holmes and Levinson in their common ideal was the salvaging, by the latter's remarkable legal acumen and astuteness, of the assets of the Community Church of New York City from complete loss in the depression of 1929. For this immense service, Levinson, with characteristic generosity, refused to accept the slightest compensation.

Changing political conditions moved the board of *Unity* in 1941 to provide for the presentation of non-pacifist opinion by giving the managing editor, Curtis W. Reese, equal control with Holmes in editorial policy, so that "*Unity* shall not be committed to movements or organizations antagonistic to liberal democracy." This editorial ambiguity continued until 1946, when Holmes withdrew from any connection with *Unity*. Reese's editorship since then has entailed no abatement of the policy of radical reform and of prophecy against social wrong, save that for Jones' and Holmes' pacifism there has been substituted support for collective security through the United Nations. A substantial endowment enables *Unity* to approach its seventy-fifth anniversary in 1953 with no apprehensions of loss either of continuance or of independence.

The same propitious outlook obtains for Abraham Lincoln

Centre, now affiliated with the American Unitarian Association as well as the Western Conference. With the aid of its endowment, as well as grants from the city's Community Fund and other civic foundations, the Centre under Dean Reese's leadership (1930 on) is nobly fulfilling the hopes of his predecessor, Jenkin Lloyd Jones. It various activities, all of them conducted on an interracial basis, include a public-library branch, a planned-parenthood clinic, a child-guidance clinic, a summer camp at Clear Lake, Wisconsin, a cultural-arts curriculum in music, design, and dancing, as well as many other educational and recreational offerings, attended in 1951 by almost 140,000 children and adults.

The prospects for the future of other educational institutions whose existence was largely due to Western Unitarians are for the most part highly encouraging. However, as a result of their plinthic non-sectarianism, Unitarian participation in their administration has been reduced well nigh to the vanishing point. The Chicago Historical Society, of which Rev. William Barry, Jr., from the Harvard Divinity School, was founder and first Secretary (1870-85), is now one of Chicago's foremost institutions, well endowed and magnificently housed in Lincoln Park. The rehabilitation of Antioch College in Yellow Springs, Ohio, by Arthur E. Morgan in 1920 has brought the "Antioch Plan" world-wide recognition, as well as abundant prosperity to the institution. Washington University – if not the Harvard of the Midwest of W. G. Eliot's dream – is one of the three great privately endowed and controlled universities in the Mississippi Valley.

Thus far the removal of the Meadville Theological School to Chicago has not resulted in a larger enrollment and quota of graduates entering the Unitarian pulpits of the Western Conference. During the presidency of Rev. Sydney B. Snow (1928-44), and owing largely to his irenic and gracious spirit, the Ryder Divinity School – the theological department of the Universalist foundation, Lombard College at Galesburg, Illinois — was merged with the School, its dean, Rev. L. Ward Brigham, becoming professor of parish administration (1928-39). The financial plight of Lombard became hopeless during the great depression, and its trustees voted in 1933 to transfer its educational activities to the Meadville School in Chicago. At the present time the personnel of the Lombard College board and the Meadville School board is the same, although the charters and the assets of the two institutions are separately administered. In 1939 Professor Carl Beth, a scholar of European reputation in the history of religion and former rector of the theological faculty of the University of Vienna, came as a refugee from Nazi persecution to the School to teach in his special field until retirement in 1944.

The Second World War bore heavily upon the enrollment as well as upon the revenues of the School, considerations that tipped the scales in favor of a proposal from the University of Chicago in 1942 for a working union of the Meadville School, the Disciples Divinity House, the Chicago Theological Seminary (Congregational), and its own Divinity School (Baptist) in a Federated Theological Faculty. Though by the terms of the Articles, ratified by all the boards in 1943, each of the institutions retained control of its own finances and plant, including its library, yet the important powers of faculty appointments and curriculum making as well as students' admission requirements were ceded to the total Federated Faculty, governed in turn by the Cabinet of Deans, one of whom is Rev. Wallace W. Robbins, of the Meadville class of 1935, who succeeded Dr. Snow as President in 1944. During the regime of Chancellor Robert M. Hutchins, the spirit of the University had been admirably free; but the trend of its educational policy is increasingly toward research methods and values rather than the humanities and technical vocational training. Whether the School will be able to defend its integrity and dignity, its freedom for radical thought and progress toward world religion beyond Christianity, its primary function as a training school for ministers, its Unitarian character and obligations, against the brass mountain of the University's great financial and academic strength – all this remains to be seen.

In the present, as in the past, the Western Unitarian churches are centers of social action, libertarian and humanitarian. Their concern for an efficient, non-sectarian public-school system and for free public libraries continues in their united efforts against Catholic and Fundamentalist efforts to get tax money for parochial schools and to use public-school class-rooms, sometimes even the teachers' time, for sectarian instruction. The early concern to liberate human beings from poverty, ignorance, intemperance, brutal treatment in prisons and insane asylums, continues in the virtually unanimous championship and publicizing by Unitarian churches of the birth-control and planned-parenthood clinics, as well as drives to get such agencies permitted by state laws. *Unity* was the first important religious periodical in the West to defend Margaret Sanger against attack. Many ministers – among them Rev. Newton Mann in Nebraska, Rev. Charles E. Snyder in Iowa, Rev. Caroline Bartlett Crane in Michigan, Rev. E. Burdette Backus in Indiana – have been leaders in efforts to introduce more humane and scientific methods into mental hospitals. A salient recent instance of such activity has been the crusade of the Minnesota Unitarians to modernize their state's medieval attitude and policies. An indignant hospital attendant, Engla Schey, persuaded them to institute a committee headed by Mrs. L. D. Steefel, later by Rev. Arthur Foote of St. Paul, to attack the problem. They prevailed upon the governor to make mental-hospital reform the first measure of his legislative program in 1949, for which the committee secured the support of leading civic organizations. After winning from the legislature increased appropriations, the committee has pressed forward, with the aid of the National Committee on Mental Hygiene, to a program of state-wide education and vigilance in lifting the preventive, remedial, and custodial treatment of mental illness in Minnesota up to the standards of the American Psychiatric Association.

Sympathy and service for the mentally ill are no longer regarded as radical attitudes by any save the most bigoted and niggardly persons. But efforts to infuse the economic order, as well as interracial and international relations, with justice and true democracy are still in need of adherents who dare to be pioneers and heretics. The temerity of Channing and Parker, of Clarke and May, of the Free Religionists, the *Unity* editors and later minor prophets, in contrasting professed religious ideals with social and economic wrongs has forfeited the support of many wealthy and prejudiced persons who, as Tolstoi said, "would do anything for the poor but get off their backs." Offense was taken when even such moderately advanced movements as Co-operation and Credit Unions were commended in sermons and seminary lectures in the eighteen-nineties. Nevertheless, with few exceptions, the Unitarians in any community where a Co-operative of any kind was sincerely undertaken have endorsed and assisted it substantially, in accord with a tradition that reaches back to the willingness of British Unitarian dissenters to join with Owenite Socialists in order to found the famous Rochdale Equitable Pioneers of 1844. In most of early Co-operative ventures – particularly of the Credit Union and Consumer type in the Midwest from 1900 on – there was a strong contingent of members from the near-by Unitarian churches.

To offset the fear of economic radicalism which inhibited the Department of Social and Public Service that the A.U.A. set up in 1907, the Unitarian Fellowship for Social Justice was founded in 1908 "to provide a fellowship for united action against all forms of social injustice and to enable its members to sustain one another in the application of their religious ideals to the needs of the present day." Since that time the Fellowship has been the militant social conscience of the denomination. Charge after charge the Fellowship has made against exploiters of labor, fomentors of racial prejudice and discrimination, imperialistic foreign policies and militarism at home, the munitions buzzards, universal military training. The Western churches have always been closer to the manual workers, the foreign-born, the salaried professional callings, than the Eastern; this may partly explain why a disproportionately large number of the Fellowship's members and officers have belonged to Western churches.

A special sense of responsibility for just treatment, legal rights, and equal opportunity for the Negroes, arising from the recent immense influx into Northern industrial centers, has marked the social action of the Unitarian churches in the Detroit and Chicago areas. They have worked with the American Civil Liberties Union, the National Association for the Advancement of Colored People, and similar bodies to educate citizens, police, and city officials in the principles and feelings of human brotherhood and American democracy. To this end the Chicago Council against Racial and Religious Discrimination was organized in 1946, Preston Bradley acting with Bishop Bernard J. Shiel as co-chairman and Rev. Homer A. Jack as executive secretary

(1944-48). With resourcefulness and courage Dr. Jack aroused the liberal forces of Chicago to the dangerous, un-American situation resulting from discrimination against the Negroes in restaurants, schools, employment, and housing. Working with civic and social agencies, Methodists, Jews, Congregationalists, and Quakers, the Council aided in persuading the police to adopt stronger methods to prevent race riots. Dr. Jack's successor, a former official of the Unitarian Service Committee, Rev. Waitstill H. Sharp, has further developed the Council's work.

A significant development of the Second World War was the formation in 1940 of the Unitarian Service Committee, an adjunct of the A.U.A. until 1948, when it became a separate corporation. Designed at the outset "to investigate opportunities for humanitarian service in America and abroad and to take action to perform such service as may seem advisable," it undertook at the outset the relief and rehabilitation of families and homes in France. Gradually its scope was broadened to aid refugees from Nazi persecution to escape to America. Among the hundreds thus aided were Franz Werfel, Heinrich Mann, Konrad Heeden, Arthur Koestler, Otto Meyerhof. Since 1946, according to a proposal made to it by Professor Maurice B. Visscher of the University of Minnesota, the Committee has broadened its work into a world-wide program of medical and public-health missions to necessitous countries, sent "to revive human initiative, knowledge and skill" and "to demonstrate and to share the best of our own heritage." The specialists of the mission have taught the latest and best skills of surgery, internal medicine, dentistry, anaesthetics, and antibiotics to medical schools and conferences of physicians. Similar missions of specialists in public health, child guidance, and democratic educational methods have been sent not only to devastated and decivilized regions in Europe but to Japan, Israel, Iran, Korea; on similar principles, work camps have been held in Mexico and in Harlem, New York; a "Neighborhood House" is maintained in Bremen, Germany. Yet only a tithe of the humanitarian beneficence of the Committee has been indicated. The funds for the work are supplied not only by the Unitarian churches and individual members throughout the country, but by many gifts from non-denominational sources, including the United Nations and the United States government. Rev. Raymond B. Bragg, who has acted as executive director of the Service Committee since 1947, served his apprenticeship for administrative work in his ministries in Evanston, Illinois; Minneapolis, Minnesota; and the secretaryship of the Western Conference.

Thus, at the end of the century, our movement has created a unique form of world-wide "foreign mission" work in which Theists and Humanists heartily collaborate and whose Statement of Purpose unites our historic principles with present action:

> To help restore human dignity where it has been violated and to strengthen it everywhere;
>
> To render service at home and abroad without regard to race, creed, color or nationality;
>
> To maintain and give expression to the unity of human kind.

CHAPTER SIXTEEN

Conclusion

PATIENT READER! Surprising as it may seem, our journey through so many chapters has acquainted us with only a small part of the life and work of the Conference! The indescribably valuable contributions of the women's groups – Ladies Aid, Sewing Circles, Women's Auxiliaries, the Women's Western Unitarian Conference, the General Alliance – have not received as such the attention they deserve. Nor has adequate citation been made of the interesting and helpful activities of the Lend-a-Hand and Harry Wadsworth Clubs and the Kings Daughters inspired by Edward Everett Hale and very numerous in the West during the eighteen-eighties and nineties. Were it not for the assurance that all they did was done for the joy and good of the doing, the historian would feel remiss indeed.

This apparent neglect has been due largely to the failure of our forerunners to keep permanent records, because of a feeling perhaps that they had left church history behind them when they departed from the venerable Puritan and Colonial churches of New England. But after the Civil War, Western Unitarianism ceased to be "a New England plant, a Boston flower," as Rev. A.D. Mayo described it in 1870. With a growing constituency of the native-born and of immigrant liberals from Europe – and to the reveille of Parker and Emerson – it awoke to a sense of identity and historic significance, the autobiographical mood. Correspondingly it acquired a central focus in Chicago, its own Secretary, periodical and other organic assets which, with wise tenacity, it has since defended against all centrifugal influences. Evidence of this vitality and of the awareness of its permanent place in the life of the Unitarian movement was the overwhelming vote by which the ninety-ninth annual meeting of the Conference at Evanston voted down the proposal of the

274

Commission on Planning that the central office be liquidated and that the Conference be subdivided.

Puzzled Reader! Have you wondered why the story of theological conflict within the Conference has been told in detail? The purpose has been to reveal the dangers of personal bias, of excessive ecclesiastical prudence, of timid distrust of the practicality of the plinthic principles of Unitarianism – freedom of thought, the sovereignty of ethics, spiritual democracy. Have we not rejoiced, however, that though serious differences have arisen, courtesy and magnanimity were not forsaken? – that the Conference has never permitted a heresy trial, nor any semblance of one, for church member, minister, or theological instructor? – and that mutual acknowledgement of the absurdity of such contentions in a fellowship dedicated to the Kingdom of God or, as others preferred to put it, to Truth, Righteousness and Love, soon brought about honest compromise and happy reconciliation? Western Unitarianism and Eastern Unitarianism, conservatives and radicals, have never been more genially and co-operatively blended than at present.

Faithful Reader! *You* are now the maker of Unitarian history for the coming century. The principal achievement of the Conference in the past century has been to prove the feasibility and to demonstrate the method of maintaining spiritual unity and charity amid diversity of opinion. Never before in recorded history, for so long a time and with such crescent vitality, has Free Religion held its own and performed its function of guarding the mind of man from bondage to any dogma, and the heart of man from any bigotry. And never before on the earth have there been such multitudes of young persons who – as graduates of schools and universities the non-sectarian climate of which has been won and defended by religious liberals – have been trained in the method of science, in humanist culture, in social values and vision. To win them for Free Religion and with them to go forth against authoritarianism in all its ominous forms – political, economic, religious – is our task on the new frontier.

Bibliographical Guide

The relationship of the bibliography of this book to its text is like that of the Great Lakes to the power house at Niagara Falls. A register of all the books, pamphlets, minutes, and periodical articles used could for the most part serve no purpose but that of pedantic vanity, since a majority of the sources used are available to the research student only in the libraries of the Meadville Theological School in Chicago, Illinois; of the Harvard Divinity School in Cambridge, Massachusetts; of the American Unitarian Association in Boston, Massachusetts; of the Starr King School for the Ministry in Berkeley, California – and in the author's own collection. For detailed guidance the curious and the critical are advised to apply to the librarians of the institutions mentioned, although questions concerning Unitarian history in specific areas might often be better directed to the city and state historical societies serving those areas. For instance, most of the data concerning the work and writings of Kristofer Janson are to be found in the Minnesota State Historical Society in St. Paul. The library of the Kansas State Historical Society is rich in Unitariana of Free Soil days. The Iowa society – whose *Palimpsest* of November, 1949, consists of a monograph by Rev. Charles E. Snyder on Unitarianism in Iowa – has many records of early liberal religious beginnings in that state. With the Missouri State Historical Society are deposited the papers of William G. Eliot, including relatively unexplored diaries of his ministry in St. Louis during Civil War days. The diary of A. H. Conant, together with copious material dealing with Unitarianism in Chicago, may be found in the accumulations of the city's Historical Society.

In some large libraries of the Midwest there may possibly be found certain general denominational histories, such as *Unitarianism in America* (Boston, 1902), by G. W. Cooke. To his painstaking factuality and broad, just estimates the author's debt is great; but Cooke's treatment of the West is necessarily lacking in consecutiveness and inclusiveness. E. M. Wilbur's *Our Unitarian Heritage* (Boston, 1925) affords a masterly panorama of denominational history, but his treatment of developments in the West, though wholly admirable in narrative and appraisal, is perforce limited. The first three volumes of Samuel A. Eliot's series, "Heralds of a Liberal Faith" (1910) – *The Prophets, The Pioneers*, and *The Preachers* – have been of inestimable value, the last volume especially. Unfortunately the information contained in the fourth volume of the series, *The Pilots*, soon to be published, has not been available to the writer. Owing to

276

the plenary coverage of the *General Catalogue of the Divinity School of Harvard University* (1898-1920), edited by E. Hale, and of the *General Catalogue of the Meadville Theological School* (1945), edited by F. L. Weis, as well as to the annual ministerial necrologies in the Year Books of the A.U.A. and the numerous entries in the *Dictionary of American Biography* (Washington, 1928-37), the lives of few of our Unitarian ministers remain obscure. As for the churches, *A List of the Unitarian Churches and Their Ministers in the United States and Canada*, compiled by F. L.Weis in 1947 but as yet available only in typescript in the Meadville School Library, has been of incalculable assistance to the writer and deserves the highest praise for its meticulous accuracy. Of similar nature and usefulness has been E. M. Wilbur's typescript *Bibliography of the Controversy in the Western Unitarian Conference*, which correlates with a Master of Theology thesis of his student, E. J. Bowden, on *The Western Issue* (1926).

Fairly available surveys and interpretations of Unitarian theological development are G. E. Ellis' *A Half-Century of the Unitarian Controversy* (1857); *Boston Unitarianism, 1820-1850* (1890), by O. B. Frothingham; *Transcendentalism in New England* (1876), by the same author; J. H. Allen's *Our Liberal Movement in Theology* (1882) and its *Sequel* (1897); J. W. Chadwick's *Old and New Unitarian Belief* (1894). The thorough scholarship of C. L. F. Gohdes' *The Periodicals of American Transcendentalism* (1931) and of Stow Persons' *Free Religion: An American Faith* (1947) ranks them as virtually definitive in their fields, although Persons' almost complete disregard of the relationship of the Western Issue and the position of the *Unity* men to Free Religion is puzzling.

Well-written autobiographies and memoirs go far toward revivifying the past. Frontier conditions along the Ohio and Mississippi rivers and in Cincinnati in the eighteen-twenties and thirties are picturesquely described by Timothy Flint in *Recollections of the Last Ten Years* (1826). The first six chapters of James Freeman Clarke's *Autobiography*, used by E. E. Hale in his memoir of Clarke (Boston, 1891), describe with arresting detail not only Clarke's years at Harvard and in Louisville, Kentucky, but the varieties and vicissitudes of travel to and from the East in the eighteen-thirties and forties. For the latter decade in Cincinnati, the *Memoir and Writings of James Handasyd Perkins*, [edited] by W. H. Channing (2 volumes, 1851), faithfully reconstructs not only a ministry but a social period. The Eliot era in St. Louis is covered in competent fashion by Charlotte C. Eliot's *William Greenleaf Eliot* (1904), with special attention to the frontier and Civil War years. Descriptions of pioneer beginnings in Meadville, Pennsylvania, are given in Francis and Nina M. Tiffany's *Harm Jan Huidekoper* (1904), which also provides delightful scenes of life at Pomona Hall and the comings and goings of young ministerial tutors from Harvard and Boston. Harm's oldest son, Alfred, supplemented these idylls by recollections of his own in *Gathered Leaves* (1866). What was being done contemporaneously in missionizing and church founding six hundred miles to the west is recounted in Robert

Collyer's life of Conant of Geneva, *A Man in Earnest* (1868). Collyer's own work in Chicago, commencing in 1858 and including dramatic narratives of Civil War days there, the Great Fire, and the burning of Unity Church, is related with pathos and humor in *Some Memories* (1908), which forms the core of J. H. Holmes' inspired *Life and Letters of Robert Collyer* (2 volumes, 1917). Another account of Chicago's Great Fire in even more vivid detail is furnished by C. W. Wendte in the first volume of his autobiography, *The Wider Fellowship* (1927), a rich mine of interesting information covering three-quarters of a century of the liberal faith across four continents. A similar reminiscential treasure is M. D. Conway's *Autobiography, Memories and Experiences* (2 volumes, 1904), whose relevance for the Western Conference lies in his brilliant description of ante-bellum Cincinnati and its growing politico-religious tensions. What a contrast is presented in *Jasper Douthit's Story* (1909) of the persecution and poverty endured by a rural prophet! Yet the one celestial incident of Christian-Unitarian comity is Chapter 4 of *Chaplain Fuller* (1863), which describes his lay-preaching sorties from Belvidere Academy through northern Illinois with Elders Walworth and Conant.

Parts of other biographies have proved useful. Chapter 3 of the *Life and Letters of Christopher Pearse Cranch*, by L. C. Scott (1917), depicts the boredom of the aesthetic young cleric from Cambridge in Louisville in the eighteen-forties; idealistic William Henry Channing, according to Chapter 7 of O. B. Frothingham's *Memoir* of him (1886), found Cincinnati uncongenial. *The Life and Letters of T. J. Mumford*, [edited] by S. J. Barrows (1879), opens with a touching description of the subject's experiences in the Meadville School and in Detroit, Michigan, as its first Unitarian minister. *Some Reminiscences* of Samuel K. Lothrop, edited by his son (1888), are revealing and explicit as to the father's attitude toward Parkerism. The *Memorial of George W. Hosmer* of Buffalo (1882) gives a glimpse of his heroic sacrifices to save the church in that city and lead it to strength and influence. A similar story for Milwaukee is told in a tribute to Rev. N. A. Staples, *Way, Truth, and Life*, by J. W. Chadwick (1870). Other tributes of this sort are extant in scores of brochures attesting the rock-like character of the ministers on which the future churches were built.

Of particular value for the opening phases of religious Humanism in the West are E. Stanton Hodgin's *Confessions of an Agnostic Clergyman* (1948) and Carleton Winston's biography of John H. Dietrich, *This Circle of Earth* (1942). The antecedents of Humanism are noted in J. M. Robertson's *Short History of Freethought* (2 volumes, 1906) and his *History of the Freethought in the Nineteenth Century* (1929). The best résumé and critique of current Humanism is that of E. A. Burtt, *Types of Religious Philosophy* (1939).

Somewhat of the same dilations of awe, expectancy, and exultant vision which the original explorers and builders of the West must have felt are likely to be experienced by one who undertakes to read his way into the great epic. The literature of the subject is immense, as F. J. Turner's famous and frequently revised *List of References on the History of the West* indicates. Of Turner's own studies, three have been especially helpful, in addition to his *The United States, 1830-50* (1935); they are "Greater New England in the Middle of the Nineteenth Century" (*Proceedings of the American Antiquarian Society*, 1919); "The Ohio Valley in American History" (*Ohio Archaeological and Historical Publications*, 1911); and "Middle Western Pioneer Democracy" (*Minnesota History Bulletin*, 1919-20). Maps and descriptions of ways and routes of travel given in A. B. Hulbert's *Historic Highways of America* (1902-05) not only provide facts but kindle the imagination.

Louisville and Cincinnati are charmingly though somewhat discursively described in W. H. Venable's *Beginnings of Literary Culture in the Ohio Valley* (1891). A more thorough coverage of all activities that might be subsumed as "literary" is given by R. L. Rusk in *The Literature of the Middle Western Frontier* (2 volumes, 1925). By an ingenious arrangement of travelers' observations the social and intellectual milieu is ably reconstructed in the first volume. Then follows information regarding the beginnings of religion, education, and journalism – as well as a review of major controversies (to 1840) in platform and pamphlet debate. The brilliant style of Van Wyck Brooks gives a technicolor enchantment to Chapter 16 of his *The World of Washington Irving* (1944), in which his correlations of New England with the beginnings of Western literature are exceedingly relevant to our subject. The sharp cultural contrasts that vexed and retarded Unitarianism in the West are further elucidated in Chapters 4 and 14 of *The Times of Melville and Whitman* (1924) and in Chapters 5 and 6 of *New England: Indian Summer* (1940). These contrasts are interpreted by Vernon Parrington in *The Romantic Revolution in America, 1800-1860* (1927), Book III, Part II ["The Rise of Liberalism"] and Part III, Chapter 1 ["The Genesis of Transcendentalism"]. The militant anti-religious trends of the Democratic party are described in Chapter 26 of *The Age of Jackson* (1946), by A. M. Schlesinger, Jr., though the whole history of Western Unitarianism refutes his minimization of the social radicalism of Channing and Parker. The Paine-Volney Deism from which early Unitarian apostles felt called to save Western souls – only to find themselves accused of it by the orthodox – is well set forth in Albert Post's *Popular Freethought in America, 1825-1850* (1943).

Within the last few years two books have been published that synopsize massively yet minutely much of the research on Western history done in preceding decades. R. A. Billington's *Westward Expansion: A History of the American Frontier* (1949) is *multum in parvo* concerning practically all phases of the Western epic save the religious and cultural. Limiting his treatment to *The Old Northwest* (2 volumes, 1950), R. C. Buley complements Billington by rare prints and by chapters on education (Volume II, Chapter 13) and religion (Chapter 14).

The latter, though not too accurate in its references to Unitarian matters, is the best general survey thus far available. Other recent studies include N. H. Sonne's *Liberal Kentucky, 1780-1828* (1939), which affords the most accurate and impartial review of the fortunes of Transylvania University under the Unitarians [Harry] Toulmin and [Horace] Holley that has yet appeared; and J. E. Morgan's *Horace Mann at Antioch* (1938), a definitive compilation of Mann and Antioch College data, though lacking the peculiar flavor of expatriate and unappreciated Unitarianism one finds in the classic *Life of Horace Mann* by his wife, Mary Peabody Mann (1865).

The fullest sources for the work of the Western Sanitary Commission, besides the two chapters (9 and 10) in his daughter's biography of W. G. Eliot, are J. G. Forman's *The Western Sanitary Commission* (1864) and W. G. Eliot's own presentation in the *North American Review* for April, 1864. For Unitarian initiative and participation in the work of the U.S. Sanitary Commission – the Eastern body – a dramatic account is given in Marjorie Barstow Greenbie, *Lincoln's Daughters of Mercy* (1944).

Our detour into the bibliography of secular history thus swings us back to the religious field and to the inquiry for authoritative and interesting reading concerning the arrival and upbuilding of the denominations in the West. Before W. W. Sweet began his memorable development of this subject, utilizing the treasure trove of itinerants' diaries, conference minutes, manuscript sermons, and other lowly records slipping into oblivion, the West had no scholarly, systematic church history. Including his *Rise of Methodism in the West* (1920), together with two books on *Circuit-Rider Days in Indiana* (1916) and *Along the Ohio* (1923), the series "Religion on the American Frontier" deals with all but one of the major denominations: (I) *The Baptists*; (II) *The Presbyterians*; (III) *The Congregationalists*.* The early story of the Disciples of Christ was told by W. E. Garrison in *Religion Follows the Frontier* (1931). The advantage of having such able authorities for guidance is underscored by the contrasting paucity of thorough studies of the Christian movement in the West. M. T. Morrill's *History of the Christian Denomination in America* (1912) is laborious but not inclusive and organic; the *History of the Christian Church* (1849), by J. R. Freese, has the cogency of a contemporary record not only of the *engorgement* of saintly Barton W. Stone by the very practical theologian and ecclesiastic, Alexander Campbell, but of the inception of the Unitarian-Christian experiment in Meadville School. Both the history of *The Cane Ridge Meeting-House*, by J. R. Rogers (1910), with the appended autobiography of Barton W. Stone, and the biography of Stone by C. C. Ware (1932) have been of great assistance. The conviction remains, however, that the historiography of the Christian movement is a sadly neglected though very worthy subject of research.

For the coming and the spread of the Religious Society of Friends in the West, there are several carefully documented regional studies, such

---

* (IV) *The Methodists* was published in 1964.

as that of H. E. Smith, "The Quakers, Their Migration to the Upper Ohio" (*Ohio Archeological and Historical Quarterly*, 1929), and Chapter 12 by Harlow Ludley in Howard Brinton's *Children of Light* (1938) ["The Quaker Contribution ot the Old Northwest"] which weaves the Ohio story in with Indiana Quakerism and its outreachings into Illinois. The non-theological "Progressive Friends" movement – organized congregationally, a separation from conservative Quakerism on the principles of anti-slavery, women's rights, temperance – which created new Yearly Meetings in Ohio, Indiana, and Michigan from 1848 to 1861, is sympathetically described by J. F. Clarke in the July, 1856, number of the *Christian Examiner*. But for neither Quakerism nor Universalism does there seem to be a recent and comprehensive synopsis of their activities in the Central West. At the tail end [of volume 2] of R. Eddy's *Universalism in America* (1886) there are useful data; and E. A. Robinson's studies of Universalism in Indiana (1917) and in Ohio (1923) have given me both reassurance and substance. For the *Gesamtansicht* one needs of these and of all the denominations together in the West, Chapter 14 of Sweet's landmark work, *The Story of Religion in America* (1939), along with the salient emphases of his article, "Religion and the Westward March" (*Ohio State Archeological and Historical Quarterly*, 1941), have served fairly well; as have W. E. Garrison's *The March of Faith* (1933) and G. G. Atkins' *Religion in Our Times* (1932) for the period after 1865.

Neither of these books, however, nor even F. H. Foster's *The Modern Movement in American Theology* (1939), for all their other merits, has an adequate treatment of the impact of evolution on American theology. That has been analyzed for the East by B. J. Loewenberg, in "The Controversy over Evolution in New England" (*New England Quarterly*, 1935), and by H. W. Schneider in "The Influence of Darwin and Spencer on American Philosophical Theology" (*Journal of the History of Ideas*, 1945). Other competent studies are R. Hofstader's *Social Darwinism in American Thought* (1944) and F. W. Conner's *Cosmic Optimism: A Study of the Interpretation of Evolution by American Poets* (1949). Evidence of the early acclimatization of evolution in Unitarian thought is to be found in Mrs. J. T. Sargent's *Sketches and Reminiscences of the Radical Club*, which was started in Boston in 1867 and whose proceedings were fully reported for years in the *New York Tribune*. The service rendered by the Eastern Unitarians, John Fiske (*Outlines of Cosmic Philosophy*, 1874), J. W. Draper (*History of the Conflict Between Religion and Science*, 1875), and A. D. White (*History of the Warfare of Science with Theology in Christendom*, 1896), in reconciling Theism with evolution and thereby forwarding the freedom of science in American colleges and universities, is given proper credit by Sidney Warren in his *American Freethought, 1860-1914*, Chapter 2; but the prior promulgation of a new theology of such reconciling nature by the immanental Theists of the Western Conference is still unacknowledged. The stages by which G. W. Cooke moved from the Universalism of boyhood in the early eighteen-seventies to the advanced positions of his *Social Evolution of Religion* (1920) are significantly outlined in his autobiography, "The Story of My Mind," which was published in *Unity* during 1925, commencing with the issue of March 3.

This reference to one of the chief periodical sources of the history of the Conference prompts a brief survey of them all. Not only have the minutes of its annual sessions been carefully kept, but the reports of them in *The Christian Register* from 1852 until about 1895 were rendered with accuracy and often pungent detail. Throughout the years its large folio pages carried correspondence, missionary reports, church news, and travel stories from the West. The same policy was followed by *The Christian Inquirer* (after 1866 *The Liberal Christian*), which H. W. Bellows founded in 1846 and used as a kind of personal medium not only of his deep concern for the Western work but of the interest of his New York constituency in religious, musical, and literary culture. Like the *New York Tribune* of those days, the *Inquirer* was deservedly popular with Western Unitarians, for it brought a weekly feast of the finest and most progressive intellectual and aesthetic culture of this country and England to farm houses in rural Michigan or Wisconsin. The weekly issues of *The Christian Inquirer* for twenty years constitute a veritable Egyptian tomb of cultural riches that thus far seem to have escaped even Van Wyck Brooks' eye.

For correspondence from the West concerning anti-slavery agitation in Unitarian churches and their neighborhoods, *The Christian World*, a weekly Boston newspaper (1843-48) founded and edited by G. G. Channing, with J. F. Clarke as a later co-editor, is particularly valuable; the same is true of the latter's little-known *Anti-Slavery Days* (1883). Many contributions from Unitarian ministers in the West are to be found in *The Christian Examiner*, the eminent organ of liberal theological scholarship published in Boston from 1824 to 1869 and rendered usable by an admirable Index (1879) prepared by W. Cushing. Similar utensils of research are desirable in the case of *The Index*, the weekly courier of the Free Religious Association from 1870 to 1886, replete with thoughtful articles and spicy news of radical stirrings in the world; in the case of *The Unitarian*, Sunderland's and Herford's monthly protest against the "Ethical Basis," which appeared from 1886 to 1896 with subject matter of distinguished quality; in the case, especially, of *Unity*, every number of which, beginning in 1878, has been vibrant with radical yet constructive criticism, poetry, reform projects, book reviews, editorials, tributes to deserving yet often defamed liberals in literature, science, philosophy, humanitarianism, and religion. The retrospect of this valiant record given in *Unity's* fortieth birthday issue (March 5, 1926) is both informative and inspiring.

Like *Unity*, the periodical *Old and New*, edited by A. M. Judy and E. E. Gordon and published from 1891 to 1908 intermittently at Daven-port, Iowa, and Chicago, Illinois, contains, besides news of the Iowa

Conference churches, well-written articles of originality and sound scholarship. Their secular progressiveness and practicality present an odd contrast to the homely Biblicism of *The Christian Palladium*, and the *Herald of Gospel Liberty*, organs of the Christians in the eighteen-forties and fifties, which I have consulted with profit in connection with the fortunes of Unitarian-Christian collaboration in Meadville School and Antioch College. In both these honest and sturdy papers there are frontier vignettes of great value for the future historian of culture of the West.

In the same category of invaluable aids where I place the Annual Reports, later the Year Books, of the A.U.A. and the Conference Directories published in *Unity* from 1878 to 1896, I place also the numerous local church histories I have been graciously furnished. Of special value because of their broad coverage and wise selection of emphasis, as well as narrative skill, I select the following: *First Congregational Church (Unitarian) of Cincinnati*, by Rev. George A. Thayer; *The First Unitarian Church of Louisville in the State of Kentucky*, by Edith F. Bodley and Gustave Breaux; *The Independent Congregational Church, Meadville, Pennsylvania*, by Rev. E. M. Wilbur; *The Church of the Messiah* in St. Louis, Missouri, by Rev. Walter S. Swisher; *The Church of the Unity, St. Louis*, by Olga R. Kayser; *The First Unitarian Society of Chicago*, by Esther Hornor; *One Hundred Years of Unitarianism in Alton, Illinois*, by W. W. Robbins; *History of St. John's Unitarian Church, Cincinnati, Ohio*, by Rev. Hugo G. Eisenlohr; *The Unitarian Church, Quincy, Illinois*, by E. B. Montgomery; *Fifty Years of Unitarian Life in Geneva, Illinois*, by Fanny LeBaron and Rev. T. H. Eddowes; *The First Unitarian Church, Milwaukee*, of composite authorship; *The First Unitarian Church of Sioux City, Iowa*, by Mrs. H. I. Brown; *The First Unitarian Church, Davenport, Iowa*, of composite authorship; *Early Unitarianism in Pittsburgh and the Story of the First Church*, by Mrs. L. Walter Mason; and *History of the Unitarian Church, Cleveland* [by Winifred Storer]. All these books and brochures, and many leaflet histories of smaller compass, bear the marks of long and patient research and by virtue of narrational skill and elegiac tenderness confer great dignity upon modest gains.

Many of these local church histories are available in printed form in the library of the Meadville School in Chicago. Typescript theses dealing with aspects of Western Conference history and accepted for the degree of Bachelor of Divinity in Church History are likewise available there. Each thesis cited is thus far the best extant treatment of the subject dealt with. Their scholarly excellence and their great usefulness in refreshing my memory on many points forbid their omission from this effort to chart the bibliographical infinite: *John White Chadwick* (1937), by Angus DeMille Cameron; *American Unitarian Interest in the Study of Non-Christian Religions* (1945) by John K. Hammon; *The Place of the Forum in the Liberal Church Program* (1940), by James Hanner; *Unitarian Women Ministers*, by Clara C. Helvie (1928);

William Channing Gannett (1928), by Alfred W. Hobart; *An Anthology of the Writings of Theodore Parker*, by J. Donald Johnston (1944); *Henry Whitney Bellows* (1938), by F. Danford Lion; *A History of the First Unitarian Society of Chicago* (1933), by Herman A. Newman; *The Life of Jasper Douthit* (1935), by Wallace W. Robbins; *Jenkin Lloyd Jones* (1929), by Richard W. Seebode; *Liberal Religion in Rockford, Illinois* (1945), by Harold K. Shelley; *John Haynes Holmes: Opponent of War* (1949), by Kenneth J. Smith; *A Sociological Study of Unitarianism in Illinois* (1948), by Walter E. Stephens; *Neo-Humanism as a Religious Philosophy* (1928), by W. Francis Swift; *The First Unitarian Society of Chicago: Its Relation to a Changing Community* (1933), by Donald A. Thompson; *The Provenance of Humanism Within the Unitarian Movement* (1930), by Melvin L. Welke; *The Religion of Humanity* (1926), by Edwin H. Wilson.

The theses of Raymond B. Bragg on *Principles and Purposes of the Free Religious Association* (1930) and that of Arnold Crompton on *Unitarianism in the Middlewest* (1939), though ultimate at the time of writing, have since been replaced by Stow Persons' *Free Religion* (1947) and by this history.

Index

292

INDEX

Index of Works Cited

Articles, Essays, Poems, Reports, Tracts, and Sermons

Books